ENDING CASH

ENDING CASH

*The Public Benefits
of Federal Electronic Currency*

DAVID R. WARWICK

QUORUM BOOKS
Westport, Connecticut • London

Library of Congress Cataloging-in-Publication Data

Warwick, David R., 1937–
    Ending cash : the public benefits of federal electronic currency /
David R. Warwick.
        p. cm.
    Includes bibliographical references and index.
    ISBN 1–56720–239–X (alk. paper)
    1. Electronic funds transfers—Government policy—United States.
2. Monetary policy—United States.   3. Cash free society.
I. Title.
HG1710.W37   1998
332.1'0285—dc21   98–20131

British Library Cataloguing in Publication Data is available.

Library of Congress Catalog Card Number: 98–20131
ISBN: 1–56720–239–X

First published in 1998

Quorum Books, 88 Post Road West, Westport, CT 06881
An imprint of Greenwood Publishing Group, Inc.

Printed in the United States of America

∞™

The paper used in this book complies with the
Permanent Paper Standard issued by the National
Information Standards Organization (Z39.48–1984).

10 9 8 7 6 5 4 3 2 1

Copyright Acknowledgments

Arthur R. Miller. *The Assault on Privacy.* Ann Arbor: University of Michigan Press, 1972.

On Nineteen Eighty-Four edited by Peter Stansky. Copyright © 1983 by Stanford Alumni Association. Reprinted with permission of W. H. Freeman and Company.

Edgar L. Feige. *The Underground Economies.* New York: Cambridge University Press, 1989.

Two quotes (Nisbet and Strasser) from *1984 Revisited* by Irving Howe. Copyright © 1983 by Foundation for the Study of Independent Social Ideas. Reprinted by permission of Harper-Collins Publishers, Inc.

Joseph Cabrelli. *Costco Connection.* August 1993. By permission of Joseph Cabrelli.

Robert D. Kaplan. "The Coming Anarchy" in *The Atlantic Monthly.* By permission of Robert D. Kaplan.

Quotes from *American Banker*, January 12, 1990, p. 4, and November 8, 1993, p. 24.

CONTENTS

PREFACE

Cash is an archaic form of money that sustains widespread crime, much of which is violent. Though only a fraction is the object of illicit activity, handling and processing of America's cash costs some $60 billion a year.[1] The cash features responsible for this—its physical form, fixed denominations, and anonymous ownership—could be eliminated in a single stroke by transforming cash into federal electronic currency. The profound benefits of this change would substantially improve American society and its economy.

Some readers may be uncomfortable with the idea of switching to a government payment medium that would electronically record all their formerly cash transactions. Fearing the cure might be worse than the disease, many would opt to leave currency and coin as they are. In the long view, however, keeping currency in circulation is not an option. Evidence mounts that tangible money is gradually being displaced by various bankcard monies and that in some distant day cash will fade out of usage entirely. The issue thus framed is whether tomorrow's electronic cash should be federally issued or should comprise some type of currency issued by private-sector institutions. Before reaching a conclusion as to which approach would serve the nation best, it is important to pit any misgivings readers may have about federal electronic money against the realities.

References to "Big Brother" are commonplace, and distrust of government runs deep in the United States. Moreover, the right to data privacy has swelled in importance. Against this background, citizens might imagine federal electronic cash transaction data being scrutinized by officials for violations of law, transacting parties being unduly grilled, data being leaked, and emergence of the dreaded personal "dossier"—the novel *1984* in the making.

Realistic individuals would recognize that the nation is hardly on the brink of becoming a totalitarian state and has a proven capability to design and maintain privacy-secure data systems for its citizens. United States mail, federally processed personal checks, and Social Security and Census files, for example, have long withstood any significant invasions of privacy—indeed, withstood them incomparably better than private-sector personal data. Federal electronic currency not only would warrant and receive high-level security but also could be operated under principles recommended by privacy advocates.

As a matter of sentiment, however, much of the public would favor a private-sector replacement for cash. The reliability of bankcard systems, familiarity of usage, and perhaps a respect for innovation and efficiency underlie this inclination. This outlook is shared by experts. A monetary school of thought, endorsed by a number of economists and officials in the United States, as well as abroad, makes strong argument for a system of multiple private currencies that would supplant fiat currencies. Profit-minded industrialists are serious, if not sanguine, about such a future. Citibank even holds a patent detailing the operation of such a system.[2]

That Americans might favor a system of private electronic currencies over federal money of any type is doubtful, and the concept raises a host of potential problems. At least one expert in electronic funds transfer terms the whole idea confusing and preposterous.[3] In a normal economy, how realistic is it to think anyone would prefer privately issued currency over strong government currency—for example, Bank of Petaluma banknotes over Federal Reserve notes? Not very. Would ordinary citizens and businessmen really prefer to negotiate, compare, and maintain accounts in a variety of currencies, which might vary in value, instead of using today's single U.S. dollar unit? Other problems loom large as well, including possible domination by larger and stronger currency issuers of an international nature, thus raising the specter of international cartels that like today's oil cartels, could impose their will on domestic economies. If all this is not problematic enough, switching from cash to private currencies would mark the end of the Federal Reserve System and require rewriting the basic lending rules for America's banking industry. Who would guarantee failed currencies, and what laws would govern them? Also, getting back to the original issue here, would privacy be better protected in these currencies? Not likely.

A caveat is that though the private-currencies route to cashlessness may prove the most problematic and the least desirable in usage, Americans, through monetary attrition and governmental acquiescence, could some day be saddled with it.

It can hardly be overemphasized that replacing cash with electronic currency holds a bountiful potential, far beyond the mere convenience and efficiency America has grown to appreciate in bankcard systems. Done properly, it promises to slash crime rates, cut the tax burden, lower business costs, and much more. Thus, cashlessness deserves to be targeted and mandated.

It is my firm belief that the most direct and least complicated path to that destination is through a staged transformation of today's cash into federal electronic currency. This would merely change the form of cash, not its issuer. It would preserve the Federal Reserve System and its monetary controls, retain most of the law and conventions governing currency, and obviate the problems encountered with private currencies. Just as important to many individuals, one's data privacy, as well as one's monetary funds, would be incomparably more secure in federal electronic cash than in any private currency.

ABBREVIATIONS

ACH	Automated Clearinghouse
BJS	Bureau of Justice Statistics
BSA	Bank Secrecy Act
CTR	currency transaction report
EBT	electronic benefits transfer
EFT	electronic funds transfer
FEDEC	federal electronic currency
FinCEN	Financial Crimes Enforcement Network
FMI	Food Marketing Institute
FNS	Food Nutrition Service (U.S. Department of Agriculture)
FOIA	Freedom of Information Act
FSTC	Financial Services Transaction Consortium
GAO	Government Accounting Office
IC	integrated circuit
IRC	Internal Revenue Code
IRS	Internal Revenue Service
LAN	local area network
MDT	mobile data terminal
MICR	magnetic-ink character recognition
NCVS	National Crime Victim Survey
NIJ	National Institute of Justice
ONDCP	Office of National Drug Control Policy

PCN	personal communication network
PDA	personal digital assistant
PIRG	U.S. Public Interest Research Group
PIV	personal identification verification
POS	point of sale
TCMP	Taxpayer Compliance Measurement Program
WAN	wide area network

ENDING CASH

INTRODUCTION

The emergence of electronic funds transfer (EFT) systems is the most important monetary development of our age. It is reforming the banking world, facilitating new ways of conducting business, and creating new financial giants, and it might divorce government from cash.

As its title indicates, this book is about making America cash-free. It postulates that fully transforming currency and coin to electronic money would yield vast social and economic benefits, including the prevention of a great deal of today's crime. It argues that while cash might ultimately disappear through attrition, it can and should be terminated much earlier by implementing an affirmative strategy. In substantiation, the book discusses key issues involved in such a transformation, including privacy, security, feasibility, cost, practicality, and monetary interchange, as well as the fundamental issue of who would run the e-currency system, the private sector or government? Several chapters analyze and estimate various economic benefits that could be generated.

Chapter 5 describes a model federal electronic currency system. This is not intended to be a blueprint for America's ideal and ultimate payment system. Rather, it demonstrates how the abstract concept might be put into practical operation.

The reader may presume that the model is based on e-cash and smart cards, perhaps similar to systems being undertaken by various European governments. To the contrary, the system would operate, basically, as a debit-card system, though e-cash and/or smart cards are options that might be given a minor and/or temporary role. While the basic message of this book is that cash should be phased out as soon as possible, it cautions against a crash conversion to e-currency and acknowledges that prudent implementation would require a span of years.

Several years ago, I confronted Milton Friedman with the idea of replacing cash with federal electronic currency. He responded that such action was unnecessary because cash would disappear "naturally." He also said replacing cash with a government electronic currency is not feasible. Yet, given the reluctance of many to give up cash, evidenced by its persistent heavy usage, cash's natural disappearance, at least in the foreseeable future, is hardly assured. Moreover, considering EFT developments in recent years, including smart cards and e-cash as well as advancements in communications systems, feasibility looks very promising.

Many would share the view, however, that it is unnecessary for government to take any action to end the use of cash. After all, isn't cash being crowded out of existence by expanding bankcard operations? Bankcard and EFT experts know better. Scott Cook, chairman of Intuit, testified before Congress in July 1995 that "My expectation is that physical cash will be with us for the rest of our lives." According to a June 1997 GAO report,[1] "The demand for coins and currency is not expected to diminish, despite past predictions to the contrary. . . . The Congressional Budget Office (CBO) estimated in 1996 that cash payments represent about $1 trillion, or 20 percent, of annual consumer expenditures." As a result, the Mint and the Bureau of Engraving and Printing are investing hundreds of millions to retool for increased production of currency and coin. Will the cashless society ever arrive of its own accord? In 1993, *American Banker* asked this question of several leading bankcard experts. They were unanimous in the opinion that cash will not disappear in our lifetime.

Cash still accounts for some 85 percent of today's payment transactions. Several factors block its disappearance, but consumer EFT access is not one of them. For example, although various bankcard systems have long been deployed at supermarket checkout stands, they are used by only about half of the public.[2] No matter how convenient bankcards, smart cards, and home banking systems may be and despite clever promotions, tens of millions of citizens cling to cash. Most simply resist change and new procedures, preferring to see and feel their money, to count and possess it. A percentage of cash usage is sinister, as where cash is used in street and drug crimes; and some is rather less sinister, as in the underground economy. One faction is very vocal in its philosophical fear of losing the privacy that cash ensures. Fringe elements seem convinced that a switch to recordable e-currency is the very device evil forces would employ to impose Orwellian government.

The predominant reason that cashlessness has been slow in coming is that neither industry nor government has made it a goal. The banking industry originally developed electronic funds transfer (EFT) technology and transaction card systems as means of increasing check-processing efficiency and, subsequently, to earn profits. Neither objective requires national cashlessness. While Visa proclaims that it wants to be the world's money, the bankcard industry of which it is a part falls short of attempting to replace every cash transaction with a credit-, debit-, or stored-value-card transaction (in this book "stored-value card," "value-stored card," "prepaid card," and "prepayment card" are used synonymously), and of shouldering the costs and tackling the problems inherent in the task. Nor does the private sector have the economic framework or legal ability to fully replace cash, at least without government assistance and cooperation.

Government has the ability to replace cash and could do so under a national mandate. However, that would go against policy. In contrast to the Federal Reserve System's early role in developing and operating the federal Automated Clearinghouse (ACH) for bank checks, it elected as far back as 1977 to take no active role in consumer electronic payments. Ever since, it has remained on the sidelines as a regulator.

Unlike the gradual establishment of credit-card and ATM/debit-card systems over the last couple of decades, accomplished in a relatively orderly fashion under the cooperative auspices of government, e-cash systems bolted on-scene in the early 1990s and engaged in virtually unregulated operations. They lacked interchange, common standards, clearing and settlement provisions, and reserves, and could transact internationally. Some not only operated outside of conventional payment systems but also clashed with each other. Philip Diehl, director of the Mint, drew an analogy between the medley of disjointed e-cash systems and the unstable private banknotes that were in use in mid-nineteenth-century America, warning of an electronic "Tower of Babel." Particularly disturbing to authorities was that the new systems facilitated transactions beyond the observation of law enforcement and taxation authorities. This remains worrisome, and officials are relieved that e-cash is not racing into high volume, as some had predicted. Of course, no one can predict whether e-cash is in pause, will die on the vine, or will accelerate upwards in the near future.

E-cash transaction anonymity stirred particular concern. DigiCash, Inc., for example, offers a patented security system that ensures anonymity to all but the transacting parties. Mondex and other e-cash companies offer similar "fire walls" against invasions of privacy. (We may ask, Privacy from whom?)

E-cash (discussed in Chapter 2) is the catalyst that precipitated activity in Washington, compelling monetary planners to consider possible changes in the nation's money system. As Congressman Michael Castle, chairman of the House Subcommittee on Domestic and International Monetary Policy, put it, "This Subcommittee bravely continues to go where no one has gone before."[3] Whereas in prior years many in the Fed and the Treasury Department seemed detached from or unknowledgeable about e-money systems, the ideas in parlance after 1995 range from comprehensive regulation of private-sector e-cash systems to the issuance of federal electronic currency.

Beginning in 1995, a flurry of activity began in various divisions of government both to educate themselves on the technology and monetary functions of e-cash and to determine what, if any, government intervention is appropriate. In July 1995, the U.S. House of Representatives Subcommittee on Domestic and International Monetary Policy commenced a series of hearings on "recent technological and market developments that will impact on the forms and creation of 'money,'—'electronic cash,' the Internet as a marketplace and other innovations."[4]

All the same, government keeps its distance from general consumer EFT operations. With the exceptions of electronic payments of benefits and government invoices (the Debt Collection Act of 1996 requires all federal payments to be made via EFT by January 1, 1999) and specialized smart-card/EFT programs, government continues to relegate the matter exclusively to the private sector. In keeping with such policy, Chairman Castle, concerned with suggestions that the government issue some form of electronic currency,[5] cautions against government competition with industry. Officials have expressed a wait-and-see attitude even as to regulating e-cash and a reluctance to move beyond current exigencies. The Fed hesitates to regulate e-cash because it "has not the slightest desire to inhibit the evolution of this emerging industry by regulation, nor to constrain its growth."[6]

In September 1996, the Treasury Department hosted a major conference entitled "Toward Electronic Money and Banking: The Role of Government." The agenda focused on four areas: consumer issues, law enforcement, issuers of e-money, and international cooperation. No mention was made, publicly at least, about the possibility of federal electronic money. The tenor was simply concern over whether or not to regulate. Speaker after speaker warned against premature regulation of electronic payment systems that might "stifle innovation," so much so that EFT innovation seems to have become an end in and of itself. Without fixing on any specific applications of its "bounty," some officials trust implicitly that industry will harness innovation in ways that will better the economy. Accordingly, some even downplay the negative history of "wildcat banking" in the United States and go so far as to suggest that creation of the federal ACH may actually have retarded development of more advanced technologies. Some officials appear willing to grant away government seignorage, which runs around $20 billion a year, to industry as a fair trade for some undefined public betterment. Such deference to the emerging e-payment industry, while paying scant attention to the idea of a federal electronic currency and the public benefits thereof, causes one to wonder if the heavy bias in favor of the private sector precludes thorough and balanced analyses of the issues.

Such a polarized governmental position, relying fully on the private sector, ignores even the need to supply lacking industrial guidance, if not leadership. Nonstop development of new technologies and e-money products, coupled with turbulence among competing companies in e-money markets, perpetuates an uncertainty among e-money users that works against its fulfillment. Europe has progressed more rapidly than the United States largely because governments there participate with industry in establishing universal systems.

That said, officials in Congress, the Federal Reserve, the Treasury, and other departments now keenly follow e-money developments, and many might be receptive to a possible government role in electronic money. This climate presents a rare opportunity to form novel monetary policies.

Some readers will react skeptically to the crime-prevention hypothesis put forth in this book. That is understandable. Considering that Americans have been subjected to the hackneyed phrase "as we approach the cashless society" for over 25 years, a degree of doubt has formed as to whether they will actually witness it. Moreover, as crime-prevention programs have had little apparent success, the prediction that cashlessness will prevent crime is somewhat unconvincing.

One does not have to spend much time reasoning out hypotheses or to rely on experts to realize that cash robbery would become impossible if cash no longer circulated. Basic logic dictates that bank robberies, cash-register robberies, and most street robberies would simply cease. One can easily appreciate the direct ramifications. It is less apparent that such effects would constitute only a portion of the overall crime-prevention benefit and that *all* crime would be impacted by a conversion to electronic currency. The more one examines the equation, the more credibility it gains—because it makes sense.

Irrespective of crime prevention and of whether or not a national mandate to end cash were set, many of the issues raised in this book are inherent in today's ongoing electronification of cash and will have to be addressed soon anyway. As a subtheme, therefore, this book discusses some of the issues raised by the increasing attrition of governmental currency. For example, though more slowly than many had predicted, the various bankcard systems, because of their efficiency, convenience, and profitability, will someday increase their transaction volume beyond that of cash. Cash will become less important. Thus, a major question presents itself: Who will operate the nation's "cash" in coming decades—the private sector or the government? As cash shifts from federal currency to e-cash and other private-sector money systems, will government's economic controls be jeopardized? How will this affect the dollar's integrity? This leads to other questions, including the practicality of private currencies and whether future annual/transaction fees for electronic payments might have an inflationary effect.

Though crime prevention is discussed herein with an eye to its fiscal impact, this subject is more than just a money-saving affair. Every day of the year some five Americans are murdered and 300 seriously injured in robberies that very likely would be prevented by ending tangible cash. Each day another 3,500 individuals, though uninjured, are put through the terror of successful or attempted robberies. Of course, thousands more are victimized in other types of cash-related/inspired crimes. Certainly, emotional impact and quality of life must be given due weight in discussing future currency systems. The proposition that today's crime can be reduced through cashlessness requires analysis of the cash-crime nexus. An appropriate place to start is by focusing on an actual cash crime, which we do in Chapter 1.

CHAPTER 1

CASH IS KILLING US

THE CANTINA ROBBERY

The evening of Sunday, March 7, 1993, marked the end of a busy weekend at a popular Mexican restaurant called the Cantina. Located in the Glenview district in the foothills of Oakland, California, the modern restaurant had become a favorite meeting place for local upper-middle-class residents of a quiet neighborhood that was appreciating in value. The community had become a model for harmonious racial integration.

At about 11 o'clock that evening, a car was parked in the shadows across the street from the restaurant. The three men sitting inside it waited patiently until almost all of the diners had paid their tabs and departed. Then they burst through the entrance of the Cantina, brandishing pistols and shouting orders to startled patrons and employees to immediately lie facedown on the floor and not to look at the robbers' faces—threatening to kill anyone who hesitated to obey.

The ten people in the dining area, mostly waiters and busboys, lay facedown on the floor while one of the robbers struck several of them with his weapon and stole their wallets. Two of the robbers rushed to the kitchen area, where they found the 38-year-old assistant manager, Scott Paddock, working his very last shift before going to a new job in San Diego; the 33-year-old bartender, Albert Hart; and the 24-year-old dishwasher, Luis Vargas. The robbers ordered the three to hand over all the cash in the till and to open the safe. They complied promptly.

The robbers then shot all three employees. Paddock and Vargas lay mortally wounded on the kitchen floor, while the robbers forced Hart, whom they had shot in the abdomen, into the restaurant's walk-in freezer along with the ten other horrified victims.

Everything proceeded perfectly for the robbers. The patrons remained compliant, immobile, and silent as the robbers ransacked the restaurant and stole several thousand dollars in cash from the safe. Uncertain as to whether the robbers had fled, the victims waited in terror inside the freezer for half an hour, until they felt it was safe to come out and call the police.

Scott Paddock died at the hospital at 12:59 A.M., leaving his bride of six months with only a shattered future. Luis Vargas died an hour later, leaving his wife and two young daughters without a husband and father or a means of support. Albert Hart survived his wound, but along with the others in the restaurant that evening, he suffered an indelible psychological trauma that has made full enjoyment of life less attainable.

Despite its familiarity with robbery and murder, the San Francisco Bay Area was shocked by the news of this violent crime. Oakland's Glenview district, an oasis in a city racked by violent crime, was thoroughly traumatized. Flowers of condolence amassed on the sidewalk outside the restaurant. Two days after the murders, a candle-light vigil was held at the restaurant's closed doors, and a crowd of over 300 filled the sidewalk and poured into the street.

Those who learned of the tragic event from newspapers, television, or radio were struck with the realization that yet another brutal and outrageous crime had occurred in their area; inwardly, they were even more disturbed by the knowledge that it would happen again and again. The story was not covered by the California or national news media because almost every urban center has its own similar tragedies to report. For a newspaper to cover all the nation's robberies for just one day (estimated at over 3,100 per day based on victimization surveys, and 1,400 formally reported to police each day)[1] would require a newspaper several inches thick and would be utterly demoralizing to read. Two valuable lives were taken in the robbery of the Cantina, eleven others were put through hell, and a whole community was made to suffer lasting depression and anger—all because vicious criminals were attracted to the cash that they knew was available at the restaurant.

With good reason, many Americans regard crime as the nation's foremost problem. In 1996, as part of the Justice Department's annual crime survey, citizens were asked, "How much do you worry about the following situations? . . . Getting murdered, to which 10.6% replied 'very frequently;' Getting beaten up, knifed, or shot, to which 12.5% replied 'very frequently,' and 'Your home being burglarized,' to which 20.4% again replied 'very frequently.' "[2]

While politicians and authorities are quick to take credit for decreases in the nation's high crime rates but search for solutions when rates again rise, about 37 million crimes are committed against individuals, their homes, and motor vehicles each year. Included are some 20,000 murders[3] and over 6 million burglaries and robberies.[4] Scores of American cities contain drug-infested neighborhoods that have become literal war zones.

Despite soaring arrest, conviction, and incarceration rates in the United States, the expenditure of about $100 billion a year by the criminal justice system,[5] and increasingly intrusive police actions that test civil liberties, the nation's crime rates continue to rival or exceed those of third-world countries. It is increasingly evident that we cannot continue addressing America's crime problem on a post facto basis. Clearly, new methods must be found besides simply making more arrests and putting more judges on the bench and more convicts in prison.

CRIME LOVES CASH

Cash is the perfect medium for transacting affairs in secret. It provides criminals huge advantages over any other payment medium, for it bears no mark of ownership. Payment by cash creates no record and leaves no trail. One can deny having taken or received it, whether to subvert criminal prosecution or to hide income from taxation. Then one can pass it on for value, no questions asked. Its tracelessness and unrestricted negotiability makes cash a criminal's most desired commodity. One need only read the familiar sign fixed to many delivery trucks, "Driver carries no cash," to realize the worst feature of cash: Simply possessing it puts one at risk of being robbed, assaulted, or worse.

Americans in the 1990s know that a lot of innocent people are killed for the cash they possess, yet the numbers are still startling. Consider employees who must handle cash in their jobs. Of the 1,004 homicides on the job in 1992, 936 were killed by strangers during robberies; just 68 were killed by coworkers or spouses, apparently emotionally motivated. While the death rate for all Americans on the job averaged 5 per 100,000, for taxi drivers, who deal in cash, it was 142 per 100,000.[6] It is no wonder that taxi companies are pioneers in using portable credit-card terminals.

Crime in America is largely interwoven with cash. Most crime consists of thefts of cash itself or of property to immediately sell for cash. Table 1.1 summarizes all crimes either reported to police (Uniform Crime Reports) or reported to the U.S. Census Bureau via its national household survey, the National Crime Victim Survey (NCVS). Although the NCVS is considered the most comprehensive accounting of crime in America (because it

Table 1.1
Crime in America, 1996

I	CRIMES REPORTED TO POLICE	
	TOTAL CRIMES	13,475,000
	VIOLENT CRIMES	1,683,000
	Murder/Manslaughter	20,000
	Rape	96,000
	Robbery	537,000
	Aggravated Assault	1,030,000
	PROPERTY CRIMES	11,792,000
	Burglary	2,502,000
	Larceny Theft	7,895,000
	Auto Theft	1,395,000
II	CRIMES REPORTED BY VICTIM	
	TOTAL CRIMES	36,794,000
	VIOLENT CRIMES	9,124,000
	Rape	307,000
	Robbery	1,134,000
	Assault	7,683,000
	PURSE SNATCHING/PICKPOCKETING	318,000
	PROPERTY CRIMES	27,352,000
	Burglary	4,845,000
	Larceny/Theft	21,120,000
	Auto Theft	1,387,000

Sources: U.S. Department of Justice, Federal Bureau of Investigation, *Crime in the United States 1996* (Washington, D.C.: U.S. Department of Justice, September 1997). U.S. Department of Justice, Bureau of Justice Statistics, *Sourcebook of Criminal Justice Statistics—1996* (Washington, D.C.: U.S. Department of Justice, 1997).

is based on surveys and includes even those crimes that are not reported to the police), both reporting systems agree that robbery, burglary, and larceny theft—crimes in which obtaining cash is the most common objective—comprise about 80 percent of all crimes.[7] Furthermore, as much as 16 percent of all property stolen in the United States consists of currency,[8] or items intended to be exchanged for currency. When one speaks of the crime problem, one is referring for the most part to the cash-crime problem.

Cash crimes are often violent. Americans are assaulted and/or murdered for their cash, no matter how small the sum. About 10 percent of all robberies (by definition violent) and thefts in the United States are for less than $10.00[9]; yet, it is common for victims to be beaten, and sometimes murdered, for even smaller sums or because the hapless victims possess no money. Robbery is most often carried out by armed criminals, 41 percent of whom employ firearms and another 9 percent of whom use knives.[10] Strong-arm and other tactics account for the balance. A government study based on robbery victimizations from 1973 through 1984 indicates that over half of all robbery victims are attacked and that about one in twelve victims suffer serious injuries such as rape, knife or gunshot wounds, broken bones, or concussions from being knocked unconscious.[11] This means that about 740,000 Americans are attacked in robberies each year and that about 123,000 are seriously injured.[12] In addition, about 2,000 are murdered in the course of robberies.[13]

One envisions a typical robbery-murder being plotted by coldhearted thugs, but it sometimes occurs otherwise. A tragic example of how quickly a simple cash theft can become violent came to the author's attention from a news item describing a purse-snatching attempt that, when resisted by the intended victim's husband and others nearby, resulted in the youthful purse snatcher's shooting one man to death and wounding two others. This incident is recorded as a homicide—which, viewed simply as a statistic and unless someone were to dig up the facts of the case, fails to illuminate the tragic role that cash played in it.

Violence results from other types of cash-related crimes as well, including household burglaries. Burglary, we know empirically, is perpetrated predominantly to take cash or items to sell or fence for cash. Unfortunately, sometimes victims of residential burglaries are home at the time. As a result, as the Bureau of Justice Statistics reports, "Three-fifths of all rapes committed in the home . . . and about a third of home aggravated and simple assaults are committed by burglars."[14]

Cash plays a major role as a payment medium in many types of crime. Murderers-for-hire, arsonists, kidnappers, and parties to bribery deal exclusively in cash. Billions of dollars' worth of stolen goods are fenced for cash each year. It is evident from television's images of bundles of confiscated U.S. currency and teenage drug dealers flush with cash that the illegal narcotics trade, running somewhere between $50 billion and $300 billion a year in the United States, is conducted exclusively in cash.[15]

PREVENTING CRIME BY ELIMINATING CASH

Aside from domestic violence, drunk driving, and most rapes, most crime in America involves U.S. currency. Cash is the common denominator. Even crimes that may not involve cash directly often have an ultimate cash connection. Wire-service, credit-card, and check scams usually end up as cash in the criminal's hand.

At the very least, transforming cash to electronic currency would prevent all bank robberies and almost all of the approximately 300,000 "commercial house" robberies committed annually in the United States.[16] Convenience-store, gas-station, and bank robberies or any other crime in which cash is a criminal's target would become history. Achieving just this much would be a stupendous accomplishment. However, even more crime can be prevented, because electronic money provides a means for record keeping.

To the extent records were accessible to law enforcement (requiring due process), e-currency could be employed to suppress a broad range of crimes that today, when conducted in cash, shroud criminals with anonymity. These include drug trafficking, bribery, receiving stolen property, and fraud. All told, conversion to traceable currency would save enormous sums in justice outlays and garner tens of billions of dollars in revenues from tax evaders. Overall, the profound social and economic potential of redesigning the nation's cash system is staggering.

Enthusiastic unveilings over the years of one crime-stopping program after another have instilled a pervasive lack of faith by the public in virtually all of today's attempts to curb crime. Indeed, if the statement were made to the average American that there is a way to reduce substantially store robberies, bank robberies, holdups, muggings, and purse snatchings, the listener would immediately suspect a joke or a trick explanation.

However, today's electronic transaction technology makes it possible for us to do even better than that. The proposal to convert cash to electronic currency is not some Buck Rogers fantasy but a feasible concept that would put an end to much of the nation's crime. As well, it promises to deliver huge pecuniary benefits to all levels of society.

The prospect of converting currency and coin to an electronic system is a bit unsettling. It is something like facing a computer for the first time, for it raises a number of imponderables, such as how the system would actually function and how one would use electronic transaction cards in particular situations. For example, how would an individual give "money" to another individual? The reaction of some when first confronted with the idea of making cash electronic is that it would result in a complicated, bothersome system preventing few crimes—and then only until crooks would begin stealing electronic money cards and finding ways around the system. To those who haven't kept up with e-money developments, this is all futuristic, "Star Wars" talk.

In truth, the required technology necessary for a national electronic money system, ranging from terminals to communications systems, has already been developed. Americans would find the new electronic money convenient, secure, and highly economical, the kind of change that causes one to ask in retrospect, "Why didn't we do this a long time ago?"

CHAPTER 2

WHERE IS THE RISING USAGE OF ELECTRONIC MONEY TAKING US?

THE ORIGINS

In 1972, financial commentator Robert Hendrickson wrote a book entitled *The Cashless Society* and thus originated the term. However, the concept was expressed nearly a century earlier by Edward Bellamy in his 1888 book, *Looking Backward*, an early science fiction work about a man who in 1887 falls into a coma and awakens in Utopia in the year 2000. Among other oddities, cash is not used because everything is purchased with "credit cards." Bellamy's credit cards are made of pasteboard and are hole-punched at each transaction until the owner's credit is exhausted. This type of card is reminiscent of the paper transfer tickets given out to passengers on urban trolley and bus systems. Today, it would be classified as a "prepaid" or "stored-value" card, the electronic form of which is used in telephone and transit systems.

In yet an earlier age, Western civilization experienced true cashlessness. During the fourth and fifth centuries A.D., the Roman economy was in a state of collapse and lacked a central authority to issue coinage. Trade routes had become so insecure that they were abandoned. Thus, trade remained local or was nonexistent, and payment was either in kind or by barter. No doubt, similar conditions existed at other times and locales.

Some historians trace the roots of the bankcard industry to the year 1914, when both Western Union and GPCC, which later became Mobil Oil, issued their first consumer bankcards. Payment of charges made with this type of card, given to preferred customers gratis, could be deferred for a limited period without incurring fees or interest.

Buying now and paying later is a practice as old as time, of course, at least where a previous face-to-face relationship exists between the buyer and seller. Purchasing this way at country and company stores has a long history in America. With the introduction of the bankcard, however, a previous acquaintanceship between the proprietor and the customer was not required. The bankcard allowed one to incur charges at any of a company's stores even though the customer was unknown in the particular establishment.

This marketing idea soon caught on with gasoline companies and hotels, which began issuing bankcards to their customers. For decades, department stores issued embossed (raised-print) metal "charge plates" that were processed through point of sale (POS) imprinters that transferred customer information onto sales invoices. These types of merchant-issued cards were used only at the issuing merchants' establishments.

The next innovation was a single card that could be negotiated with diverse merchants. The term "credit card" is attributed to Frank McNamara. In 1950, Diner's Club was the first to organize individual merchants who would accept a common credit card. As with the earlier bankcards, customers were given free credit for the initial billing period, at the end of which they were expected to pay in full. However, the customers paid Diner's Club, and the merchants submitted invoices to Diner's Club, which paid them about a month later, less a fee of between 5 percent and 10 percent, called a "discount," a term that is still with us. By 1954, Diner's Club earned additional revenues from a $5 annual fee charged to cardholders. Despite being nearly drowned in paperwork during the initial years, the scheme came to be a great success.

Banks immediately expanded on this model. As early as 1951, Franklin National Bank of Long Island began enlisting local merchants and issued its own "universal" credit card, which functioned similarly to the Diner's Club card, yet included a variety of merchants, not just restaurants. Other banks, including Chase Manhattan, followed suit, but the local and isolated nature of their early operations, in an industry that requires high volume for efficiency, left them with small, unprofitable bases. Most quickly exited the credit-card business.

Conditions were different in California, however, where Bank of America had hundreds of branches throughout the state. In 1958, the same year that American Express introduced its first bankcard, Bank of America issued the milestone BankAmericard. In addition to its acceptability by thousands of merchants statewide, this card offered an important new feature: Cardholders, upon receipt of their monthly statements, could elect to pay the balance in installments, with a finance charge of 1.5 percent per month added to the unpaid balance. The BankAmericard was immediately popular. By the end of 1959 some two million BankAmericards were in use. For over seven years, Bank of America had a virtual monopoly in the bankcard business.

In 1966, four large Illinois banks, ultimately joined by various others across the states, formed a bankcard alliance to issue and mutually honor bankcards. Thus, the Interbankcard Association came into existence, later known as Master Charge and then as MasterCard. This novel interbank arrangement prompted Bank of America to expand in similar fashion. Thus, in 1967 it began franchising the BankAmericard trademark and system. For a fee of only $25,000, within a year some 100 banks had signed on.

By 1970, some 1,400 banks were issuing either BankAmericard or Master Charge cards, and the combined total outstanding credit stood at $3.8 billion. That same year, Bank of America spun off BankAmericard to the newly formed National BankAmericard, Inc. (NBI), a private, nonstock corporation. Bank of America had licensed banks in some 15 foreign countries as well. In parallel, BankAmericard's foreign operations were transferred to another private, nonstock corporation called IBANCO. Ultimately, in 1977, both organizations were renamed: NBI was given the name Visa U.S.A., and IBANCO became Visa International. Today, these Visa organizations, as well as MasterCard, serve as nonprofit processing and utility systems for the card-issuing companies, mostly banks, that own them.

Although challenged by American Express, Discover, and General Motors credit-card systems, Visa and MasterCard together process the lion's share of transactions. In an ironic twist, over the years, nonbankers, including GE Capital, First Data Corporation, EDS, FiServe, CheckFree, and others, as processors and lenders, came to play greater roles in credit-card activity than bankers. By 1996, credit-card debt had reached $340 billion in the United States, and the credit-card transaction had entrenched itself, worldwide, as a new form of payment.

BANKCARDS BECOME ELECTRONIC

It seems incredible that until the early 1970s credit cards were not electronic. (Early bankcards are collectibles, drawing as much as $500 from dealers.) Transaction authorizations, required for purchases over an amount coded in the bankcards, were obtained verbally over the telephone. Transaction records, in the form of thin charge slips, had to be sent between banks by courier or the mail. Merchants' banks usually paid their merchants on time but then looked to cardholders' banks for remittance, a system that not only lacked presentment and payment deadlines but was also dependent on much physical processing. With increasing volume, it soon bogged down and left many bankers upset.

The first step taken to remedy this situation was the employment of a computerized switch to speed up authorizations, thus eliminating the expensive and time-consuming phone calls. Later steps included replacing physical transfer of charge slips with electronic data transfer. Today, the credit-card transaction, from beginning to end, is totally electronic; the only purpose for those paper charge slips that customers sign is to verify sales, should someone protest a charge. Incidentally, a significant portion of protested charges are waived simply because merchants cannot find the charge slips in question.

The addition of electronics dramatically improved credit-card procedure. First, it reduced credit-card fraud by speeding authorization, keeping account records current, and ensuring accuracy. It slashed operational costs, which, among other advantages, allowed reduction in "discount" fees imposed on merchants. Also important, it provided prompt settlement of credit-card charges between banks—indeed, faster than for checks.

The birth of credit cards had a lot to do with the checking world. Of concern to bankers in the late 1960s was a growing glut of checks. Prior to World War II, personal checking accounts were used mostly by the affluent, with the average American typically paying bills and making purchases in cash. In a more sophisticated America after the war, the use of checking accounts became popular with all but the lowest socioeconomic class. By the late 1960s, paper checks flowing through the banking system in the United States were increasing at an unprecedented rate. It was clear that the mechanical check process in use at the time would become incapable of handling the load.

To address this problem, the Federal Reserve Bank in San Francisco, along with ten California banks, established the first electronic system for clearing and settlement of checks. Today's electronically automated check clearinghouse, the federal ACH, had its origins in 1968, when the San Francisco and Los Angeles Clearing House Associations formed a committee to look into the possibility of setting up a "paperless" check-clearing system. In 1970, California banks formed the Special Committee on Paperless Entries (SCOPE), which applied computers to check processing. Although the American Bankers Association was contemporaneously studying an independent, industry-controlled, automated clearinghouse system, the Federal Reserve Board took an active role in the matter by offering space, equipment, and management for a local electronic facility. In October 1972, the Federal Reserve Bank of San Francisco and the Los Angeles branch started up the first automated clearinghouse. Seven months later, the Federal Reserve Board started up a second ACH in Atlanta, Georgia. By 1973, some 23 SCOPE committees had formed across the country, and more ACH facilities were put into operation. These ACH systems were electronic only within their local regions. Interregional transactions required the physical transfer of data tapes. Interregional electronic interchange was introduced in 1978, ultimately resulting in the current fully electronic nationwide federal ACH system.

At about the same time, NBI, Visa U.S.A.'s forerunner, headquartered just south of San Francisco and adjacent to what came to be known as Silicon Valley, was applying electronics to credit-card authorization and settlement. The two developments were more than coincidental, for both were motivated, in large part, by the tremendous growth in the usage of checks.

In the early days, many bankers viewed credit-card transactions as a load-relieving alternative to the use of checks. By aggressively promoting credit-card usage, they sought to shift a portion of their burdensome checking transactions to the new, relatively efficient payment medium. Although their efforts did not halt the growth of check transactions in absolute numbers, in relative terms they were successful. As the economy continued to grow over the following decades, more and more Americans purchased with credit cards rather than by check, and thus the rate of growth of checking transactions fell substantially. As things turned out, the clever innovation of the electronic credit-card system not only provided banks an answer to the growing problem of processing paper checks but also generated interest revenues, discounts charged to merchants, and various fees charged to cardholders.

In contrast to its active role in processing the nation's checks through the federally operated ACH, the Fed refrained from operational involvement in bankcard operations, opting instead merely to regulate. There was growing reason for the Fed to get involved: The pre-electronic days of bankcards experienced serious bankcard fraud. As there were no federal regulations restricting cardholder liability, many a cardholder got burned. Moreover, a growing backlog in settlement between banks demanded intervention. The government's response was limited to enactment of laws and regulation. Payment schedules were established for interbank payment, and Regulation E, limiting consumer liability, requiring receipt issuance, and the like, was put into effect. The National Commission of Electronic Fund Transfers issued a report in October 1977 stating that (1) consumers could benefit from EFTS (electronic funds transfer systems), and that (2) it recommended the federal government not get involved in the operation of any POS (point of sale) system, and that (3) the private sector should operate such systems. It is time for officials to reconsider points (2) and (3).

As commonly happens with competing technologies, when one form advances, outmoded forms tend to catch up. That is what happened with check-processing technology. It was not long before magnetic ink character recognition (MICR) was invented. Printed in magnetic ink, these familiar routing and account numbers are imprinted on the face of checks, thus allowing them to be handled by high-speed machines. The cost of processing checks soon fell dramatically, and one of the early motivations for increasing credit-card volume declined in importance. During this same period, the Federal Reserve's Automated Clearinghouse for bank checks came into operation, providing yet further efficiencies.

The lucrative nature of credit-card lending, as well as the ancillary opportunities these operations provided, drew nonbankers into the business, players who had different motivations. Sears Roebuck, American Telephone and Telegraph (AT&T), General Electric, General Motors, Ford, and others soon got into the act. What bothers bankers about the entrance of these nonbankers is the advantages they have over bankers because of their disparate motivations. For example, AT&T's primary motivation for issuing credit cards may be to protect its calling-card business, and it might therefore offer bankcard services at little or no direct profit. "A bank may need a 3% return on assets, while a non-bank might need 1%, or even break-even, if that device helps protect or expand a primary business," says Donald Auriemma, of Auriemma Consulting Group of Garden City, New York.

New check-handling technology continues to unfold: One of the greatest tools in banking (and in other industries) has been *imaging*. The process uses scanners to "read" documents—checks, for example—and to capture their "pictures" in computer memory. Not just the data from the check, but the entire check—borders, handwriting, and all—is seen electronically. To save computer-memory capacity, the checks are compressed and miniaturized. Imaging handles a minimum of 40 checks a second, about twice that of MICR processing, and provides a number of additional advantages. First, checks stored in memory can be instantly brought up and viewed on a computer screen. Then, if desired, the image on screen may be printed into "hard copy." Moreover, viewing and/or printing an imaged check stored in a facility's computer may be done remotely.

Of particular significance to bankers, imaging has the potential to eliminate the need to freight checks and physically run them through processing centers, which usually takes days. Thus, as a check is presented for payment at a branch, it can be transmitted instantaneously to a processing center. By efficiently printing imaged canceled checks in miniature for return to account holders, banks can save additional handling, mail, and other costs. Imaging could generate even greater efficiencies but for the fact that the Fed's ACH doesn't accept images; the Fed insists on itself capturing the images from paper checks, which means that checks still have to be transported to the Fed's processing plants, an inefficient requirement that irritates many bankers.

Imaging is used in bankcard processing as well. Thus, credit- and debit-card sales drafts are imaged, transmitted, and filed electronically. In the bankcard industry, the handling of chargebacks can be expensive. These occur when customers dispute billings and request copies of original sales drafts. The industry spends over $200 million a year settling these disputes, plus an additional $140 million in filling requests for sales records. By converting to imaging, the bankcard industry can decrease its handling and mailing expense by up to 25 percent. Beneficiaries will include merchants who have difficulty finding bankcard slips when charges are protested.

The paper check is on a road to obsolescence, and bankers are encouraging this (although they will lose their biggest fee earner, the bounced-check charge, which runs as high as $25). The relatively lower processing costs of electronic payment devices, float, increasing counterfeiting of checks, and other risks motivate bankers to find electronic alternatives. Merchants welcome checks' demise as well, and the day may soon come when "checks not accepted" will be common at point-of-sale (POS).

Various payment devices, including credit and debit cards, compete with check volume. Smart cards have the potential of displacing a significant percentage, at least in face-to-face transactions. For remote payments, however, replacements are not as available. Home-banking systems have failed to catch on, largely because they are generally user unfriendly, require prearrangement procedures to list payees, and, surprisingly, are often slower in effecting payment than paper checks. Despite electronic input by account holders, payment is sometimes made by mailing checks! Moreover, home-banking systems must be accessed via computers, which are possessed by only 40 percent of Americans—and only half of these are equipped with the necessary modems. Screen phones, far easier to use than computers, could increase home banking, but they are not in general use. Bill payment via ATM machines, still on the horizon in the United States (though used in Europe), could hasten the demise of checks as well.

The "electronic check," a computer-based system that emulates the paper-check transaction, has been under development for several years. Its protocol, interchange, security codes, and other features have been worked out for use in banking networks, and it is being tested in pilot programs. The electronic check is but one of several e-payment devices that bankers hope will gradually overtake checking in volume. Payment schemes abound, some on drawing boards, some in trials, and a few in usage. Most do not exactly parallel the paper check, with each system having a diverse set of features. A particular scheme might be geared for business-to-business purchasing/bill presentment/bill payment, while another might be designed for consumer transactions, perhaps as an adjunct to Internet shopping. Some systems incorporate computer messaging (of purchase orders/shipping data) and effect multiparty communication/payment functions. Thus, new payment systems not only include counterparts of today's paper-based systems, ranging from checks to letters of credit, but couple features that surpass the capability of today's paper instruments.

Though government and industry are fast converting to electronic replacements for checks, getting individuals to change habits is a different matter. It is not just a matter of having the equipment and expertise. Even if all of today's check writers were provided electronic access via computers, screen phones, personal digital assistants (PDAs), or other means, many would not take advantage of them, for old habits die hard. In contrast, some third-world countries are skipping the check experience altogether and going straight from cash to e-monies. Certain European nations have all but phased out checks.

DEBIT CARDS AND AUTOMATIC TELLER MACHINES

The debit card is more modern than the credit card, for it was born in the electronic age. Yet, it is generally auxiliary to a checking account. Indeed, it is sometimes described as an "electronic checkbook." Debit-card systems allow customers at point of sale (POS) to make immediate payment, remotely and electronically, from their checking accounts. Credit is not involved, and the transaction is instantaneous, although often the actual debit and credit messages between banks may be delayed for a period of hours or days. Some economists classify this medium as an "accounting payment system."

Credit-card systems, in contrast, are devices for using preexisting lines of credit and have nothing to do with the funds in users' bank accounts. It is merely incidental that credit-card bills are typically satisfied by checks drawn on cardholders' bank accounts.

The earliest and most vociferous proponents of true debit-card systems were American retail merchants. In the late 1970s, they recognized the potential advantages of debit-card transactions over both checks and cash. Not only is a debit-card transaction much faster, on the average, than a transaction in which the customer writes a check and the merchant goes through a verification and handling process, but debit-card transactions do not bounce. In supermarkets, where some 70 percent of the nation's checks are negotiated and where profits can run under 1 percent of gross, bad-check losses can be critical. Two percent of all checks bounce.

Cash attracts crime. The argument is sometimes heard that by switching customers from cash to electronic money, retailers—particularly convenience-store chains and oil companies—would reduce the incidence of pilferage and robbery. This would, in turn, help lower insurance premiums and forestall costly security measures, which sometimes include restricting hours of operation and even ceasing operations in high-crime areas. However, actually to reduce the chance of robbery, cash would have to be almost totally replaced by debit cards so that virtually no cash would be kept on premises; the prospect is poor that this will occur soon.

Merchants also favor debit-card usage as a way of reducing cash-handling expense, which involves stocking cash registers, repeated count-ing, packaging, storage in local safes, and then transportation to banks or armored-car company vaults. In some businesses, merchants are required to fill out time-consuming currency transaction reports (CTRs), which are then used by Treasury officials in tracking money launderers.

Despite urgings by merchants in the early days, banks were slow to join and/or form debit-card networks. What made a great deal of sense to merchants did not appeal to bankers. Consequently, some major retailers, particularly on the West Coast, including the Von's supermarket chain and Lucky Stores, long ago lost patience and started their own debit-card systems. Using the Fed's Automated Clearinghouse (ACH), they were able to process retail transactions made on store-supplied cards against funds in customers' bank accounts. Subsequently, the four largest banks in Cal-ifornia formed a debit-card system called Interlink. By 1991, it was serv-icing over seven million transactions per month for several statewide merchants, including Atlantic Richfield and Lucky Stores. That marked the beginning of an era of local and regional debit-card system startups, bank membership drives, system alliances, intersystem contractual ar-rangements, and organizational maneuvering.

Early attempts to establish debit-card systems were caught in a chicken-and-egg situation between bankers and merchants. Bankers asked, what was in debit-card systems for them? There were mixed motivations. ATMs promised to reduce labor costs by providing "tellerless" transactions and facilitating freestanding minibranches. Furthermore, debit-card services could be used to attract new checking accounts. However, merchants wanted debit-card systems only if nearly all local banks were included. That is, they wanted a system that all of their customers could use. From the banker's point of view, however, having all local banks in the same system negated any individual bank's advantage in attracting new ac-counts.

Revenues from debit-card operations were paltry alongside the lucrative interest income produced by credit cards. Moreover, they depended on exacting discount fees from protesting merchants and charging transaction fees to reluctant customers. If it were not for the development of ATM networks, debit-card systems might have disappeared altogether.

Many Americans still do not understand what a debit-card transaction is, but all know about automatic teller machines (ATMs). Ironically, one of the earliest applications of modern EFT technology was to make it easier to obtain and use the ancient medium of physical cash. The advantage of being able to withdraw cash at any hour, any day of the week, without having to enter the bank or wait in line made the ATM card instantly popular. Soon tens of millions of Americans would regularly withdraw cash from their banks' branch ATMs, from other banks' ATMs, or even from freestanding ATMs in supermarkets and elsewhere. Today, there are some 160,000 ATMs in the United States. By 1996, the public was making some nine billion withdrawals a year.

Banks promoted ATMs, both to earn fees and to cut costs in tellerless transactions. Initially, ATMs were singular units used only with the bank owning them. This gave bigger banks the advantage. In time, switches provided interbank operations, which ultimately expanded to local, then regional, networks, including Pulse, Honor, NYCE, Cash Station, Star, and many others. Added to these are the MasterCard and Visa networks, Cirrus, and Plus. Service providers, such as First Data, EDS, and Traveller's Express, continue to play a role as well. The result is a virtual international ATM network allowing almost any ATM card to be used anywhere. These networks, which tie in with POS, also support debit cards. Thus, you can buy groceries with your ATM card, and you can also walk across the aisle of most supermarkets and use the same card to withdraw cash from an ATM. You can usually get "cash back" at the checkstand.

When ATMs were first being introduced, some banks were able to get ahead of others by offering ATM cards gratis with new checking accounts. As the networks grew, all these gimmicks eventually fell by the wayside, and the ATM has become a required customer service. As it turns out, overall, ATM operations cost banks some $28 million a year. However, once the savings from displaced tellers are taken into account, the bottom line becomes positive.

Virtually every bank belongs to interconnected ATM/POS networks, thus allowing its customers to use their debit cards across the country, if not around the globe. Slowly, the numbers of true debit transactions is increasing—but very slowly. The double-function card carried by tens of millions of Americans is still used almost exclusively for withdrawing cash. In recent years, industry has promoted the pure debit usage by mailing out bankcards described on their face as debit cards.

Almost every year, beginning in the early 1980s, great predictions have been made for increased debit-card usage. For example, the Electronic Funds Transfer Association declared that 1988 would be the year of the debit card. Another proclamation stated that 1994 would be the turning point for debit cards. Still others predict that debit-card usage will surpass that of credit cards by the year 2000. However, a more conservative report estimates that only 3 percent of consumer purchases will be converted to debit cards by the decade's end. Despite the debit card's many advantages over checks and cash, persuading people to transact with it has been an uphill struggle. Cash, available at convenient ATM machines, is a dominant competitor, while credit cards remain far more popular.

The role of debit-card schemes in the overall progress of electronic payment media in the United States is seen by some as transitional. In a banking world leaning heavily toward payment fees as income, some see the debit card as a vehicle for banks to capture a share of the coming e-cash market.[1] The idea is to gradually shift credit-card users to debit cards by offering enhancements like price guarantees and notary service, while making credit cards less attractive by limiting the float period and charging higher and additional fees. Some banks have begun imposing fees on credit-card holders who pay "on time."

In a reenergized campaign to increase debit-card usage, banks are employing new tactics. First, because many of the public confuse "debit" with "debt," banks are avoiding use of the term and instead advertise the "cash card," the "check card," and "the credit card you can use like a check." Second, the functional emphasis of the dual-purpose card (the old ATM card) is being changed: Instead of labeling cards "ATM cards"—that incidentally serve as debit cards—many newer cards being issued are dubbed "money cards" or "master money cards" or are given nondescript titles—all of which incidentally allow their owners to withdraw cash from ATMs.

Once the public has become comfortable with debit-card payment, then it can be introduced to the wonders of the Internet as well as to smart/prepaid cards, all of which would be tied to bank accounts. The public would then be able to enjoy "more choices, an expanded market, and decreased shopping time," while bankers would reap transaction fees.

Having lost some half of the credit-card market over the last decade to nonbankers like First Data Resources and AT&T, bankers now worriedly face a new threat—e-cash, which could serve as an avenue for nonbankers to wrest away even more banking business. The future of e-cash is unclear, and everyone is trying to figure out its long-term consequences. The unveiling of clever electronic payment innovations, almost monthly, does not help. Many bankers are caught in the dilemma of taking a wait-and-see position and being left behind. A few risk investment in new payment schemes, while most remain disabled by indecision.

E-CASH

E-cash made its debut in the United States in the early 1990s. "E-cash" is a category of money systems employing a common element: locally stored electronic units of value. Paid for in advance in conventional money and representing equivalent units in real currency, these units can be transferred between vendors and individuals using compatible electronic systems. E-cash has two basic divisions: smart card e-cash and computer e-cash.

This form of "money" is typically downloaded from its system through special terminals (e.g., at specially equipped ATM machines, computers, or cell-phone terminals) onto smart cards or via modem onto personal computer hard disks. The "money" remains stored until the user spends it—in the case of smart cards, by transacting it in vending machines, turnstiles, toll-collecting devices, or retailer's terminals; in the case of computer e-cash (cybercash), over the Internet

Some systems provide interchange between one's computer and one's smart card. Newer products permit downloading of e-cash via wireless communication to a mobile terminal and from there onto the user's smart card. Each e-cash transaction reduces the amount of "money" stored. Some types of e-cash cards are simply tossed when depleted; others can be reloaded for reuse.

The computer-based form of e-cash, often called "cybercash," is the newest payment medium, having made its appearance, primarily in the United States, around 1995. It is transacted in non-face-to-face transactions over the Internet. So far, its users consist of a small but affluent segment of society that shops on the Internet. The popularity of the medium is hampered by perceived security and privacy issues, as well as by the basic difficulty in getting even sophisticated computer jockeys to change old money habits. Shopping on the "Net" is also hindered by disorganization and slow communication. It is still too much like wandering through an endless garage sale. As a result, Internet e-cash remains incipient. Coming communication systems, using fiber optic and/or radio, should eliminate frustrating delays and see an upturn in the use of cybercash. Providing Internet access via television sets or other innovative devices, projects now underway, promises an even more dramatic effect, for the Internet, no longer tied to computers with modems, would be at the disposal of virtually the entire population.

Smart-card e-cash is generally used in face-to-face transactions (although the other "face" may comprise a parking meter, vending machine, or bill-payment kiosk). In basic form, it can be viewed as the electronic version of a very old idea. Recall bus transfers and pasteboard punch cards. Modified versions of these media are in widespread use today. Some, still made of paper, have magnetic stripes across their back sides so that the "punch" feature is replaced by an electronic reduction, or "decrementation," to use a mathematics term. What began some 20 years ago at about the time that Jerome Svigals invented an electronic fare card for use in the then-new San Francisco Bay Area Rapid Transit System—a paper mag-stripe card that subtracted value as it was used for each ride and to which value could be added in coin-operated machines—has grown exponentially. This type of card has been adopted by transit systems around the world.

In a historical analog, the same functional element that transformed the early merchant charge card (usable only in a single retailer's establishments) to the credit card (transactable with a variety of merchants) has advanced the status of prepaid cards into today's e-cash. E-cash brings it all together, combining the prepaid feature with the diversity of vendors. Thus, today's e-cash can be used to transact with any of a variety of merchants who have joined the particular e-cash network. The variations of smart cards are myriad. The Tower Group, a consultancy, is assembling a compendium of the hundreds of smart-card schemes underway around the world. Smart-card e-cash usage in the United States remains insignificant. Because America is blessed with faster and cheaper communications systems than most other countries, its future would seem to favor credit-card, debit-card, and perhaps Internet payment systems.

Some confusion exists about "smart cards" and "e-cash." They are not synonymous. E-cash systems typically employ the smart (as opposed to mag-stripe) type of card. Yet, smart cards are used for diverse functions, many having nothing to do with money payments. For example, governments and industries commonly use them for identity authentication in controlling access to secure areas, equipment, and software systems. Moreover, they can function as and are commonly used for both credit and debit cards.

The smart card, or "chip card," saw its first use as a payment medium in Europe. The world's first widespread smart-card payment application began in France in the 1980s. At that time, mag-stripe card usage was accompanied by a high incidence of fraud. To provide better security, a joint governmental-industrial decision was implemented by which smart cards gradually replaced mag-stripe cards. This change saw French card fraud plummet to near zero. In Europe, the smart card has since expanded to pay transit fares, highway tolls, vending machine fares, and virtually all types of retail payments. About 100 million smart cards are in use worldwide. However, few are used in the United States, and Europeans are quick to declare that America is ten to twelve years behind the trend.

Because of contrasting politicoeconomic environments, sea changes are sometimes easier to accomplish in Europe than in America. Banking and government officials in Europe, as a vestige of oligarchy and monarchy, find it convenient to confer on national and/or European concerns and are often successful in working out joint policies. They have been able to designate, coordinate, and implement and impose payment systems, to the exclusion of other systems, on a compliant public. The same is unthinkable in the United States. Here, innovation and competition are expected to produce the greatest efficiency and utility, while a laissez faire policy keeps the race open to all. Moreover, the American public has a voice in the products it uses.

With merit on both sides of the Atlantic, Europe's bankcards will shortly comprise 100 percent smart cards, which are far superior, technologically, to America's standard mag-stripe cards. Smart-card proponents blame America's failure to implement smart-card systems on a lack of leadership and a slowness to recognize the country's bankcard needs. Others point out that European smart-card technology was developed in part at least because Europe lacks the relatively efficient communication system of the

United States. Whatever the history, smart cards have remarkable advantages over mag-stripe cards. The ability of Europeans to launch smart cards, as they have, should cause officials in Washington to consider whether government should remain on the sidelines as a referee in consumer EFT (electronic funds transfer) or whether it should begin setting standards and taking a position as to the choice of payment technologies.

The use of a smart card's integrated circuit (IC) chip simply to add and subtract value is a bit of overkill; a far less expensive mag-stripe card works as well. Some refer to cards limited to such usage as "token memory cards." The ability of an IC chip to calculate, sort, and more often is wasted. But, for some purposes, the smart card is chosen because it can store up to 500 times more data than a typical mag-stripe card.

A prime feature of smart-card technology is security. Software installed in them can prevent their unauthorized usage, making smart cards valuable whether used as prepaid, credit, or debit cards. For example, some keypad-equipped smart cards must be activated by the entry of a personal identification number (PIN).

Again, smart cards and e-cash are separate concepts. While 95 percent of today's smart-card activity occurs in Europe, most of this does not involve e-cash. Europe's purely e-cash card companies include Proton, Danmont, and Mondex. The Geldkarte, a German bank product, issues a multiuse card that incorporates a debit system with prepaid functions.

Smart cards are often used in "closed-environment" systems. This category covers a variety of card payment systems that operate within limited locales—such as college campuses, factories, even prisons—for identification, meal payments, library fines, toiletries, parking fees, and other transactions. Some closed environment systems employ prepaid cards, while others lack this feature. Almost all are multipurpose, incorporating access to several systems via a single card. To accomplish this, some smart cards include multiple chips, plus mag stripes, and even a bar code. College campuses have become proving grounds for new chip cards.

Despite predictions of tremendous e-cash usage, often emanating from marketing personnel, some critics paint a dim future for this medium in the United States, where e-cash remains at the trial or pilot-project level, with no major rollouts expected for at least several years. Except for certain niche functions, such as nonstop toll payments, phone cards, and transit fares, and perhaps in closed environments, Americans have not yet been subjected to the election to use smart cards.

The most prominent impediment to public acceptance of stored-value cards, according to a recent in-depth study, lies in the requirement that consumers pay card issuers in advance. The "rational consumer," states the author, faced with a choice of debit, prepayment, and credit methods, would opt for the latter.[2] In the abstract, this analysis makes sense. Why give the issuers free advances when they can be paid later? In practice, however, things are not that clear.

Convenience holds a much higher priority with the bulk of Americans than incidental payment of fees and costs. The public is resigned to paying convenience fees and accepts that there is no free lunch. Most already keep general operating funds in noninterest-bearing or extremely-low-interest-bearing checking accounts, and many also pay per-check charges and other transaction fees. There is a grumbling acceptance of the fact that as fee-based banking creeps ahead in the United States, free-usage payment media are fast disappearing—including cash. ATM cash-withdrawal and check-cashing fees are well established. Coin-counting machines charge fees. How long can it be before a fee will be imposed for "cash back" service in retail stores? Given this trend, the negative float in prepaid e-cash card systems, particularly if they do not charge for off-line payments, will hardly halt consumer acceptance. Indeed, such systems could prove to be the most economic of consumer EFT.

Stored-value system proponents sometimes assert that massive volumes of small-ticket transactions (below $5) would hopelessly overload debit-card bank operations, and they emphasize the adaptability of smart cards to low-value transactions. Yet, with computer speed and memory capacity constantly on the rise and with prices falling, and as dramatic communications improvements lie just around the corner, the assertion rings dubious and suspiciously self-serving. If one is considering a system to replace cash, obviously, on-line debit systems would have to invest in equipment capable of handling the load. Yet, e-cash carries similar infrastructure requirements.

Indeed, the initial hurdle to widespread e-cash card usage in the United States lies in the cost of switching from mag-stripe to smart cards. Smart cards themselves cost some ten times the price of mag-stripe cards (roughly $4 versus 40 cents), with the total outlay for, say, 100 million cards running around half a billion dollars. Retailers would have to fork out another huge sum for smart-card terminals. Altogether, including promotional expenses, the undertaking could easily cost billions of dollars. Why do it? What would e-cash issuers get in return?

Not new accounts and new deposit assets—for banks already hold the deposits of prospective smart-card users. Improved security and reduced fraud losses? Perhaps. However, this is manageable now. Credit-card losses are covered by interest revenues. Besides, improving security means employing the most advanced smart-card technologies, including self-authentication and biometrics, which necessitates smart cards with keypads and higher-capacity chips, all costing a premium. Thus, despite European successes with smart cards, American card issuers are hesitant to make the investment.

Only in narrow transaction scenarios are smart cards making inroads in America. Lacking conventional bankcard competition, smart cards are being used for toll collections, with enthusiastic public acceptance. This application is spreading across the country. Parking meter and telephone payments are targets as well. A number of major transit authorities are testing smart-card payment systems. Yet, these diverse applications are not interoperative. They do not comprise e-cash.

Investment in such applications has not generally been made by banks; the moving parties are smart-card developers, gasoline companies, transit authorities, and municipalities. Efficiency and cost savings support these investments, while the very meaningful convenience to motorists and commuters of not having to wait in line or to undergo exasperating telephone keypad number drills makes these schemes winners.

So, what is the future of e-cash? This is a question that has many nervous bankers speculating—a task made difficult by promotional hyperbole, shifting technologies, and the constant unveiling of improved products. In Europe, e-cash issuance is generally limited by law to banks. This proposal is still being considered in the United States, but some consultants seem to think America will not follow Europe's lead. Indeed, research firms predict that nonbanks will capture some 50 percent of the coming smart-card market (which is far broader than just e-cash).[3] Preparing for the future, therefore, big banks have formed alliances with payment software companies, terminal and data-processing firms, companies including Microsoft, Hewlett-Packard, Oracle, Verifone, Motorola, DigiCash, CyberCash, First Virtual Corporation, and others. Wells Fargo is running an in-house e-cash pilot program. Yet, an air of uncertainty plagues even the big guys, and no one has a grip on the overall direction that consumer EFT might take.

Clearer is that special-usage smart-card payment systems, such as for toll payments, will increasingly provide those products a foothold in the United States. From that point, one can envision a sequence of developments something like this: Smart-card companies, dominated by combines of superbanks and powerful computer-based interests, emphasizing to retailers that virtually all commuters (will) carry smart toll cards and perhaps pointing out that off-line payments cost retailers no discount fees, would enlist gas-station chains, fast-food chains, and vending machine companies into their systems. Smaller smart-card contractors/e-cash startups would combine, merge, and ultimately be bought up. At some point, consumers, plagued with multiple smart cards, would welcome single multi-application cards. Thus, smart-card usage would metamorphose into true e-cash with vendor networks and multivendor card acceptance. In the meanwhile, dual-system terminals, able to process both mag-stripe and smart cards, would find their place in convenience stores and supermarkets. All this would see a gradual shift of deposits from banks into the coffers of a few superbanks and nonbanks.

Mindful of these prospects, a caveat heard in banking circles is, "Get on board with e-cash, or you'll be left behind!" What startled American bankers about e-cash from the outset—the loss of deposits to that new industry—may be the factor that forces them into it. Thus, if e-cash ever becomes a major payment medium in the United States, it may do so in large part, from bankers' defensive action to retain threatened deposit assets rather than from profit-motivated strategies.

Mondex, having tested its e-cash system at sites in various countries, is trying to deploy it in the United States as well. This promises to be a difficult task. Even in Swindon, England, Mondex's first test site, where its e-cash products were promoted extensively and where 70 percent of merchants accept such payments, fewer than 0.5 percent of sales are conducted via Mondex. Continental Europe has shown little interest in Mondex.[4] Other e-cash systems include Visa Cash, Proton, Danmont, and DigiCash. The latter, headquartered in Amsterdam, is also engaged with U.S. Operations with the Mark Twain Bank. Giants, including Microsoft, Citibank, Wells Fargo, and Bank of America, are probing as well. E-cash is insignificant in the United States. Both the card and computer forms of e-cash are still in the pioneering stage. Basic hurdles, including security, shared protocols, regulation, communications, and terminal standards, are just now being crossed.

Despite its currently negligible impact as a payment medium, the emergence of e-cash has sounded an alarm in government. And well it should—especially about traceless e-cash systems that provide payers and payees more anonymity than they would have with paper currency. Currency can at least be marked or videotaped in sting operations; further, its movement is reported in currency transaction reports (CTRs). Advertisements for e-cash systems that play to antisocial elements are disturbing, as is the prevalence of e-cash vendors on the Internet selling X-rated movies, gambling, and currency exchange services. One e-cash system caters to "freedom-oriented individuals" seeking to avoid "bureaucratic snoops, nasty ex-spouses, and lawsuit-hungry lawyers."[5]

It is ironic that Jeffrey Rothfelder's book *Privacy for Sale*, published in 1992, abhorring the widespread dissemination of personal data, could as well today be taken as a reference to anonymous e-cash systems. Thus, while private data is a marketable commodity, so is the tool for blocking access to it. But, do we want to block all access to private transaction data—from law enforcement investigators, judgment creditors, and the IRS?

Perhaps the best thing about e-cash, so far, is that it has wakened government officials to possible economic and social perils of certain consumer EFT developments. Thus, concern has been raised about protecting the public from potentially abusive practices of e-cash companies and about their financial responsibility. Officials question how government will detect and audit transactions in the new medium to determine tax liability and track illegal activities. Fearing that e-cash may outpace regulation, the Office of Thrift Supervision, the Treasury Department, and Congress are looking into these issues.

It is interesting that Director of the Mint Diehl suggested in the 1995 congressional "The Future of Money" hearings that a study "be implemented to determine the feasibility of a private/federal partnership to develop a currency smart card." As described later, e-cash technologies, in both computer and prepaid-card forms, might have a role in some future replacement for cash.

INTERNET PAYMENTS AND WIRELESS MONEY—THE COMING GENERATION

Cybercash systems are limited to payments between modem-accessible vendors and proficient computer owners, the latter of whom must be willing to immobilize themselves before monitors, endure advertisement gibberish, and wait for product pictures to be transmitted through snail-paced analog bottlenecks. Speedier modems are finally being marketed, but a drastic improvement is coming about from another quarter.

The Internet is a breeding ground for tomorrow's money media. Though it supports incipient e-cash systems, particularly for sales on the Internet, it more importantly underlies novel credit and debit devices. Surpassing home banking, it is generating wholly new types of payment arrangements, including some that are adjunct to bill presentation and/or third-party participation.

Roughly 40 million Americans have computers, and about ten million of them have modem connections to the Internet. This growing segment is the target of on-line retailers, bankers, and nonbankers, such as credit-card-issuing AT&T, First Data Corporation, and many others. This has spawned a subindustry with Internet payments as its nucleus. Included are companies like CyberCash, Inc., which acts as a gateway between the Internet and credit-card authorization networks; First Virtual, which provides consumer credit verification to Internet information providers, and others, each of which offers a different twist or fills a particular niche. The importance of good security in this area has produced a wave of software developers, as well as novel cryptological products.

Industry spokespeople expect that some 100 million Americans will have Internet access by the year 2000. Although purchases on the Internet today are sparse, some predict $500 billion in annual sales within six years,[6] which, incredibly, would amount to about 8 percent of today's worldwide purchases! The Fed and other cautious observers, in contrast, downplay this prospect, pointing out with some accuracy that in the past many grand but fallacious predictions have been made about consumer EFT. Whatever the rate of growth, encroachment by nonbankers in the e-money arena muddies the future of banking and causes a degree of anxiety. Relying on such prophecies, banks have thrown billions of dollars into home banking schemes, almost all of which have yet to draw significant volume.

The expectation that Internet payments will increase dramatically rests on the assumption that computer ownership and usage will rise sharply. However, communication advancements may facilitate a different payment scenario, one in which the computer is not central.

In just a few years "wireless money" will make its debut in the United States. The significance of the event lies in the history of consumer EFT systems, which have been limited by slow and costly communication links, relative to those on the horizon. This new money classification, defined by the communications systems supporting it rather than by how payments are stored or transferred, will employ all-digital and nearly instantaneous communication. There is no need even to pause for dial up, because one is always on line. Just as important is that everyone, not just Internet users, will use it.

A number of communication companies have acquired bandwidth allocations from the FCC and have begun rolling out networks supplying all-digital unitary service covering television, computer, and telephone. These wireless networks can be used for payment communication as well. Verifone, Inc., and Motorola, Inc., world leaders in payment terminals and wireless communication, recently formed an alliance that will support end-to-end payments over the airwaves. Access to such payment communication will hardly be limited to computer owners. It can easily be put at the disposal of anyone who owns a telephone.

Digital consumer payment communication itself marks a systemic breakthrough because EFT progress has long been restrained by the cost and time requirements of the analog telephone. Historically, these impediments fostered the development of several deviant techniques. One of them has been to defer EFT accounting. Thus, the off-line payment transaction was devised, by which data accumulated from multiple transactions are bundled into "batches" that are subsequently transmitted in single telephone calls. An additional advantage of batch transmissions is that they can be made at a time of day when lines are clear and rates are lower. This device saw its first usage for clearing bank checks. When applied to POS electronic payments, postponing of data transmission also has the advantage of speeding up the sales process at sales counters (by not taking time to dial up during the sale), vending machines, and toll collection points. It is used in both credit-and debit-card payments.

Another technique to avert the cost and delay of analog telephone communication involves the use of stored-value cards. If value can be transferred between payer and payee without contacting an intermediary, such as a bank, the need for immediate communication is obviated. In some systems, prepaid "money" can pass through several hands, or through several computers, before it is submitted to the issuer for payment in conventional money. Numerous technologies and products support off-line stored-value payment and have been put to use in e-cash systems. However, their legal and practical pitfalls have financial institutions and government officials grappling for safeguards. Moreover, the mere proliferation of schemes, running into the hundreds worldwide, has heads spinning with indecision as to which will survive.

Delay in accounting opens the door to fraud and abuse. One method used to counter this is to identify troublesome accounts. This entails compiling account numbers of cardholders who have exceeded their borrowing limits or whose accounts have been breached by some third party or are problematic in some other way. For years, cards issuers supplied "blacklist" pamphlets to vendors, listing all such accounts in fine print. They were usually sent out on a weekly basis. Clerks, instructed to confiscate listed cards, dutifully checked proffered customer bankcards against such lists before consummating sales. Gradually, the paper blacklists were replaced by computer-stored lists, still in usage, which are maintained in electronic form at vendor sites and revised daily by downloading new data from a central computer. Thus, when a customer's card is swiped, the vendor's local computer first looks for a match with its blacklist. This system is popular in Europe. Blacklists in the United States, except for small sales, have largely been replaced by on-line authorizations.

Wireless payment networks can not only extend electronic payments access to virtually every household but also render obsolete the various circumventions of analog-based problems. Delayed accounting, with required local accumulating of payment data, downloading of blacklists and bad-account matching, and batch transmissions, will have become unnecessary. Also gone would be the utility of off-line smart cards. However, the most salient feature of wireless money lies in its lack of need for a computer.

Absent a computer, what device would one use to access wireless payment networks? Several possibilities exist. The telephone itself has long been used for similar purposes, as in home banking, and would of course remain available. Even today, Mondex markets a bankcard-reading telephone that has several payment options. BankSys and others also offer such devices. Today, however, most are still geared to interchange with stored-value technologies and systems, in either bankcard or hard disk formats, and are further limited to relatively slow and expensive analog communications.

Wireless communication eliminates the dialup and connection process, and one is always on line. Payment-data transmission is typically running at less than a tenth of a second. Newer products continue to be developed. Digital television-computers are on the market. Digital terminals, some combined with telephones, include inexpensive bankcard readers that link individuals with banks and payment networks.

Although described as "wireless," some systems employ radio only in the links between the sender or receiver and their respective local servers. Between servers, the signal travels via optic cable. In other configurations, the middle link comprises a satellite communication. Either route provides all-digital service from sender to receiver and eliminates the necessity of connecting a terminal directly to a land line. Though local power is still necessary for operation, it can be supplied by battery; thus, wireless payment terminals are inherently portable and are limited only by radio-transmission range.

As wireless payment systems become popular, equipment and service costs will fall. It is plausible that data communication will become so quick, efficient, and universally accessible that the on-line method will become standard for all payments.

Today's struggling home-banking schemes, limited as they are by telephone response systems and computer modem users, could blossom into systems far grander than the original planners could have imagined. Direct-debit remote payment, conducted via user-friendly low-cost home terminals, could become a common way for individuals to pay their bills. Coming terminals, for example, might allow individuals first to swipe their card and then to swipe one supplied by the payee that contained the payee's routing and bank account number. (The latter "card" might consist of a bill with a mag-stripe across one end.) The entire transaction, including keying in the payment amount, would take place in a few seconds—less time than it takes to warm up a computer. An inexpensive built-in printer would provide the individual with a paper record. There are many possibilities.

This brings us back to this book's theme, that payments conducted today in tangible cash could be replaced by fast, cheap, and incomparably more secure electronic transactions.

THE GREAT CASHLESS-SOCIETY NO-SHOW

Electronic transactions account for only a 4 percent share of volume so far, with cash at some 87 percent.[7] Even e-cash enthusiasts, predicting a vast payment volume in coming years, concede that cash will be around for a long time.

In support of his prediction that cash will disappear "naturally," economist Milton Friedman points out that cash in circulation has already dropped from 13 percent of the GNP at the end of World War II to about 4 percent today. (He also believes that replacing cash with a government electronic system is not feasible.) It is true that the United States uses less cash today, relative to the GDP, than it did in 1945—but circulating cash actually increased sixteen-fold from 1945 to 1996, from $25 billion to about $400 billion.[8] During that same period there was a volcanic rise in illegal drug trafficking, conducted almost exclusively in cash. As acknowledged by most economists, the underground economy, conducted largely in cash, has grown dramatically.[9] Larry E. Rolufs, director of the Bureau of Engraving and Printing which produces Federal Reserve notes, reports that "currency demand has tended to increase on the average 3–5% per year over the past decade."[10] As noted earlier, the Treasury Department is retooling to handle the increasing demand for currency and coin.

In 1993, *American Banker* surveyed a number of the nation's prominent observers of bankcard and other payment trends, asking "Is there a 'Cashless Society' in the future?" H. Spencer Nilson, publisher of *The Nilson Report*, a leading bank news and advisory service for credit/debit card executives, answered, "Nobody reading this paper will ever live in a cashless society, in this country or any other. . . . Even by the middle of next century, cash will still account for over 35% of dollar volume on all types of consumer-payment systems." Mike Shade, marketing director of Verifone, Inc., the nation's largest manufacturer of bankcard terminals and related devices, replied, "I don't believe we can expect a 'cashless society,' but we will definitely see a 'less-cash' society." And Paul Martaus, of Martaus and Associates, responded, "It has been a practice of mine never to say never about anything, but I feel extremely comfortable about going on the record as believing that we will never see a checkless, cashless society in this country."[11]

Cash cannot be disappearing when about 34 percent of all violent crime has a strong causal connection with cash.[12] It is not fading away when money laundering, mostly from drug trafficking, runs year after year between $50 and $300 billion (obviously, estimates vary by a wide margin) and when the underground economy, equal to about 10 percent of the GDP, or roughly $750 billion, operates predominantly in cash.

This is not to say that cash is utilized predominantly as an instrument of crime or mostly in illicit dealings. Indeed, in total dollar value, cash represents some 30 percent of all media of exchange in the United States.[13] In numbers of legitimate consumer payments, cash easily holds the lead. That cash may gradually be substantially displaced in coming years by debit cards and e-cash does not mean that cash crime will diminish on a concomitant gradient. Crime will remain somewhat constant. Illicit use of cash will simply represent a larger percentage of total cash transactions.

The incidence of crime is declining in the United States. The Justice Department reports that general rates are the lowest since 1973, the year that victim-of-crime statistics were first compiled.[14] Though the reasons for the decline are unclear, it is a welcome relief. It would be unrealistic to expect the trend to continue and then to remain at some reduced level. Historically, crime rates have fluctuated. In the mid-1980s crime rates had descended almost to today's levels, but then climbed again for more than half a dozen years. It is noteworthy that today's decline is not as "across the board" as is often portrayed in the media. For example, in 1996, robberies had actually increased in thirteen states and was up by 59 percent in seven of them.[15] Bank robbery increased by 14 percent.[16]

Most misleading about reported overall trends in crime rates, and of particular concern to parents with teenaged sons and daughters, is that the reports usually do not include illegal drug crimes. Oft-quoted standard crime tables produced by the FBI and in the National Crime Victim Survey do not include lines for drug crime statistics. The latter are reported in separate tables. Unfortunately, crimes involving marijuana, cocaine, crack, and other illegal drugs have increased steadily from 1980 to today. Arrests for sale, manufacture, and possession of illegal substances rose from 256 per 100,000 population in 1980 to 536.6 per 100,000 in 1995.[17]

In 1995, the nation recorded its highest drug arrest total; an estimated 1.5 million people were arrested for either the sale and/or manufacture or possession of illegal narcotics. Furthermore, . . . since 1980, the number of arrests for all drug types rose substantially, with those of heroin/cocaine showing the highest increase, 741 percent. In comparing arrests for specific drug types from 1990 to 1995, marijuana arrests have increased 80 percent and heroin/cocaine arrests 6 percent.[18]

Focusing on a longer period of time, one also observes that violent crime is four times greater and property crime almost three times greater today than in 1950. As FBI Director Freeh told a Chicago audience in 1996, violent crime, despite recent decreases, has doubled over the last 20 years. While it is true that victimization rates for most noncommercial cash-related crimes have fallen steadily since 1973 (the inception of the National Crime Victimization Survey), by 1996 we still experienced 42 violent crimes per 1,000 people, 32 percent of which were robberies.[19] Theft and its attempts, even allowing for recent decreases, still stand at the intolerable rate of about 200 crimes per 1,000 persons, which means that one American of every five is a victim![20] As these are national averages, the chances of being robbed and attacked are even higher for persons living in higher-crime areas. Crime rates vary between town and country as well. In 1996, there were 9.7 robberies per 1,000 people in cities, but only 2.9 robberies per 1,000 in rural areas.[21]

Across-the-board crime statistics also fail to reveal that crime is increasingly concentrated in inner cities, where it is a disproportionate problem for African-American and other minorities[22] and where aggressive law enforcement methods may exacerbate racial tensions. Such broad statistics say little about upward trends in crack babies, AIDS, increased sales of lethal firearms, and the other insoluble social problems linked to the cash-dominated, illegal drug trade.

Falling crime rates could be the result of a better economy, more and better policing, or perhaps social programs that have finally kicked in. Many liberals are loath to acknowledge that stiffer criminal laws and sentences have been effective. To the extent that they have been, however, they exact a price. By 1995, some 5.4 million adults in the United States, or 2.8 percent of the population, were under some form of correctional supervision. This represents a 7 percent increase over 1985.[23] As tragic as this social condition is, it also places tremendous fiscal pressure on the country. Justice outlays between 1982 and 1993 alone rose some 126 percent; the corrections portion alone rose 250.3 percent![24]

The crimes in which cash plays a key role continue to plague America. The Bureau of Justice Statistics notes that "the decline in rates [in 1996] for robbery . . . and burglary . . . were not statistically significant."[25] But why does America continue using cash as its primary payment medium? A variety of reasons, legal and illegal, underlie the continued popularity of cash. While criminals, drug addicts, employers of illegal immigrants, and tax cheaters depend upon cash, so do millions of law-abiding Americans who lack the creditworthiness to obtain bankcards and/or to have their checks honored and who therefore must transact in cash. Moreover, there are those who by force of familiarity, lack of sophistication, or distrust of financial institutions elect to deal exclusively in currency and coin. Tens of millions of Americans still conduct nearly all their transactions in cash: According to a Federal Reserve Board survey of consumer finances for the year 1995, some 15 percent of U.S. households did not have checking accounts. Of this 15 percent, 84 percent stated that they did not write enough checks to make an account worthwhile, and 23 percent said they simply did "not like dealing with banks." The unbanked receive some ten million checks a month worth $5 billion. The typical family income in this group runs less than $25,000 a year, and apparently, virtually all of this group's payments are made using cash or money orders or bank checks. By 1996, a quarter of U.S. households had no bank account, and the number was rising.[26]

In order effectively to reduce crime by obstructing the cash-crime relationship, cash must not circulate at all. A mere reduction in the nation's cash supply, no matter how substantial, is insufficient: Even a relatively small amount of cash will sustain widespread crime. Robbers of convenience stores, gas stations, and ATM patrons typically get away with only $487 to $567 in cash, while purse snatchers average $296.[27]

It is difficult to imagine how a truly cashless society can evolve by increased bankcard and/or e-cash usage alone. Bankers would have to per-suade criminals and tax evaders voluntarily to give up the use of cash. Most cash payments are small, with 80 percent being for less than $2.[28] Many cash transactions are occasional and do not occur in commercial settings, making it difficult for the bankcard industry to service or profit from them.

Bankcard companies acknowledge this limitation. Although Visa International states that "it is and wants to be the world's common currency," it has no intention of replacing the United States monetary system and admits that its future plans "may not mean that Americans will live in a completely cashless society."[29] Bankers, across the board, are recanting premature predictions of cash's demise.

If the use of e-money increases at its current rate, cash will ultimately be completely displaced. Harvey Rosenblum of the Dallas Federal Reserve Bank points out that "[e]-money is an important technological and financial innovation. It will happen," but, he adds, in an evolutionary rather than a revolutionary process.[30] That day will not occur for at least several decades, during which time the cash-crime syndrome will continue exacting its toll. This cost is so heavy in lost lives, grief, physical pain, economic loss, and social disruption—matching the impact of actual war—that its perpetuation cannot be justified.

On the other hand, the e-money industry has shown the way. Almost every cash transaction can now be accomplished electronically. Bankcard and e-cash companies continue to demonstrate and prove this point. They have recently moved into the fast-food market, where payments had previously been exclusively in cash, averaging less than $5. E-money can be used in vending machines, for personal exchanges of "money," and for transfers over the Internet. Toll roads that collect fares electronically as cars drive through at high speeds are already operational in the United States. There can be little doubt that the technology is available to make ourselves completely cashless.

The *American Banker* article mentioned earlier about the prospect of a cashless society did not discuss the possibility of a system created specifically to replace cash; it merely surveyed opinions about the impact of current private-sector e-money systems on cash. In June of 1994, *POS NEWS*,[31] a debit-card industry publication, published an article about a research booklet this author wrote entitled "Reducing Crime by Eliminating Cash." In preparing that article, *POS NEWS* contacted several EFT industry experts, including Thomas Tremain, vice president for electronic banking at First National Bank of Chicago. Although Mr. Tremain questioned the article's proposed federal electronic money system, he responded that "[Warwick's plan] should not be dismissed out of hand." Liam Carmody, president of New Jersey–based Carmody and Bloom, an

EFT consulting firm, apparently intrigued with the idea of replacing cash, commented that "within 10 years, we could make it happen. We could eliminate cash if it were a national mandate."

Absent such a mandate, our near future may look like this: The growing usage of credit and debit cards, as well as e-cash, will gradually usurp a greater portion of cash activity, yet never eliminate it. Capitalizing on the preference for convenience, industry will continue picking off limited types of cash payments from which it can profit, as it has done in the fast-food industry. It will leave untouched certain unprofitable and/or undesirable cash areas, including drug trafficking and the huge underground economy. Thus, Americans may be left to suffer the continued prevalence of cash crimes and the inequities of the underground economy. Not to be overlooked in this scenario is the economic discrimination that increasingly concentrates the perils of cash in the lowest socioeconomic groups. Moreover, any significant shift of cash to e-cash systems might infuse a raft of other economic concerns.

MONEY LAUNDERING

The amount of cash generated from crime in the United States is so enormous that handling it is a problem. U.S. currency notes weigh about one gram each, with about 450 bills to the pound. A week's take for a local drug distributor, perhaps $227,000 in $10 bills, weighs about 50 pounds and is not easily transported, stored, or negotiated without the risk of flagging attention.

Thus, criminals launder cash to make it look legitimately derived. The process has become a specialized activity in itself, often conducted by independent money-laundering experts. These service providers typically work on a percentage basis for laundering the funds. Law enforcement officials estimate that up to $300 billion in U.S. currency is laundered each year.[32] This not only indicates the high cost of crime in the United States but also underscores the insidious relationship of cash and crime.

Money laundering begins with dirty money; money is dirty either because it is generated through illegal acts—for example, drug sales, receiving stolen property, prostitution, and bribery—or because, even if generated legally, it is the subject of tax evasion.

Although money laundering is a felony, this law is actually aimed at halting the crimes that produce the cash in the first place. A report to the president on organized crimes states that "drug sales, gambling, or other crimes that generate cash are pointless if the cash cannot be spent. Without laundering, the risk/reward ratio for the underlying crime is unattractive."[33] Money-laundering analysts at the Government Accounting Office (GAO) point out that "[a]side from perpetuating crime, money laundering deprives the nation of billions in tax revenues. Further, laundered funds can be used to undermine and manipulate legitimate businesses, corrupt public officials and institutions, and threaten the stability of governments."[34]

Choking off the avenues through which criminals legitimize illicit cash is very difficult. Anti–money-laundering strategies are reminiscent of urban police crackdowns on drug activity, which often result in drug dealers moving to the next block or adjacent neighborhood and taking up business as usual. When drug traffickers, under pressure from law enforcement in southern Florida, moved much of their money laundering operations to California, it was soon reported that California was suddenly swimming in cash. [35]

Analogous to the police-pressure-and-relocation cycle is the series of legislative crackdowns on money laundering and the innovative reactions of criminals, who merely design new schemes to avoid being snared. This legislative-action and dodging routine began with the Bank Secrecy Act of 1970 (BSA), Congress's first major assault against money laundering. It required financial institutions to file a Currency Transaction Report (CTR) for each deposit, withdrawal, or other transaction involving cash in an amount exceeding $10,000. (The amount is now $3,000.) As an additional measure to help track the flow of illicit cash, the government required that a Report of International Transportation of Currency or Monetary Instruments (CMIR) be completed when currency or monetary instruments exceeding $10,000 are transported into or out of the United States. A Report of Foreign Bank and Financial Accounts must also be filed by owners of, or persons with authority over, foreign bank accounts exceeding $10,000. Casinos must report large cash transactions on a special IRS form as well.

To avoid detection through CTRs, criminals began using businesses as fronts to purchase and sell various expensive items, such as cars, jewelry, and real estate, as a means of legitimizing illicit cash. In response to such circumvention, Section 6050I was added to the Internal Revenue Code (IRC) in 1984. It requires any person engaged in a trade or business who receives more than $10,000 in cash payments in a single transaction or series of related transactions to file a report on an IRS Form 8300 giving details and the identity of the payer. Thus, car dealers, jewelers, and other specified businesses must also report cash transactions. Willful failure to comply with IRC Section 6050I, as with the BSA reporting requirement, is a felony. Although originally intended as a means of identifying tax evaders, the use of Form 8300 has been extended to any federal law enforcement agency (even for non–tax-related purposes).

During this same period, drug traffickers began laundering money by sending it offshore. To check this flow, Congress enacted the Anti–Drug Abuse Act (1988), which includes Section 4702, known as the "Kerry Amendment," aimed at combating international narcotics trafficking. This section provides for cash transaction reporting to the United States by foreign countries. It calls for negotiation of agreements with target countries, coordination with the respective law enforcement, customs, and other pertinent factions of such countries. It also provides, if necessary, the imposition of sanctions against such countries for failure to cooperate with the United States. However, a GAO report states, "Some countries may view section 4702 as an extraterritorial action and decline to negotiate on this basis" and (quoting "Treasury"), " 'It is virtually impossible to assure that countries that negotiate 4702 agreements will take adequate measures to assure full and accurate currency reporting. Our experience with the Bank Secrecy Act has demonstrated that without rigorous enforcement compliance is elusive.' "[36]

More recent government legislation dealing with tracking of illicit cash focuses on domestic cash purchases of bank checks and drafts, cashier's checks, money orders, and traveler's checks.[37] It requires the issuer of any of these instruments, if made for $3,000 or more in cash, to keep a chronological log with entries detailing each issuance and verifying the identity of each purchaser. Among other requirements, if the purchaser is not a previous account holder of the issuer, the latter must log the purchaser's Social Security number or alien ID number and date of birth.

Not every cash transaction of $3,000 or more must be reported by banks. A bank may unilaterally exempt itself from reporting cash proceeds generated by certain types of business operations. This includes retail businesses, sports arenas, racetracks, amusement parks, bars, restaurants, hotels, vending-machine companies, theaters, and public utilities. Special exemptions can be obtained for other businesses, including auto repair shops, bowling alleys, car washes, dry cleaners, golf courses, and ski resorts. However, certain types of business are never exempted, including dealerships that buy and sell cars, boats, or aircraft.[38]

Some states have enacted their own antilaundering statutes. However, these laws often define the reporting requirements and elements of the offense in discordant ways. As of June 1992, some 22 states had such legislation. To date, the complexities of interstate activity and federal reporting make such statutes, at least for prosecuting money laundering, of questionable value.

Until 1985, the volume of CTRs filed with the Treasury Department amounted to only a few hundred thousand a year. That was before a $500,000 penalty was levied against the Bank of Boston for failure to file CTRs to cover the forwarding of $1.16 billion in cash to several European banks. Word of the stiff penalty spread quickly among bankers, and filings of CTRs shot up to 3.6 million the next year. In 1986, new legislation made such omissions by financial institutions a crime. Faced with the possibility of being heavily fined, as well as prosecuted, banks are reluctant to avail themselves of the exemption provisions. The penalties remain stiff:

In 1994, a $100 million penalty was levied against a bank for money laundering.

After the Bank of Boston fine, when almost all financial institutions began complying with BSA requirements, bankers noticed a pandemic army of runners making cash deposits of just under the $10,000 threshold. Someone likened them to the little blue cartoon characters called "smurfs," and the name stuck. In 1987, Congress enacted antismurfing legislation making it a crime to "structure" cash transactions so as to evade the cash-reporting laws.

In 1990, the Treasury Department established the Financial Crimes Enforcement Network (FinCEN) to support law enforcement agencies, both domestic and foreign. Its job was to analyze cash data. This comprehensive network has enlisted all segments of private industry that deal in cash and employs virtually every division of law enforcement. It also works with foreign law enforcement agencies, Interpol, the Financial Action Task Force, the Basle Committee, and the United Nations. Thus, massive amounts of cash transaction data is funneled from these various sources (although 95 percent is from CTRs) to FinCEN, where, using advanced computers, it is scrutinized and analyzed in sophisticated profiling programs.

In 1992 alone, nine million CTRs were filed, representing $417.6 billion in currency transactions. As of April 1993, 49.8 million CTRs had been filed. The GAO reports that the number of CTRs being filed increases yearly and that the number on file by 1997 could exceed 92 million. At the average cost to banks of $9 for preparing and filing each CTR, this will have cost them and their customers almost $1 billion. The federal government can hardly process the vast harvest of CTRs, Forms 8300, and other cash transaction reports it has accumulated over the years. Consequently, it has reversed gears and is now urging financial institutions to make full use of the exemption provisions for filing CTRs.

Money-laundering cases can be highly complex and time consuming. "Certain prosecutors assert that because money laundering cases often require an extensive amount of analysis, once prosecutors are assigned, they are unable to work on other cases."[39] The GAO reports that "federal resources may be insufficient to address the problem of money laundering on the scale that is required."[40] Much of the problem centers on the lack of reporting by businesses and trades, as required by IRC Section 6050I, and on incompleteness and errors in such reports when they are filed. Moreover, information from 6050I reports, until recently, was not generally available to states. The GAO recommends greater dissemination of such data to, and involvement of, state law enforcement agencies and comments that "combating money laundering is going to require a long-term, sustained effort by federal authorities."[41]

It is difficult to find a "body count" in the form of money-laundering convictions that would presumably measure the success of antilaundering laws. Between 1987 and 1989, IRS prosecutions alone resulted in convictions of over 1,000 money launderers. However, the true impact of anti–money-laundering efforts is hard to measure. Money laundering is not prosecuted as a separate law enforcement priority by the Justice Department; it is treated as part of the overall activities involved in drug, white-collar, and other crimes. These are attacked in a number of ways, including narcotics crimes charges and seizure of illicit profits. While the primary objective is to immobilize underlying crime by making laundering impossible, a variety of criminal charges, including money laundering as well as seizures, are used to achieve this end.

Law enforcement agencies assert that financial data supplied through cash transaction reports are extremely valuable investigative and prosecutive tools in the war on crime. Some say anti–money-laundering efforts are beginning to pay off. However, if such efforts are aimed at reducing the nation's drug-abuse problem, this claim is unsupported by evidence. Pronouncements from recent administrations that the war on drugs is being won are put in question by emergency-room statistics showing increases in the numbers of drug addicts. As the years pass, more and more Americans dismayingly conclude that America's illegal drug problems are permanent.

Beginning with enactment of the BSA in 1970 and with the addition of subsequent antilaundering legislation, including Treasury, IRS, and other regulation, as well as with foreign data-sharing agreements and treaties, the federal government has constructed an elaborate, worldwide cash observation system. Yet, for all the government's effort to counter it, money laundering is a bigger business than ever.[42] Illegal drug sales, which account for the overwhelming percentage of laundered cash, are clearly flourishing in America. It is arguable that crime would be worse without antilaundering efforts, but it is dubious whether the antilaundering approach to stopping underlying crime can ever overcome a basic barrier, namely, the lack of any direct recordation in the currency transaction itself.

This obtuse approach leaves law enforcement twice or more removed from underlying crimes, making the global antilaundering scheme reminiscent of U.S. listening posts that surrounded the former Soviet Union— listening posts that often failed at detection. The government's observation system suffers from incomplete and erroneous reporting, a horrendous amount of data that even the fastest computers cannot process, leaks through international electronic funds transfers, and criminals who often remain one devious step ahead of law enforcement. To follow the analogy, if cash were transformed into a record-producing electronic payment medium, it would be tantamount to another perestroika. Currency, money laundering, and government countermeasures would fall by the wayside as historical phenomena. New e-money records, available to law enforcement within legal constraints, would facilitate direct investigation and prosecution of underlying crimes.

THE UNDERGROUND ECONOMY

The underground economy is a problem of major proportions in the United States that saps tens of billions of dollars in annual revenues from administrations at all levels. In an ongoing gross injustice, it burdens responsible U.S. taxpayers with the obligations of tax evaders. Yet, despite huge unrealized revenues and inequity, it is not the subject of a government "war" and receives little coverage in news media. The reason, of course, is that no one knows what to do about it.

The average citizen has little comprehension of the problem. Many undergrounders themselves do not realize the collective gravity of their omissions, typically considering their roles too small to have much effect, and moral restraint is easily cast aside. Researchers on income-tax compliance report:

It also became clear that there is a general belief that on-the-side vendors are evading tax obligations. Furthermore, the generally expressed view was that such tax evasion was only a little wrong: like driving 60 miles an hour [when the speed limit was 55]. If one gets caught, one pays the fine, but it is a minor and technical violation of an unjust law. Indeed, the view was frequently expressed that taxes were unjustly distributed because "loop holes" allowed persons with large incomes to avoid paying their fair share. Informal economy transactions were seen by some as do-it-yourself tax reform. (*Income Tax Compliance Research*, Internal Revenue Publication 1415: Appendix G, p. 7)

Cash is the chief lubricant for the gears of America's vast underground economy. Concurrently referred to as the "irregular," "informal,"or "subterranean" economy, this is a world of "moonlighting," "working off the books," and "working on the side." Most economists term it the "unobserved," "unreported," or "unrecorded" economy. Whatever its title, conversion from our currency and coin system to an auditable electronic system is likely to throw a wrench in the works.

Undergrounders avoid documentation and recordation of business dealings by transacting mostly in cash. They typically omit filing required forms and reports or sales reports; and most notoriously, of course, they fail to report income on tax returns. All of us have had some contact with undergrounders, via domestics, contractors, informal salespeople, and others requesting payment in cash.[43]

Investigations reveal that laundromat owners often keep two sets of books and hide up to half of their income, while hotel agents commonly fail to report commissions received for booking reservations with tour companies. IRS officials comment that a lot of underground activity occurs in construction, auto repair, restaurants, hair and nail shops, and farming. IRS studies indicate that many professionals, self-employed, and small business owners report less than half their incomes. "The most obvious way to evade tax is you sell 2,000 bucks worth of stuff, take $500 out of the till, and start your tax accounting with $1,500 of sales," says a tax official.[44]

The underground economy has been studied in depth, and much has been written about it. Yet, no one claims to know its actual size or can accurately determine the proportion of "legal" (aside from tax evasion) versus "illegal" (e.g., sales of stolen property) activity conducted in it. It is difficult to assemble statistics, for, as the IRS reports, "Part of the fundamental problem is the extreme, almost unmanageable diversity of this sector, which covers transactions ranging from the sale of deer hides or fox pelts to the informal distribution of minicomputer software."[45]

Analyzing the structure of the underground economy is impeded by an absence of normal bookkeeping. According to the IRS,

Enterprises in the informal sphere will seldom, if ever, involve more than a handful of close associates; very frequently, the going concern will consist of a lone entrepreneur who has built up a small clientele from personal networks. Thus, the extent of participation in the informal sector can rarely be directly gleaned from formal business records. Furthermore, tax evasion aside, the nature of such an entrepreneur's activity is typically not conducive to the keeping of books and records. For example, having few employees and no formal organization to maintain, this entrepreneur has little self-induced motivation to keep accurate books and records; internal controls have no meaning for such a business. In a cash intensive operation, there may also be minimal incentive to keep more than a very general track of business success.[46]

This is not just a world of small deals. Transactions in real estate, precious gems, luxury automobiles, major construction equipment, art, and other big-ticket items are commonly subjects of tax evasion, and the transactions are often carried out in cash.[47]

Little attention was paid to tax evasion and covert cash transactions in the United States until World War II, when price controls, rationing, and higher income tax rates gave rise to the "black market." The first size estimates for the underground economy appeared in the late 1950s. Almost all studies of the underground economy in the United States have focused on its effect on federal income tax revenues; few note how it impacts state income and sales taxes or how it shortchanges local regulatory fees—areas accounting for additional billions of dollars in lost revenues.

CHAPTER 3

REPLACING CASH WITH
ELECTRONIC MONEY

INITIAL CONSIDERATIONS

Implementing a central plan to make America's currency electronic is
clearly at odds with the way electronic payment media developed in the
United States. Today's diverse EFT systems are hardly the result of a grand
plan. Rather, they are the products of competing enterprises that capital-
ized on incremental technological advancements. They represent investments in a variety of novel payment systems, an innovative process that
continues today. Yet, for reasons stated earlier, that process will not displace all cash in America, at least not in the near future. Thus, if cashlessness is made a national objective, it is incumbent on government to
take the reins and lead from above. Otherwise, the nation will lose out
on profound potential benefits.

Some would regard federal electronic currency as an undue governmental interference with industry. Some officials have already voiced as
much. Yet, issuance of money has been a governmental prerogative from
time immemorial. Any assertion that government has no legitimate role
in electronic money is as spurious as the assertion that federal electronic
currency would "stifle innovation."

The common tripartite definition of money as "a system of exchange,
a unit of value, and a repository of value" is still valid, of course. But, this
definition best fits money in tangible form, especially in coinage. With e-
money in mind, it becomes more difficult to conceptualize. As tangible
currency disappears, this old definition of money could become useless.

Electronic payment technology and the older concept of money are at
a crossroads, for we are in a period of monetary transition. It seems in-

evitable that some day money will become completely electronic. Our grandchildren may have as much use for the word "money" as we do for "buttonhook." Instead of "money," perhaps in the future people will simple refer to their "credits" or "payment assets." Other words associated with cash transactions may go by the wayside as well. For example, the word "change" as used in a cash transaction. On the other hand, these terms might take on new meanings or retain limited aspects of today's meanings. "Cash," for example, in an all-electronic-payment world, might refer only to an immediate payment, as opposed to a credit transaction.

Martin Meyer likes to say that one of the greatest achievements of capitalism is the invention of titles to money. Titles to species, titles on conditions, letters of credit, and other negotiable instruments paved the way to modern banking. Electronic money, however, can incorporate all the features of these instruments and easily surpass them with incomparable flexibility, options, security, and speed. The advent of EFT is at least as great a milestone as the invention of titles to money. Indeed, it underlies a new genre of methods to keep, exchange, and transfer value.

Forerunners emerged as wire-transfer operations and interbank electronic payment networks. Consumer-oriented credit, debit, and ATM networks followed. E-cash is inchoate. Future EFT-based systems are on the drawing boards or have yet to be invented. Money as we have known it is being transformed.

The established forms of money are not simply being replaced by a new kind of money; they are being replaced by software. Software engineers write payment programs, programs that follow keypad, keyboard, voice, and other biometric input. They read bankcards and checks, count dollar amounts, debit and credit accounts, send messages to other computers to do the same, and more. One's value resides as credits in software—and not necessarily just in one software program. Interactive software programs that link computers give new dimensions to financial values. Defining the values that are processed in modern EFT systems in terms of traditional money does not seem to fit.

Definitions of money typically state its base truths, yet a definition of money is not some formula found in the rules of nature. Like numbers themselves, money is man-made. Moreover, money is not static; it tends to transform over time. Money's metamorphosis from a thing to an intangible, dispels an earlier reality as to what money comprises. Now we find ourselves in the midst of a quantum leap. In this era of monetary transition, any attempt to establish a definition of tomorrow's ultimate monetary systems is mere speculation. Moreover, as interesting as this digression may be, it is of little utility in determining how best to achieve cashlessness.

What kind of electronic system would best be employed to replace a nation's cash—e-cash, debit-card money, a combination, or something yet to be devised? Who would run it—the private sector, government, or both? These are the fundamental questions that face planners. Some have already come up with answers. (More on this in "Organizing Private-Sector E-currencies," in Chapter 4). Before delving into these issues, however, perhaps it is worth considering whether today's cash payments would automatically flow into any newly devised electronic currency system or whether events might take some unexpected turn.

Several years back, I contacted an internationally renowned bankcard expert and propounded the idea to him of making all currency electronic. I wanted to know whether computers could be designed to handle the huge number of transactions negotiated in cash—at that time about $300 billion annually.[1] He assured me that computer capacity is nearly limitless. But I was surprised by his skepticism about the prospect of converting everyone from cash to electronic currency. He commented that from his experience in continental Europe at the end of World War II, at a point when cash was nearly nonexistent, he would expect that in a cashless environment all sorts of physical objects, ranging from gold to food, would emerge to be used as alternative money.

The warning, from the lips of this respected EFT expert, that such a rudimentary form of exchange might compete with electronic money alarmed me; perhaps I had neglected an important possibility. Upon reflection, however, I realized his comment was spurious; that he failed to distinguish the collapsed economies of Europe, where money of any sort was virtually nonexistent, from a healthy modern setting in which electronic money would be ubiquitous, stable, and easily negotiated.

He was not alone in his opinion. Others with whom I have discussed the matter have also queried whether alternative money and barter might emerge in a cashless environment. One pointed out that despite its official replacement, czarist currency remained in use long after the Bolshevik Revolution and suggested the same might occur in the United States. Therefore, let us take a look at cash alternatives and barter and imagine the roles each might play in a post-cash environment.

CASH ALTERNATIVES

Cash alternatives, by historic definition, are chattels used in lieu of cash. Cigarette money used in prisons is a good example. A cash alternative is an unconventional form of money used in multisequential transactions, typically created out of necessity by individuals lacking the normal payment media.

Widespread use of cash alternatives emerges when commercial and official currencies are in short supply or unavailable or have become worthless. Such conditions can occur because of inadequate minting, printing, or distribution of currency or because of inflation or the collapse of a government.

Carpenter's nails served as alternative money in colonial America. Beaver skins (generally worth two English shillings), wampum, tobacco, and many other items were also popular as money. Merchant's tokens were used on a large scale in the United States as early as 1837. Although gold was plentiful during the California gold rush, there was a dire shortage of small coinage, hence the use of merchant's tokens such as "Jackson Tokens" and "Hard Times Tokens." These also served as advertising vehicles, and many bore inscriptions such as "Good for One Beer at Smitty's Tavern."

Cash-alternative chattels are poor substitutes for real cash because they suffer inexact value and often are physically inconvenient. They also might fail to emerge in a cashless world because the conditions that would evoke them would not exist: The new electronic money would itself serve as a dependable, convenient payment medium meeting everyone's transaction requirements. Merchants in the cashless society would refuse to accept cash alternatives just as they would today. Clearly, if merchants refuse to accept such devices as payment, they would have little value to the public in general.

Nor would criminals accept them. Crime would not come to a halt upon the removal of currency and coin from circulation. However, criminals would not begin to use some unconventional form of money or somehow continue to use defunct currency, because the ultimate application of all payment media is the legitimate marketplace. An all-criminal economy in which some unique currency can be used to fulfil criminals' needs does not exist. Criminals, like everyone else, seek and acquire money so that they can spend it: They buy cars, food, housing, clothing, and other goods and services in the open market just as law-abiding citizens do.

BARTER

In the original cashless society, when the concept of ownership was nonexistent or at best vague, individuals hunted for or simply took possession of what they needed or desired. In a purely communist system, according to theory, private ownership does not exist; goods are simply handed to those in need of them, without any exchange or the use of money. Simple barter is one stage up from that arrangement.

To barter is to trade by exchange of goods or services without the use of money. Informal barter requires a close matching of people's needs. It commonly involves items of uncertain value. Thus, barter has two basic drawbacks: First, the seller of goods must also be a buyer of goods. Second, it lacks a common denominator by which to evaluate goods. Historically, the first defect was solved by the use of "primitive money," or an item, that, although not desired for use by a seller, would be accepted by him because he could use it in a subsequent barter with some third party. Thus, weapons, rings, barley, and livestock were commonly used as "primitive money" to facilitate barter. In some cases, references to market values, in terms of currency, serve as a denominator. Five gallons of gasoline and a movie ticket may be dollar equivalents, for example. This is less clear when the items bartered consist of used/homemade goods and, particularly, services.

An IRS report, based on surveys of households across the United States during the years 1981, 1985, and 1986, indicates that barters by individuals, carried out independently of any organized barter club or association, averaged $9.8 billion annually during the mid-1980s.[2] Examples of informal barters include a used car for an outboard motor, bushels of apples for pruning services, and a hot meal for chopping wood.

Simple barter, because it is patently impractical for general commerce, would hardly emerge as a significant replacement for cash. It is difficult to imagine how the typical American would pay his rent, utility bills, groceries, and other expenses by means of barter, even with the aid of primitive money. Criminals and undergrounders would find barter just as unusable as anyone else. Simple barter, in a cashless environment, would simply remain at its present activity level.

Formal organized barter is quite a different operation. Moreover, it is high volume and big business. According to the International Reciprocal Trade Association, based in Great Falls, Virginia, barter trade in North America reached $9.1 billion in 1996. This is up from only $930 million in 1974 and $5.9 billion in 1991. Formal barter in the United States is growing at a rate 15 percent per year.[3] It is expanding around the globe.

In contrast to the backyard deals the term "barter" brings to mind, this type of formal barter is conducted through for-profit barter exchanges whose business members use it as a financial tool and marketing device. Members usually pay a retainer fee to join and pay a percentage of each barter as a commission, typically 10 percent. As of 1996, some 686 barter exchanges in the United States were serving 408,000 business clients. The average formal trade volume per trade exchange client is $3,500.[4]

Barter exchanges play the role of third-party accommodators by issuing transferable credits in exchange for goods and/or services. In this manner, barters can involve more than two parties. In one case, a landscaper who owed money to a hardware store offered to pay the debt in lawn services. The store owner was not interested. The landscaper consulted a barter exchange, and ultimately the store owner let the landscaper off the hook in exchange for barter credits that could be used to acquire whatever other goods or services were available through the exchange. In another case, a florist provided flower arrangements to a financially troubled hotel in exchange for a bank of rooms. The florist then transferred the hotel accommodations to a trucking company in exchange for billboard advertising on the latter's trucks.

For a number of reasons, formal barter is not a medium likely to be used in lieu of cash. First, the types of barters conducted through for-profit exchanges are negotiated deals sometimes requiring weeks or months to put together. Such barter involves commercial sales that, even if consummated in nonbarter form, would almost always involve noncash payment media such as checks, drafts, or wire transfers. This has little in common with and would hardly serve to replace the typical cash transaction. Moreover, as formal barter provides no protection in evading income taxes, it would not serve tax cheats who today use cash for that purpose. "The IRS has full access to all the records and transactions of all the barter exchanges, and we do periodically check the barter exchange records," says Larry Wright, an IRS spokesman.[5] Barter exchanges must submit returns to the IRS on the barter sales of their clients.

The last couple of decades have also witnessed the emergence of a different breed of barter exchanges. Better described as clubs, these are typically small and local, and they operate on a nonprofit basis for the benefit of their trading members. In theory, at least, they are more a challenge to cash than other forms of barter. Proponents explain, rather defiantly, that the prime purpose of such exchanges is to provide an alternative to fiat currency, in particular, the U.S. dollar, which they assert is often "manipulated" by government as "a fraud on the populace."[6] This category of barter includes diverse media of exchange that are designed to be independent, to a greater or lesser extent, of conventional currency. To accomplish such independence, these "local currencies" generally employ local units of value that can be negotiated. Thus, goods and services provided by or available from exchange members are appraised in terms of such units.

One of the earliest of such nonprofit barter exchanges is known as LETS (Local Employment and Trading System) and began in Vancouver Island, British Columbia, Canada, in 1983. Some ten LETS systems operate in the United States. It has seen far greater success in Australia, New Zealand, and England, which cumulatively account for several hundred chapters. This system uses a computer bulletin board on which members can request or offer goods of services. Each member has an account that is credited for goods or services given or performed and is debited for those received. Thus, a member may have a credit balance or a debit balance, the latter of which imposes an obligation for future performance. Values are negotiated directly between parties.

At variance is the nonprofit barter exchange called "Ithaca Hours," a system established in New York in 1991. In lieu of the LETS computer, this system employs a paper currency, Ithaca Hours, pegged to the U.S. dollar. An Ithaca Hour generally equals the average hourly wage for the county where it is negotiated. Goods and services sought and offered are published in an exchange newsletter. This system is being emulated in several other cities around the United States.

In the same vein, other nonprofit barter exchanges issue scrip, or "discount coupons," that are used in place of currency. One innovator, Ralph Borsodi, attempted to establish a currency not pegged to the dollar; more with a purpose of averting inflation, it was based on the aggregate of a "basket" of commodities.

All these nonprofit systems combined involve insignificant activity. By 1994, Ithaca Hours had issued only the equivalent of $48,000. Clearly, these operations appeal to a distinct minority of individuals, particularly those with a lot of time on their hands. Though it may be the dream of some "local currency" advocates that such barter and other alternative money systems might some day displace the use of government currency, that is all it amounts to.

SIMPLY ABOLISHING CASH

It is sometimes suggested, usually flippantly, that cash be abolished, with the conjecture that other existing payment media, particularly e-monies, would somehow fill in for it.[7] That is a rather unlikely outcome, for cash performs unique functions. It cannot be summarily withdrawn from circulation without disastrous consequences.

Granted, if cash were suddenly to become nonexistent, some percentage of cash volume would immediately shift to and be absorbed by checking and bankcard systems. However, a quarter of American households have no bank relationship at all. Tens of millions of Americans do not carry bankcards, and e-cash systems are, as yet, incipient. Moreover, bankcard systems operate only through EFT terminals deployed only at POS. Many merchants with very small or infrequent receipts, such as newspaper vendors and handymen, are not equipped for bankcard payments, because it is uneconomical to invest in a terminal and pay the higher discount percentages that banks charge small merchants. Moreover, no established electronic payment system is available by which individuals, for example, family members and friends, can transfer funds from one to the other.

Absent some sort of government subsidy, it is unclear whether banks or card issuers will ever equip and service very low volume and/or noncommercial transactions, for it is difficult to profit from them. EFT devices necessary to replace cash payments at toll gates, parking meters, and in vending machines are just now coming into service. A decade or two could easily elapse before the entire country converts to such payment methods.

That said, private-sector e-money systems could be modified so that cash could be abolished. Some two decades ago, recognizing the dark role cash plays in crime, Leon M. Lederman, noted physicist and director of the Fermi Laboratory, and Stuart Speiser, a New York aviation attorney, separately espoused replacement of cash with private-sector debit-card systems.[8] Because their proposals were made when EFT was still in its infancy and before the use of bankcards had penetrated the consciousness of most Americans, their recommendations were not seriously considered.

Neither proponent explained exactly how private-sector debit-card systems would replace cash. Both merely pointed out that such systems had already been developed and suggested they could be adapted to replace cash. They were on the right track.

ADOPTING A CASH-FREE POLICY

For government to adopt a policy of making America cash free, officials clearly would first have to be convinced of the forthcoming benefits. Yet, this is the easiest hurdle. The more difficult aspects of persuading government lie in addressing other basics.

One is unlikely to find anyone in government who would defend the perpetual use of cash or who opposes the idea of a cashless America. However, many officials seem fixed in their exclusive commitment to the private sector to develop and deploy EFT money systems; if they think about cashlessness at all, they think of it only in an evolutionary context. Much more on their minds are deep concerns about government "stifling innovation" or impeding progress in industry.

Companies in the consumer EFT industry, properly geared as they are to earning profits, do not need to make America cashless to achieve their goals. To the contrary, costs involved in doing so, such as servicing the poor, infrequent users, and remote locales, tend to work against profits. If true cashlessness ultimately results from industry's innovations, which might be a very long time from now, that is all right with industry; if some cash remains in circulation, that is all right, too. Indeed, if such cash is used in illicit activities or if the types of transactions would be uneconomical for industry to replace electronically, then all the better. Ignore those areas, or let government deal with them. Industry enjoys its freedom to pick and choose.

Nor does industry have the ability to stop the public from using today's cash. To make America truly cashless, cash would have to be either deliberately removed from circulation or effectively displaced by electronic money systems so attractive that the public totally abandoned the use of cash. Clearly, only government can halt the printing, minting, and distribution of cash. Only it can remove its legal-tender status.

It is also unlikely that industry, even if motivated to do so, could convince the twelve million American households that lack a bank relationship to switch from cash to e-money. As well, the nontraceability of cash, unique amongst payment systems, gives it a value to criminals and tax evaders that puts other transaction modes out of the running. (This assumes that government will not tolerate deployment of anonymous types of e-cash.) Thus, no matter how popular various forms of e-money might become at large, elements of society will persist in using cash. Retailers will continue accepting it, most citizens will continue carrying at least a little of it, criminals will continue robbing for it and transacting in it, and the public, particularly cash-handling businesses, will continue paying the profound cost.

This hardly means that America lacks the means to make itself cashless. The necessary products and systems are at its disposal. Surpassing the ubiquitous bankcard terminals that Americans have used for decades, new contactless e-cash systems are being utilized for payments of auto tolls and bus and subway fares. Wireless terminals are used in taxis and boats and at vendor stands; with minimal modification, they could be used for interpersonal transactions as well.

Several years ago, I speculated that in a cashless world some uses of tangible cash would simply have to be foregone, citing the familiar Salvation Army kettle as an example. I've had to revise this, for I discovered that the Akron, Ohio, branch of the Salvation Army developed a kettle with a transaction terminal alongside, thus allowing donations via credit card. This device is not only safer for the bell-ringing worker, but it generates a receipt that the donor can use for tax purposes! Coincidentally, just two days later, I ran across a news article about of a rash of cash robberies from other Salvation Army kettles.

GOVERNMENT IS THE KEY

Until several years ago, many federal officials still remained detached from technical developments in credit, debit, and other consumer-oriented EFT systems. At least one reporter expressed dismay that officials in the Fed and the Treasury Department were oblivious to remarkable new e-cash payment systems being deployed internationally. Recent developments may be changing interest and attitudes.

E-cash, in both smart-card and computer-based forms, made its debut in the United States around 1995 and continues to unfold. In the smart-card version, e-cash emulates and targets currency and coin. Having finally penetrated government's thick walls, news of these payment systems sounded alarm in the Treasury Department and, to a lesser degree, in the Federal Reserve. Underlying their concern was, and is, that e-cash systems can operate outside the regulated banking arena, as well as internationally. Some e-cash systems generate few, if any, transaction records, thus providing fertile ground for criminals, tax evaders, and fraudulent businesses.

This inspired a series of congressional and Treasury Department hearings and conferences. A task force, composed of delegates from various units of government, was also established to study e-cash issues and to form responses. Today, a great deal of attention is being given by particular committees in Congress as well as in the Fed and the Treasury Department to electronic currency. Government, in general, has become quite cognizant of, if not active in, a variety of EFT payment applications. Washington's comprehension of EFT systems and the possibilities they offer, of course, is a prerequisite for any discussion of policy change about its active participation in consumer EFT.

Yet, in discussing this matter, it would be difficult for some officials to accept that government should take the lead in designing and deploying an electronic payment system, particularly one that would bump heads with elements of the payments industry. The long-standing policy relegating consumer EFT exclusively to the private sector shows no signs of fading. To the contrary, it is fortified by the current administration's zealous campaign to embrace the "information superhighway," which, in familiar refrain, cautions against government interference that might "stifle innovation." Vice President Gore's "A Framework for Global Electronic Commerce" states in bold (literally) that "the private sector should lead" and that "where government involvement is needed, its aim should be to support . . . an environment for electronic commerce. . . . its goal should be to ensure competition" (Internet website address: *http:// www.iitf.nist.gov/eleccomm/ecomm.htm*). Though this document is directed primarily at the Internet, it states under the heading "Electronic Payment Systems" that "[s]ome of the methods would link existing electronic banking and payment systems, including credit and debit card networks, with new retail interfaces via the Internet. 'Electronic money,' based on stored-value, smart card, or other technologies, is also under development." However, from this author's perspective, the most significant sentence in this document acknowledges that "[from] a longer term perspective, however, the marketplace and industry self-regulation alone may not fully address all issues. For example, government action may be necessary to ensure the safety and soundness of electronic payment systems, to protect consumers, or to respond to important law enforcement objectives."

CHAPTER 4

FEDERAL OR PRIVATE CURRENCIES?

Even if government officials were sufficiently convinced of the potential benefits of cashlessness to delve into the methods of bringing it into reality, many would remain unclear as to whether government should itself engage in e-currency operations or merely orchestrate industry to replace cash. It might, for example, follow Finland's approach by designating several of the nation's large banks to issue a common e-cash structured to replace cash. (Finland's e-cash, incidentally, is transacted anonymously, and fees are incurred for loading and unloading value to and from the cards). *Avant* electronic cash was launched in 1993 by Finland's central bank. This e-cash is issued and operated by Automatia Ltd., owned by Finland's three largest banks, which together have 90 percent of the market there (Internet website address: *http://www.avant.fi/newsline.html*).

The direct approach, that is, devising a federal e-currency system and gradually withdrawing cash from circulation, would not so much replace cash as it would transform it from a physical to an electronic payment medium. This is the most practical method, the least confusing, and one that would involve the fewest unknowns. A major advantage would be keeping the Federal Reserve System intact. This should, logically, ensure strong Fed support. Law enforcement divisions at all levels would be likely to endorse it. Members of Congress, perpetually in search of revenues, would highly value a system that could generate tens, if not hundreds, of billions each year. How such a system might work is illustrated by use of the model "Federal Electronic Currency" (FEDEC) later in this book (FEDEC, as used in this book, refers exclusively to Federal Electronic Currency, and has nothing to do with any other coincidental usage of the word.)

Even without a comprehensive scheme to make America cashless, the Treasury Department could conceivably issue some limited form of electronic currency. This possibility has already been voiced in Congress. But it would be more of an experiment, the purpose of which is unclear. (The implication from the suggestion, made during congressional hearings in 1995 dealing with private e-cash systems was that federal electronic currency would preempt private e-cash and avert the problematic monetary threat.) Yet, before any general-use electronic currency could be issued and, certainly, for it ever to grow and completely displace cash, basic components would have to be in place, including interchange with current payment systems, end-to-end security, and so on. If the merits of cashlessness are appreciated and sought by Congress, it seems prudent first to design those components for use in an overall plan before issuing any e-currency whatsoever. Once all the components for a full replacement system were designed, an initial limited issuance could be kept at that level or, optionally, used as pilot project for a subsequent expansion.

Many would argue that best and "natural" route to cashlessness, as well as the stream of EFT progress, lies in the private sector. Though it seems highly unlikely to many, including this author, that Americans could ever be persuaded that NationsBank banknotes or Mark Twain Bank banknotes, for example, were more stable, practical, and desirable than Federal Reserve notes, the concept of private currencies is held in high regard by influential factions. Urged by industries fearing a negative impact from federal e-currency, many legislators might find this approach more consistent with existing government consumer-EFT policy. They might opt for federal leadership and laws enabling the formation of a private-sector system, perhaps a consortium of bankcard companies, that would issue private e-currency and allow government to withdraw cash. Some of the general public, being familiar with bankcard money and lacking comprehension of some novel federal e-currency, might be persuaded to share this outlook.

Additional support for a private-sector approach would come from privacy advocates. In today's political atmosphere, apprehension about loss of privacy could well be the greatest hurdle in achieving cashlessness. Fear of Big Brother snooping by government is a common theme, if not politically correct. Recently discovered/created rights of privacy are zealously guarded on both political extremes. Moderate privacy advocates, in contrast, would balance social interests and give due weight to the argument that privacy is abused incomparably more by the private sector than by government. Thus, if support for e-currency is found among privacy advocates at all, at least a few might favor the federal-currency option.

Private-currencies proponents, especially banking and e-money industries, might sully the waters by denigrating federal policies and illuminating the bureaucratic inefficiency of the Fed. They would assert that industry created EFT, has the necessary experience to replace cash, can accomplish it faster and better, and, in fact, is already in the process of doing so. It might be typical to hear the testimony of spokespeople like EFT consultant Liam Carmody, who has no doubt that under a national mandate cash can be replaced by a national e-money system.[1] However, he believes that the private sector should be delegated the job, emphasizing the private sector's "necessary experience" and the danger of "serious privacy intrusions" by government. Probably the overwhelming majority of electronic payment experts who would be relied on by Congress would have financial stakes in the issue.

Of course, one can view industry, rather than government, as the encroaching party. The U.S. currency system, having been seasoned over the past century and a half, is a public asset. Government earns substantial income from it. Moreover, as we shall see, it is a far less complex undertaking merely to change the form of money than also to switch its operators.

The true threat that FEDEC would pose to industry depends on its design and scope, which might not be as all-dominant as some would imagine. FEDEC, as this author envisions it, would be limited to emulating today's currency and coin. In its optimal state it would comprise a government debit-card system in which everyone would have an account (termed by some economists an "accounting system of exchange"). FEDEC would interchange with private banking systems, and FEDEC reserves would be kept. With an open-frame construction, the federal system might also incorporate smart cards, perhaps like the dual system currently deployed by Holland's group of banks. It might employ combination cards like Germany's Geldkarte, which supports both value-stored transactions and online debit. Several systemic variations are possible.

FEDEC would not, however, provide credit, nor would it pay interest or operate over the Internet or in other non-face-to-face transactions—at least, not initially. Thus, the impact on credit-card and checking systems should be limited. Only e-cash, still an insignificant operation in the United States, would take a direct hit. Demand balances would not flood into government electronic currency, any more than they are converted to cash today. Indeed, retailers' FEDEC receipts and individuals' FEDEC funds would remain in FEDEC accounts for less time than it takes to deposit today's physical currency in banks, that is, before they were electronically shifted to various interest-bearing private-sector accounts.

PRIVATE-CURRENCY ADVOCACY

Aside from the motivations of certain interested factions for replacing cash with private currencies, as described above, the idea of switching to private currencies in lieu of government fiat monies is a popular economic theme. The most eminent theorist in this area was Nobel laureate F. A. Hayek, whose works are widely respected and who has influenced many economists, including some in government. Inasmuch as we live in a transitional period in which private EFT systems are positioned to usurp governmental cash, some might deem it an appropriate time to put theory into practice, an opportunity that comes around only every few centuries or so. Thus, the pros and cons of the theory come into play as it pertains to the choice of methods of ending government currency.

As implausible as it is that Americans would ever favor, accept, and use a variety of bank-issued currencies in place of government currency, private-currency theory could easily play a role in blocking plans for federal electronic currency—as an element of uncertainty, as fuel for endless discussion and studies, and as fodder for indecision and delay. Thus, the tenets of the theory require examination and are discussed in several of the following sections.

This theory holds that currency stability can best be achieved by market forces in a world of privately issued currencies that are free from government manipulation. "Stability" here generally refers to control of inflation. The idea, in an overly simplified summary, is that mechanisms in such a world would restrain overissuance of currency and thus also inflation. Overissuing would be checked by negative clearing (as issuers would have to honor other issuers' notes). This safety mechanism would be made more acute by today's fast electronic communications. Consumer selection and competition in the marketplace would assure that only the most efficient money systems survive, according to the theory.

Proponents often find it necessary to explain away the troublesome 1837–1863 "wildcat banking era" in the United States, when the nation's only domestic currency consisted of private bank notes. The United States National Bank had been dissolved, and government had not (since the Continental Currency fiasco) begun issuing currency again. A fundamental problem developed with these private currencies in that their market value often was something less than face value, because of the lack of supporting specie or other backing. Merchants typically kept lists, called banknote detectors, indicating which notes were worthless or stating the percentage by which particular notes should be discounted. Bankruptcies of issuers was not uncommon, and fraud, as well as a lack of quick communication and transportation in those days, left many a note holder short.

Free banking proponents remind us that, historically, private currencies have been used in over 60 countries, pointing out periods in China, Sweden, and Scotland during which private monies allegedly functioned well. However, it is noteworthy that these currencies were generally specie backed. Just how pertinent these examples are to the issue at hand is thus questionable, for the likelihood of issuers of modern private-currency notes offering gold backing appears slight.

A few economists, "gold bugs," advocate a return to a gold standard. At least one e-cash company, World Trade Clearinghouse, has advertised that its money is "100% gold-backed." Species-based currency raises a number of old issues, including possible insufficiency of the gold supply, the effect of new gold-mining technologies, Bre-x frauds (in which the discovery of huge new goldfields proved false), and so on. Little enthusiasm is expressed among economists for a return to a gold standard. Gold is becoming less relevant in the 1990s, with a number of central banks selling off sizable percentages of their stocks.

Alternatively, government bonds might substitute for specie backing; or private insurance, analogous to FDIC coverage, or both might provide adequate guarantees. During the American 1863–1930 banking period, private bank-issued currencies were required by federal law to be 111 percent backed by U.S. bonds. This backing quelled the earlier instability. The state bank currencies of this period ultimately failed only because they suffered from reserve inadequacies during regional contractions. Ultimately, in 1913, the Federal Reserve System was established and gradually phased out state currencies. Yet, assuming that adequate security might be developed for modern private currencies, other concerns remain.

The argument that private-currency managers are more likely than central banks to produce stable currency systems is contestable. It assumes that private managers will be prudent and efficient in their currency operations. Yet, researchers recently concluded that profit-motivated institutions and governments tend to view risk differently. In "Do Markets and Regulators View Bank Risk Similarly,"[2] Professor John R. Hall and Federal Reserve economists Andrew P. Meyer and Mark D. Vaughan found that bank holding companies tend to accept nearly any risk if the anticipated return is sufficiently high. Governments (regulators), in contrast, stop short of any risk that might cause an institution to fail. Thus, facing the same options, a profit-dominated policy might lead to failure of a private currency, whereas the government system might survive. Further, as David A. Balto of the Federal Trade Commission observed, the profit motive sometimes drives banks to opt for the least-efficient money system. He noted that in the choice between on-line debit and riskier off-line debit, banks invest or promote off-line debit because they earn bigger transaction fees from it—2 percent of the transaction in off-line, as against a $.10 flat fee on-line.[3]

If the principal advantage of switching from public to private currencies is in checking inflation, then this is a poor period, historically, to argue the point. In 1998, it is not uncommon to hear some economists speculate that the United States may soon experience deflation. As Thomas C. Melzer, president of the Federal Reserve Bank of St. Louis, points out, the closer America gets to zero inflation, the less the private sector will be motivated to invest in alternative types of money. Also, the additional cost of using private currencies could itself be inflationary, for they would very likely require consumers to pay fees that generate profits, a factor absent in government currency. Thus, private currencies, for example, electronic debit and e-cash, carry with them a burden that, in effect, diminishes their net value.

Private-currency theory is often discussed in an abstract global scenario in which inherent counterbalances tend to ensure currency stability and make sense. Yet, if private currencies were to be transacted internationally, how and by whom would fee fixing, cartels, and other abusive practices be checked?

Even on the domestic scene, questions arise as to practicality, particularly as to fluctuations in relative value among multiple currencies. Suppose America had only private currencies at its disposal, each varying or having a propensity to vary from one another as to their relative accepted value. Would this require transacting parties always to designate a particular currency for payment? Would every security document, promissory note, agreement, and purchase on credit have to specify payment via one of several available currencies? Would currency exchanges be necessary? The common cash-using citizen, having to make choices among privately issued currencies and having to keep abreast of the latest monetary data as well as to switch accounts about, would find it all, relative to today, a big, time-consuming nuisance. Selecting from myriad payment structures, with the options, enhancements, and tie-ins that surely would be offered to consumers, would make today's choosing of telephone carriers seem like child's play. These collateral inefficiencies would more than offset any gains from no longer handling tangible cash.

One can argue that this objection can be rectified by referencing a neutral constant value. Some historical precedent exists: Variations in value between private currencies were sometimes adjusted by using an abstract denominator. In medieval Europe, diverse coinages (as many as 50 in Milan) found common ground by equating each to a nonexistent standard pound, lire, or livre.[4] Perhaps a "dollar" denominator could be used to adjust values between future private e-currencies in the United States. Computers could do the job automatically. But the idea of resorting to an imaginary dollar as part of a scheme to decommission the real thing verges on the absurd.

Absent federal currency, questions would also arise as to how government would replace its former resource for generating money in times of need, for instance, to raise funds in times of crisis or if such action were necessary in steering the economy. It is worth recalling that, although through acts of last resort, the American Revolution and the Civil War were partially financed through the issuance of government fiat currency. Government might never again employ such methods, but the idea of permanently giving up its power to do so could prove imprudent.

It is worth noting that employing FEDEC as a means of ending cash does not necessitate an exclusive and/or permanent election between government and private currencies. Thus, private-sector EFT systems might be allowed to compete; and as demonstrated in the following pages, FEDEC could coexist with credit- and debit-card systems and e-cash (the latter at least in its computer-based form). For various possible reasons, perhaps because certain private currencies might offer attractive features, such as payment of interest, they might prove more popular than the FEDEC with the public. Further, the election to transform cash to FEDEC does not necessarily preclude some future decision to dismantle it and to rely exclusively on private currencies.

Currency stability, the focal point of private currency advocates, is but a single, albeit major, attribute in organizing a nation's payment systems. Another attribute is the propensity of currencies for use in or, conversely, their facility to prevent crime and tax evasion. Also to be considered are their relative integrity in maintaining data privacy, cost and ease of usage, practicality of legal structure, and overall operational efficiency. Thus, even if private currencies might prove to be a superior check on inflation, these other attributes may favor a government payment system and, collectively at least, outweigh mere stability.

ORGANIZING PRIVATE-SECTOR E-CURRENCIES

America can be weaned away from cash in a variety of ways. The federal government has already taken advantage of EFT in its own affairs. Until recently, this has been aimed at eliminating payments and receipts by checks. The Treasury Department has also begun making arrangements with financial institutions to service those of the nation's previously unbanked individuals who currently receive federal checks so that they may be paid electronically. This will have the effect of reducing cash usage by most of these individuals, for their common habit is to negotiate government checks for currency. This practice feeds the vast check-cashing business in the United States. However laudable, the Treasury Department's effort to switch check recipients to EFT is limited to government payees.

Measures aimed at discouraging the general public from using cash could be taken, such as taxing cash transactions. For example, a federal tax could be levied directly on ATM cash withdrawals and on "cash back" as it is dispensed at POS. Government might also provide various tax incentives and subsidies for cash-replacing devices and systems, as well as remove legal tender from cash in targeted settings. Yet, as successful as such proddings might be, they would not bring an end to cash. For a variety of personal reasons, many individuals would continue using cash.

Part of the resistance would lie in the fact that available credit-, debit-, and smart-card systems do not yet provide practical counterparts for all cash transactions. For instance, they do not provide a way for individuals to make interpersonal electronic payments. Bankcards are not universally accepted by all merchants. Millions of small merchants, not to mention vending machines, are not EFT equipped. The various bankcard payment media do not always share interchange. Indeed, any premature effort to end the use of cash would likely result in increased usage of checks and money orders, decrease general payment efficiency, and create problems for banks.

In the 1990s, the bankcard EFT industry is not currently organized enough and lacks sufficient cohesion to replace federal currency. A creature of capitalism, it suffers fierce competition, periodic reformation of alliances, changing standards, and a lack of centralized leadership. It is hardly in a position to begin processing the several hundred billions of payments now conducted in cash. Even if it could overcome these obstacles, tooling up to handle the more than 85 percent of the nation's payments that cash represents would require substantial investment, and it could prove challenging to allocate the necessary contributions.

An initial approach to coordinating industry to handle the job would be for government to assemble a task force of representatives from various EFT firms. Clearly, many would be eager to participate in the potentially lucrative undertaking. The representatives could focus on the objective, coordinate ideas with government, and ultimately establish a team of designers, technicians, economists, and the like that would, in turn, structure a plan of operation. As part of the framework, for example, Visa USA and MasterCard might provide an initial network and services.

Privatizing a government-run enterprise is hardly novel. Governments around the world, expecially former socialist governments, have set precedents and established guidelines for the process. Though many such operations are unique, some are more difficult than others to privatize in a manner benefitting the public. For example, telecommunication companies (telecoms) are more difficult in this regard than mail operations. A nation's fundamental payment system is particularly difficult.

The objective a task force would face would involve far more than just taking cash issuance and operations out of government hands; that could be accomplished by chartering a single private bank, that is, by granting a monopoly, something akin to the old United States Bank. The objective requires creation of a system that ensures competition, efficiency, interchangeability, and value stability among multiple currency issuers. Against a background of missed goals in deregulating telecoms and cable

TV in the United States and given the gravity of the nation's basic money system, the job could prove daunting.

A means of approaching this endeavor might be to form a consortium of EFT firms, each providing the elements required for a framework within which multiple issuers could operate. Of course, this raises a raft of systemic and economic questions: Would the consortium act as a central issuer of independent e-currencies, thus doing the accounting for all such currencies, or would it merely act as a clearinghouse and governing body for its members, who would issue and manage their own currencies? Would each private currency somehow employ a new unit value, gold, for example; or would its value reference a nonexistent dollar; or would each be free to do its own thing? How would the consortium's e-currency(ies) interact and interchange with coexisting (nonconsortium) bankcard and checking systems? Would private e-currencies be self-governed by consortium specifications and/or by federal laws and regulations? Would the consortium comprise a giant bank with member branches, replicating the Federal Reserve System, or would it act more as a charterer of currency issuers? Who would underwrite the organizational costs?

Sholom Rosen has developed answers to at least some of these questions. In several patents, assigned to Citibank, N.A., he illustrates how an "electronic monetary system" would function. In an abstract to one of his patents (U.S. Patent Number 5,455,407, issued October 3, 1995), the idea is described as

an improved monetary system using electronic media to exchange economic value securely and reliably. The invention provides a complete monetary system having electronic money that is interchangeable with conventional paper money comprising (1) issuing banks or financial institutions that are coupled to a money generator device for generating and issuing to subscribing customers electronic money including electronic currency backed by demand deposits, or electronic credit authorizations; (2) correspondent banks that accept and distribute the electronic money; (3) a plurality of transaction devices that are used by subscribers for storing electronic money, for performing money transactions with the on-line systems of the participating banks or for exchanging electronic money with other like transaction devices; (4) teller devices, associated with the issuing and correspondent banks, for process handling and interfacing the transaction devices to the issuing and correspondent banks, and for interfacing between the issuing and correspondent banks themselves; (5) a security arrangement for maintaining the integrity of the system; and (6) reconciliation and clearing processes to monitor and balance the monetary system.

This elaborate monetary scheme is remarkable, among other of its features, because it comprises a system of multiple issuers and goes beyond the single-operator aspect of money systems exemplified by Mondex,

DigiCash, and others. Indeed, its paramount purpose appears to be the organization of multiple e-currency issuers into a network that would facilitate interchange and provide currency integrity as well as security. By its description, it integrates "conventional paper money," yet its breadth of design lends the system to a virtual replacement of such money. If Citibank is developing such e-currency schemes, its a good bet that virtually all other leading banks have similar blueprints in the making. Whether this type of scheme would provide meaningful competition between the e-currencies it encompasses forms a crucial issue in choosing between private and government currency systems.

Advocates of private currencies argue that the efficiency of competition between private currencies underlies their much-touted anti-inflationary attributes. Competition, however, requires that individual e-money issuers be allowed a degree of latitude vis-à-vis other currencies and freedom from rigid uniformity. The goals of universally negotiable currency and competition are at odds with one another. Maintaining an atmosphere of competition within an organized currency-issuer network, or consortium, could prove difficult.

One might argue that employing a currency consortium would create unnecessary organizational and operational issues. After all, an incipient infrastructure for replacing cash can be found in today's integrated ATM/POS networks, Internet accords, and mutual standards for smart cards. Protocols, interchange, and high-level security tools are increasingly being agreed upon by members of EFT industries. In a few years, with adjustments, extensions of service, and perhaps an infusion of government funding, existing e-systems might become capable of replacing cash.

Many would favor privatizing cash in this manner, that is, without a grand overall plan, but by infusing energy into the existing continuum and expanding new payment schemes and networks. This would simply speed up what many regard as an inevitable, progressive, and innocuous march toward cashlessness.

This discussion about private-sector mechanisms for supplanting cash has so far not addressed many fundamental economic changes that would concern citizens. Ending goverment money goes against convention and raises a number of red flags. Allowing the basic unit of measure to fall into the grip of the private sector, even with regulation and close governmental oversight, could mean the end of the federal monetary controls, of uniform money values, and of the legal and economic structures built on Federal Reserve notes. It raises questions as to whether the dollar would survive as an abstract unit of account for private currencies and, if so, for how long; and would the abstract dollar maintain its significance internationally?

Many economists are less than sanguine about the future impact of private e-monies on economies. Some point out that, even today, credit and liquidity risks threaten EFT payment networks. Such risks are capable of spreading worldwide in chain reaction and causing economic havoc. As a greater percentage of transaction volume finds its way into today's electronic money, government loses more control over it and becomes less effective in governing the national economy. With diminishing control over its currency, the Federal Reserve could conceivably lose the ability to exercise leadership or even to cooperate in adjusting international monetary policy to meet international economic exigencies. Some economists express concern that this trend undermines U.S. sovereignty.[5]

Concern rises as to whether the private e-currencies replacing cash would be subject to relatively easy manipulation by currency traders, or even by foreign governments. Conceivably, such currencies could become dominated through international mergers and acquisitions beyond the control of the American government, thus dashing the competition benefit of private currencies in checking inflation. Might a cartel of currencies, operating internationally, as do the world's oil companies, manipulate national economies?

The choice between government and private electronic currencies is far more than a question of whether the government can do a better job of servicing transactions than the private sector or an issue of which can do it more efficiently, check inflation best, or offer more user convenience, all of which many assume the private sector would excel in. Other important issues must be weighed in, including privacy, crime prevention, cost, and the impact of the dollar's integrity, matters to which FEDEC may be better suited.

PRIVACY EXPOSURE

The specter of the U.S. government closing down federal cash operations in favor of private e-money systems should alarm privacy advocates. While beards grow longer and whiter in the quixotic wait for "Big Brother" to wrest away personal liberties, it is evident, on the other hand, that bankcard payment data easily finds its way into private-sector databanks and into the general information stream, where it sometimes works adversely to the interests of citizens. Thus, placing today's cash transaction data in the hands of industry could compromise privacy by channeling transaction data to super credit bureaus, prospective employers, insurers, and others. Privacy advocates, looking to the future, have already expressed concern that if private-sector debit-card systems were to replace cash, banks would have an unprecedented opportunity to observe the financial affairs of their customers.[6]

This would not be a worry with some e-cash systems. DigiCash and Mondex, for example, offer far greater privacy than typical credit- and debit-card systems—indeed, greater than tangible currency, which can be marked and be observed changing hands. It is unlikely the U.S. government will condone the degree of privacy that such payment media offer. E-cash issuers might be required to maintain a verified identification record for each account holder and operational records showing the amounts of e-cash purchased, dates, and so on. After all, similar record keeping is already required in sales of traveler's checks and money orders.

E-cash might be reined in further by requiring traceability. With the use of stored-value smart cards that permit sequential off-line transactions, however, systemic and/or technological barriers would have to be overcome. This is an area being studied intensely by industry and government, both of which are concerned not only with secrecy from law enforcement but also with fraud that might be accomplished through multiple payments using the same unit of stored value. One of the ideas mentioned is a smart-card chip that keeps a record of transactions, something like an abstract of title that accompanies the card.

Some big players in electronic money concede they are not concerned about privacy. Demographics developed from bankcard data have long been utilized for sales of various services and products. Some smart-card promoters emphasize this potential when selling their systems to banks, touting that data-gathering software can be embedded in smart cards for use in compiling marketing databases.

Today's objectionable leaks and dissemination of private data are concentrated in the private sector. In contrast, and notwithstanding the oft-cited doomsday threat of Big Brother, privacy advocates can point to relatively few actual breaches of privacy by government. Data acquisition, access, and usage by government in a future government-operated system, judging from Census and Social Security experience, promise to be radically more confidential than in private-sector money systems.

Granted that if a private-sector money consortium were established under government auspices, intrusive practices would be proscribed. Yet, with industry's possible concurrent processing of a new e-currency along with common bankcard payments, travelling via common terminals, computers, and communications systems, and given the commercial atmosphere, an opportunity for dissemination of confidential data from the new currency would exist. The relatively greater complexity of a private-sector operation, with more institutions, switching, databanks, and personnel involved, makes the private-sector utility option more conducive to privacy leakage than a federally operated system.

Virtually everyone pays lip service to the threat of invasion of privacy, but actions belie words. Vociferous privacy advocates issue regular warnings lest the nation let fall its guard against invaders of privacy and quote polls in which Americans have indicated (in the abstract) that they put a high value on privacy, but this is at odds with public behavior.

The overwhelming majority of Americans have eagerly swapped their privacy-affording cash for the convenience and credit of bankcards. It is normal practice to give one's credit card to a waiter or waitress who carries it off out of sight while one's bill is prepared. The giving out of bankcard numbers on the telephone and Internet is on the upswing. Apparently, few perceive significant danger of their transaction privacy being invaded. Indeed, the cases of one's "identity being stolen," which quickly finds headlines, are quite rare. Significant monetary loss by consumers from bankcard fraud (which falls under the penumbra of invasion of privacy), even though capped by law, is also very uncommon. The public knows this. A recent poll indicates that the public would not be inclined to spend more than 3 percent in increased transaction costs for improved privacy security.

Americans are pestered by privacy advocates who instill public apprehension by holding the threat of Big Brother over their heads, some making wild references to Hitler's use of ID cards and emphasizing the use of Social Security numbers in rounding up Japanese Americans during World War II. Their pronouncements often wind up in the press, which, apparently, keeps invasion-of-privacy pieces, along with nursing-home abuses and UFO investigations, on the "hot" list. Thus, misuse of one's transaction data always flickers in one's mind. It is hardly surprising that privacy-sensitive individuals would feel uncomfortable with the concept of government operating an electronic currency system. A following section is dedicated to this subject—"Privacy in an Electronic Currency System."

However, the instant issue is simply this: In choosing between government and private-sector electronic currency systems, which system would protect privacy best? For reasons stated, it would seem that a government system is the easy winner.

LIMITED CRIME PREVENTION

E-money records that match parties to money transactions are an important potential tool for identifying suspects, witnesses, and victims. Indeed, public awareness that such data was available to justice officials would deter many crimes. A key issue in choosing between a federal or a private-sector replacement for cash, therefore, is the relative extent to which data can be accessed by law enforcement officials from the respective systems.

Denying criminals a safe payment medium turns, largely, on the payment system's ability correctly to identify account holders. It is important to get the identity of an account holder right in the first place, at the time his or her account is first opened. Error in private-sector identification data has been a common and persistent complaint.

The best identification verification data is kept by government, that is, in the files of law-enforcement agencies, the Social Security Administration, the IRS, HEW, and other divisions of government. It would be out of the question to allow financial institutions and e-money firms direct access to such databanks in order to verify identities of account applicants or for any other purpose. Conceivably, a procedure might be established so that, upon request, government might provide ID verification to private currency issuers. This would involve a time-consuming procedure beset by security impediments and a probable leakage of data and would incur expense both to requesters and to government. In contrast, intergovernmental ID verification is a relatively fast, everyday practice; it could easily be adapted to opening new federal currency accounts as well.

In like manner, payment-tracing inquiries by justice officials could be handled far more efficiently in a government-to-government scenario. In contrast, if officials had to glean investigative data from private currency systems, the procedure would be relatively slow, if not undependable. Moreover, the best types of personal identification verification (PIV) employ biometrics, including fingerprints, voice prints, hand geometry, and other biometric data. Because accuracy is critical in justice matters, these technologies might be utilized by FEDEC, whereas lesser and/or incompatible systems might be used in a private-sector system of currencies. In general, personal identification inquiries would likely employ a uniform ID technology and be more efficient and secure, and operating procedures would be easier to tailor to anticrime needs in a government-operated e-currency system than in any private-sector system. Government, overall, would be in an incomparably better position to manage ID verification than would industry.

PUBLIC COST, PRIVATE PROFIT

Loss of the federal currency system to private-sector currencies could cost the public as much as $20 billion a year in lost seignorage. Alan S. Blinder, former vice chairman of the Board of Governors of the Federal Reserve System, in his statement to the House Subcommittee on Domestic and International Monetary Policy on October 11, 1995, as part of its series of hearings on "The Future of Money," outlined the likely loss of government revenue if private sector e-money replaces cash to any extent:

Let me start with a potential revenue issue that will arise if the stored-value industry grows large. The federal government currently earns substantial revenue from what is sometimes referred to as "seigniorage" on its currency issue. In effect, holders of the roughly $400 billion of U.S. Currency are lending interest-free to the government. In 1994, for example, the Federal Reserve turned over about $20 billion of its earnings to the Treasury, most of which was derived from seigniorage on Federal Reserve notes.

To the degree that U.S. currency is replaced by privately issued currencies, government seignorage declines. Indeed, one of the motives for institutions to issue prepaid payment instruments is to capture seigniorage, or "float," just as issuers of traveler's checks do now.[7] Although some officials express concern over possible loss of seignorage, others seem ready to accept it as a cost of "progress."

While in theory replacing cash with private sector currencies could cost the public some $20 billion a year, inasmuch as some 65 percent of U.S. currency would remain in circulation in foreign countries, this figure would actually be closer to $7 billion. For several reasons, however, industry might not reap full benefit of this float. First, competition might force payment of interest on new e-currency accounts. If such is the case, the benefit would flow to account holders. Second, reserves in relatively low-average-balance, high-activity accounts might not be sufficient to offset the expense of maintaining them.

A private-sector replacement of cash, whether by means of extending current e-money systems or by creating an entirely new e-currency system, requires revenues to at least cover operating expenses. Putting aside float-based income, possible sources include transaction fees paid by consumers, merchant fees, and government subsidy. As the system would likely comprise a debit-card system (more on this later), today's similar systems suggest answers.

Debit-card systems generate direct revenues from two principal sources: transaction fees and merchant discount fees. According to the Food Marketing Institute, the average consumer fee at POS runs $.19, while fees charged grocers average $.30. Though refuted by most bankers, consumer advocate organizations report that banks earn huge profits from transaction fees. If ATM cash withdrawal fees are any indicator, e-money transaction fees will continue to be targeted by financial institutions. A pattern has developed in the roll-outs of new electronic payment structures. For example, during the last decade, banks lured millions into ATM card usage by offering free home-bank ATM cash disbursements; today 11.7 percent of banks impose a charge on their customers ranging from $.25 to $2. In 1993, banks took in $2.9 billion in ATM transaction fees, $2 billion of which (according to consumer advocates) was profit—this, on top of a saving of $2.34 billion by not using human tellers. The Consumers Federation of America says banks make as much as $.98 of every $1 in transaction fees. Many ATM transactions bear double fees—one levied by the "foreign" bank and one by the home bank, a trend on the increase, according to recent research. Moreover, the Justice Department is looking into possible antitrust violations in how ATM fees are set.[8]

A study by the Federal Reserve Board found that bank service charges on savings and checking accounts rose 50 percent between 1989 and 1993, for a total of $15 billion a year.[9] The U.S. Public Interest Research

Group (PIRG) conducted a study of consumer bank fees based on 271 banks in 25 states for the period 1993–1995 that indicates that fees increased at twice the rate of inflation. Regular checking account fees rose 22 percent, while no-frills accounts rose 6 percent. ATM transaction fees rose about 6.5 percent. These consumer costs rose as banks made record profits of $32, $42, and $44.7 billion in 1992, 1993, and 1994 respectively. A PIRG consultant remarked "that banks have a three-pronged strategy to gouge consumers. They raise existing fees, invent new ones, and make it harder to avoid fees."[10] The average ATM surcharge in 1997 stood at $1.15.

Bankers challenge these attacks, asserting that they actually suffer a net loss on ATM operations. Senator Alfonse D'Amato, chairman of the Senate Banking Committee, disputes this: "Banks are posting record profits, yet they are crying poverty when it comes to ATMS. That just doesn't wash. If they cannot afford ATMs, why did they put up over 100,000 of them?" Indeed, ATM cash is becoming a profitable subindustry itself. Curiously, several such networks, like Bank of America's ATM Cash and Wells Fargo's Cash Center, are not branded. Could such generic titles be designed to distance their owners and avoid criticism of high bank fees?

Although ATMs themselves would be rendered obsolete by disuse of cash, these allegedly exorbitant fees—defended as a fair exchange for "convenience"—highlight the tendency of the private sector to tax payment transactions whatever the market will bear. What occurred with ATM fees—low at first, until the public was on board, and then high—is bound to recur with debit cards. We can expect annual debit-card fees of $15 to $30 a year, plus a $.20 fee on all transactions. Complaints to the banking industry are typically met with, "We believe we provide a good service. Shop around for better rates."

Government regulations may result in even more Americans paying bank fees. Effective January 1, 1999, all government benefit payments must be made electronically to an "authorized payment agent." As a result, more than ten million Americans who now lack bank accounts, mostly seniors who receive monthly Social Security checks, may be forced to pay transaction and/or account maintenance fees. This has prompted the AARP and others to seek regulation restricting the amount of fees that such agents can charge.

Enormous profits from fees drive industry to develop new EFT payment devices even for low-value transactions. With computer-based forms of e-cash, industry seeks in addition to garner high-balance reserves from relatively affluent computer owners. In any case, if only a quarter of today's cash transactions were usurped by private-sector e-money systems, the cost in transaction fees alone to Americans could be astronomical.

User fees are a major income item in banking, accounting for over half the revenues of some banks. Payment transaction fees, even if otherwise justified as defraying a system's operating costs, are regressive, for they are imposed indiscriminately on consumers at all economic levels. Today's cash system, which future private currencies could conceivably replace, is supported by government's general treasury, which is funded largely by progressive income taxes. Regressivity and the anticipated unpopularity of paying fees for using "cash" could draw a groundswell of protest.

Merchants' fees might continue to be imposed in private e-currency systems. The practice of charging discounts to merchants began with the Diner's Club card. Merchants did not object to paying the fee because the card's convenience to customers bought the merchants new business. Moreover, merchants had a guarantee from Diner's Club that their tabs would be paid, a significant advantage over checks. When banks began issuing debit cards, they continued to charge practically the same discount rate to merchants as they did for credit cards. Merchants were quick to object that this was unjustified because debit operations do not extend credit and therefore banks do not suffer bad debts and the relatively higher costs of credit-card operations. Banks glibly maintain that new business brought to merchants as a result of debit-card usage offsets the discount— and herein lies the dispute. Whether debit-card issuers are allowed to continue such fee practices is currently the basis of a class-action suit brought by retailers.

As unpopular as these fees are with merchants, they might have a rational place in future e-currencies. If future e-currencies relieve merchants of the bother and expense of dealing in cash, the benefit would be worth billions of dollars; perhaps they should pay something for it. Yet, discount fees ultimately find their way into increased prices and fall on the shoulders of consumers.

Despite revenues from various fees and income derived from new reserves, the total might prove insufficient to offset expenses, and government might be called upon to help defray private-sector costs of absorbing or replacing cash transactions. Many new accounts in the government-mandated money system would be held by economically undesirable customers who would keep low average balances and require undue and time-consuming personal services, for example, lengthy verbal explanations of charges, beyond-normal correspondence, and matters such as levies by judgement creditors.

The Treasury Department has already requested banks to open special bare-bones accounts, labeled "Direct Deposit Two," to service low-income government beneficiaries who currently receive federal checks. One way suggested to compensate banks is to allow Community Reinvestment Act credit to cover the cost of such accounts.

The cost of privatizing cash would include public expense for government oversight, which, considering the more than 550 billion annual cash transactions in the United States and the 71,000 banks and other financial institutions that might be linked in the new system, would not be a small undertaking. Moreover, watchdog units have a way of growing. A classic example is the wage-and-price-control bureau that started out at the beginning of World War II with just 50 employees and ended up with a staff of some 17,000 by the war's end.

Some critics would reply that FEDEC would cost more to operate because government is generally inefficient. Yet, as pointed out by Indianapolis mayor Stephen Goldsmith, government workers can be as efficient as anyone else. Indeed, as a result of typical fiscal budget restraints, in many instances they have been forced to be more efficient than their private-sector counterparts. Governmental inefficiency is often the result of outmoded, if not antiquated, equipment and technologies. The IRS, with its defective computers, is a case in point. Properly equipped, FEDEC would be at least as efficient as any private-sector EFT system.

It is rather difficult to develop any operational cost figures without a specific design for a system of private currencies. However, in comparing operational costs between private and public currency systems, several factors emerge: First, privatizing currency would cost the public much of its seignorage—something between $7 billion and $20 billion a year. Second, the public would likely outlay most of the required capital. And, third, consumers would be saddled with private-sector profits. These points cause any thinking citizen to ask, why designate industry to run the nation's currency system when government can issue its own e-currency?

Private-currency concepts may well have been developed that are far superior to the rough FEDEC scheme outlined in this book, and some economists may have sound counterarguments. Yet, even assuming all this, how realistic is it to imagine that a system of privately issued currencies would be accepted by the public in lieu of federal cash and that it would be implemented in our lifetime? Clearly, employing FEDEC would be a far faster, if not smoother, route to cashlessness and would deliver public benefits sooner.

In order for officials to overcome their reluctance to involve the federal government in retail EFT payment operations, it is crucial that they recognize the U.S. currency system as a vital public utility. They must observe that it is a utility in danger of being overtaken by new technologies and products, one rapidly becoming relatively inconvenient, inefficient, and antiquated, and one that could become obsolete.

It seems too obvious that this vital public utility, upon which the bulk of the economy turns, cannot be allowed to decay while the nation waits indolently to find out whether the private sector might provide a better substitute. While growing retail EFT payment systems tend to undermine the currency system, they also demonstrate how the technologies employed in them could be utilized in U.S. currency. Government must meet its responsibility to provide the nation with a basic money system as efficient as modern methods and technology allow, one designed to support optimum economic and social conditions.

CHAPTER 5

FEDERAL ELECTRONIC CURRENCY (FEDEC)

SELECTING AN ELECTRONIC PAYMENT STRUCTURE

Which electronic payment structure is best suited to FEDEC? The choices include debit-card, prepaid-card, and e-cash systems. Bear in mind that the objective of the entire undertaking is limited to replacing and emulating currency and coin and that the new electronic currency would coexist with other payment media, just as tangible cash does today. Credit cards, checks, wire service, and perhaps money orders and traveler's checks would continue in operation, though specific payment systems would be negatively impacted and some types might not survive.

While credit-card transactions have captured a significant percentage of cash transaction volume and, indeed, would retain their share even after the transformation of federal currency, the credit-card transaction is not parallel to, and therefore, not a candidate for replacing cash. When goods or services are purchased by credit card, the cardholder exercises a pre-established line of credit by borrowing money from the issuer and becomes its debtor. It requires a subsequent transaction, which today is usually by a mailed check, for the credit-card holder to pay the debt. Even if the credit-card structure were otherwise functionally acceptable, the creation of massive consumer debt would render it an unacceptable method for replacing cash.

The computer-based type of e-cash, alone, is patently unsuitable as a general replacement for cash, although unfolding radio-based technologies and products are erasing distinctions between card- and computer-based forms of e-cash.

Many envision the stored-value-card version as the coming replacement for cash. Yet, it is a hybrid that retains some of cash's deficiencies. For example, because the value in these cards decreases with spending, there is the repeated bother of downloading more dollars onto them. Moreover, the cards are occasionally lost and destroyed, and their owners are not always compensated by the issuing companies. Compensation is usually made only after a prescribed period of time and then often without interest. (This might be cured by a Regulation-E-type guarantee).

Stored-value money is also a potential instrument for illicit activity. Ranging in design from totally anonymous stored-value systems to those which record transactions, a particular system might leave no audit trail or a trail that is limited and difficult to follow. Transaction records in prepaid-card systems, if kept at all, might be difficult for both consumers and authorities to access. For example, tracking down the perpetrator of a fraud via an audit trail might be impossible. E-cash could be also negotiated between the buyer and the seller of illegal drugs without the data ever passing through an intermediary, such as a bank. The recipient of such stored value could then repeat the transaction with a different party for some other illicit purpose, and so on, until finally the "money" was presented to its issuer in exchange for real dollars. This scenario, which indeed may be occurring in the United States today, worries officials.

The "cash" in e-cash is a misnomer. The smart card or computer disc used to store e-cash contains no money. It is closer to accurate to use the term "e-letter of credit." Contrary to the portrayal of "cash" being downloaded onto value-stored cards and to the use of language such as "electronic coins" and "electronic wallets," the value downloaded onto a card amounts only to a promise by the bank to pay the debt incurred by the consumer via the card. In reality, when a consumer purchases a prepaid card, funds are transferred from the consumer's account to the bank's account, where they earn the bank interest until ultimate settlement— thus the analogy to letters of credit, at least those based on cash deposits.[1]

Visa International has developed a smart-card system called Chip Offline Pre-Authorized Card (COPAC) that employs a different funds arrangement between bank and cardholder. First deployed in Russia in 1998 under the name "Visa Roskart," this system allows the cardholder to download "pre-authorized spending power" onto the smart card. Unlike other smart-card downloads, at this point no funds are transferred from the cardholder's bank account. The bank either freezes the authorized funds in the cardholder's account or moves the funds into a shadow account. To use the card the cardholder inserts the COPAC card into a terminal which also contains the retailer's card and enters a PIN. In this offline procedure a transaction amount entered on a terminal is deducted from the card, and transferred to the retailer's card. However, what is transferred is the power to conduct a subsequent debit transaction against the cardholder's bank account. "This is an important differentiation from stored value or pre-paid cards where monetary value is loaded to the chip and settled against an aggregate issuer funds pool. Utilizing this pre-authorization approach with a PIN, the cardholder's funds are protected if the card is properly reported lost or stolen."[2] The retailer compiles data on its card from multiple transactions and subsequently effects on-line debit transactions from the accounts of its customers.

The term "e-cash" is also misleading as to the law controlling it. E-cash systems are based on agreements among cardholders, merchants, card issuers, and banks. If you want to know your rights, read the fine print. Cash, meaning U.S. currency, is governed by the rules of personal property and statutes. Your rights are universally understood, for they are founded in well-settled law. When you tender cash, for example, it must be accepted as payment, for currency and coin are legal tender. Moreover, cash is a unique type of personal property that, for example, carries a special exception to the general personal property rule that one cannot give what one does not own. Thus, when a merchant accepts a payment in cash, the title he acquires is not in question, even though the cash may have been stolen by some prior possessor. Who knows what the case is in a parallel e-cash transaction?

While the stored-value-card system may not serve as well as other EFT structures in an overall cash-replacement scheme, it is well suited to small payments. This brings up the point that a cash-replacement system can integrate two or more types of payment structures. Thus, stored-value cards might be used in conjunction with a dominant debit-card system, the former playing the role of token devices used, for example, in parking meters and at vehicle tolls, where communication and other systemic requirements might otherwise be uneconomical. They might also serve as a payment medium for foreign visitors.

As a transitional alternative, some small-ticket transactions might be serviced in a less expensive manner. Stored-value card systems require compatible card readers. To delay the tremendous investment of retrofiting every parking meter, vending machine, and turnstile, the quarter, or perhaps the dime and the quarter, could be kept in limited circulation. They could be made available, say, only from machines. At the same time, their legal-tender status could be repealed so that counter merchants and banks would not be required to accept them, thus saving industry their handling expense.

A debit card contains no stored value; its function is simply to provide system and account access. Indeed, the need for the card itself might be dispensed with altogether by use of biometric identification. For example, one might gain access via one's fingerprint, optical iris pattern, or other biometric.

Debit-card systems are sometimes referred to as "electronic checkbooks," the analogy being that both the check and the debit card are instruments for directing a bank to transfer funds. Debit-card systems, occasionally labeled "notational digital cash," are also referred to by some economists as "accounting money systems."

Debit-card networks have been around in the United States for nearly two decades. With the advantages of the existing infrastructure, communication devices, networks, and merchant-bank and interbank protocols, this type of system is well suited to become a replacement for cash. However, it is available only at the merchant's counter. Aside from filling in for unserviced transactions, such as interpersonal transactions, with smart cards, which might be necessary in the short run, debit-card access could be extended via portable wireless terminals by which individuals could transact anywhere. Thus, one would use the merchant's terminal for purchases at the retail counter; for personal transactions, one would use a portable wireless terminal, an at-home terminal, or a fixed public terminal.

Ongoing development of EFT technologies and products promises to service the entire spectrum of consumer payment scenarios. For example, Mondex offers telephones with built-in prepaid card readers, allowing one to transact remotely with compatible telephones. Light, palm-sized cell and wireless telephones demonstrate the ease with which e-currency might be used from practically any location. Indeed, Motorola is creating a new type of mobile phone service with this in mind. According to Chris Jackson, vice president and director of marketing for Motorola's Cellular Subscriber Group, the company has added "an additional small GSM SIM card reader to the StarTAC phone . . . one potentially capable of converging the world of mobile communication and the world of the Smart Card. Just imagine—no more queuing for currency or travel tickets—do it on the move and anticipate a new convenience for buying goods and services. In the future, simply insert the relevant Smart Card into the Motorola Smart Card phone, then dial-up, book and pay for the item; access bank account details; and even download money onto your smart cash card." Production units are scheduled to be available as of the end of 1998.[3]

This prospect, however, would alter the monetary picture a bit and requires reflection. Making payments via telephone-type terminals would exceed the limitations of today's cash, for today one cannot use cash in non-face-to-face transactions, except by mailing it. If this feature were incorporated in an e-currency system, it might have significant economic ramifications, as discussed more fully in following sections.

The debit card is clearly the best structure for a federal e-currency system because it eliminates the possessory element of prepaid and smart cards and provides easily accessed transaction records. Yet, if government seeks to put cash to rest as early as possible, it cannot delay the undertaking until the optimum technologies, products, and systems are in place.

Compromises may have to be made initially, with improvements postponed to the future.

HOW A GOVERNMENT SYSTEM WOULD WORK

The following sections demonstrate how federal electronic currency would function and "feel" in usage and how it would benefit the public.

Federal currency would replace only cash. Credit-card, Internet, and other electronic payment systems such as value-stored systems would continue to operate. Checks, drafts, money orders, traveler's checks, letters of credit, acceptances, and other instruments would remain in usage. Of course, one could still use promissory notes, IOUs, scrip, tokens, tickets, or chips. ATM cash transactions, of course, would become a thing of the past.

The FEDEC system would comprise a government-operated depository over which its administrator, likely the Fed, would act as a keeper of everyone's electronic currency. Operating as a debit-card system, electronic cash would flow between FEDEC accounts. Virtually every individual and commercial entity in the United States would have an account in the new system. Because everyone's electronic currency, including that of financial institutions, would remain in FEDEC accounts, the nation's new currency would be totally accounted for.

Noncash money stock represented by balances in institutional accounts would remain valid and functional. Thus, one could continue making payments via paper checks, Fed Wire, ATM/POS, Internet, and other electronic systems.

Interchange between federal electronic cash and institutional money is exemplified as follows: A bank customer wishing to "deposit" his FEDEC dollars into his commercial checking account would conduct a FEDEC transaction by which funds from the customer's FEDEC account would be transferred to the bank's FEDEC account; the bank would then credit the customer's bank account by the same amount. The customer could then, as today, make payments out of the funds in that bank account, using any of the bank's payment devices. Thus, the customer could pay the IRS by direct debit or a landlord by personal check, or the customer could obtain a cashier's check from the bank. Should the customer wish to "withdraw cash" from the bank account, the process would be accomplished by another FEDEC transaction: Funds from the bank's FEDEC account would be transferred to that of the customer, which would be accompanied by a debit of the customer's bank account.

Though the FEDEC system would operate predominantly as a debit-card system, it would be open-framed to allow adaptation of diverse components. Subsequently, newer and/or specialized technologies and products could be plugged in. Multiple protocols could operate under its mantle. On-line and off-line debit might be used contemporaneously. The overall system might also employ a variety of personal identification verification (PIV) devices, each geared to various security levels. Such flexibility would allow customization of transaction procedures, provide smooth incorporation of auxiliary devices and methodologies, permit staged implementation, and leave the door open for further innovation. Indeed, the FEDEC system would be a lucrative market for new products. Perhaps, in a distant phase, Internet or parallel wireless-network payments might be added. As pointed out earlier, however, this might exceed the mandate for making cash electronic.

From a consumer's point of view, FEDEC dollars would be transacted at POS in the same manner as bankcards are today. Thus, a customer would extract a transaction card from wallet or purse and engage it with the merchant's terminal. An electronic communication would check the customer's account balance and immediately transfer funds from the customer's FEDEC account to the merchant's FEDEC account.

For interpersonal (i.e., noncommercial) transactions, individuals might use home terminals, perhaps models incorporated in their telephones, or terminals built into public telephones. They would also own and use pocket or purse-sized personal terminals, just as Americans increasingly own and use cellular telephones. As mentioned earlier, products combining a cell phone and a payment terminal are already in production. Their cost, when manufactured in the tens of millions, would surely plummet, just as pocket calculators did in their early years. Pagers and their satellite networks could be adapted to electronic payments as well.

A typical interpersonal transaction might occur like this:

Bob drives Alice to her house after their dinner date, and says to her, "I hate to ask you this, Alice, but could you loan me a few dollars? I'm just about out of gas."

"Don't you have a credit card?" she asks.

"Nah, my folks took it away after I charged my new stereo."

"Sure. We can use my term."

Alice withdraws a compact-sized combination telephone-terminal from her purse, keys in "$5.00," and engages her card. Then she enters her PIN (or enters a biometric such as her fingerprint). Then Bob swipes his card and enters his PIN (or biometric). The data is transmitted to a processing center in a few microseconds. An instant later, the "Transaction Complete" indicator flashes. Bob now has money for gas in his account and owes Alice five dollars.

The FEDEC system would employ terminals, individual accounts, and, initially at least, electronically encoded cards. Its features include the following:

- FEDEC would be federally operated.
- FEDEC dollars would constitute legal tender.
- Individual account holders would be able to receive as well as pay out funds by use of their accounts.
- FEDEC system funds would be transferable between individual account holders as well as between merchants and individual account holders.
- FEDEC accounts would have no checking feature.
- As an optional feature, FEDEC dollars might be transacted in non-face-to-face transactions.

The FEDEC system might provide commercial service features beyond simple retail sale transactions. For example, business operators might employ FEDEC to pay invoices and payroll. It would remain to be seen whether these applications would be more or less efficient than using private-sector payment systems, particularly systems like those being devised by the Financial Services Technology Consortium (FSTC). Again, however, non-face-to-face applications would widen the FEDEC payment arena beyond that of the cash it had replaced. To the extent this is problematic, these types of payments might be controlled or limited in some way. The issue of whether government electronic currency would shift funds away from commercial accounts is discussed in Chapter 10.

In today's bankcard transaction, only the customer's card needs to be swiped or engaged. The merchant does not use a card of any sort because the merchant's identification and banking data is preprogrammed into the terminal and is automatically transmitted along with the other transaction data. Nothing different would occur in a FEDEC retail transaction.

For use with FEDEC, certain types of terminals would not be preprogrammed with either party's identification because any two parties might use them, as was the case with Bob and Alice in the example. With terminals for public use or terminals kept and used by members of a household or staff, both parties would enter their identifications. Thus, each would swipe a FEDEC card and enter a PIN, press a fingerprint on the terminal's sensor, or provide whatever particular personal-identification verification (PIV) might be required for that transaction.

Today's cash withdrawal would have no counterpart because tangible cash would no longer exist, the possible exception being pseudo-cash in the form of stored-value cards. Deposits into one's FEDEC account would be made directly from a variety of other FEDEC accounts. For instance, a FEDEC account might be credited in a payment from an employer's

FEDEC account, from a friend's FEDEC account, or as a refund from a merchant's FEDEC account.

One of FEDEC's crime prevention features lies in the settlement of transactions within the system, where accurate identification of the transacting parties would be kept. The identities of both the payer and the payee would be instantly available to authorities. Thus, when necessary and as limited by due process, such persons might be located and contacted.

Data recording and its access by justice workers would not only deter direct theft of FEDEC funds (as technically difficult as that would be), but would also render it an undesirable medium for illicit transactions. Bribers and tax evaders, for example, would hardly use this medium. Moreover, FEDEC records would provide a means for reaching transacting parties for many non–crime-related purposes, for example, to correct mistakes in amounts paid, to warn consumers about defective products they had purchased, to identify and charge vendors with civil fraud, to locate missing persons, or to notify people that they are entitled to awards in class-action suits.

Foreign visitors or residents in the United States might be permitted to open FEDEC accounts on presentation of required identification. Of course, foreign visitors would still be able to pay for goods and services using credit cards, private debit cards, prepaid cards, and traveler's checks, just as is done today. However, without cash available, a problem might be encountered in making change for traveler's checks and other fixed-denomination instruments. This could be obviated by making FEDEC stored-value cards available to foreigners at points of entry or at banks, post offices, or other government outlets. FEDEC dollars could be downloaded onto such cards in exchange for foreign currency, bankcard payment, traveler's checks, or other documented money.

FEDEC stored-value cards issued to foreigners might vary from the types of smart cards used by regular FEDEC System account holders. To accommodate travelers, the former might be made transactable at higher dollar amounts and not limited to just small-ticket parking-meter and toll-crossing types of transactions. Furthermore, they might reference passport IDs and have built-in expiration dates, perhaps made to coincide with visa expiration dates, or immigration hearing dates.

Although military bases abroad and U.S. embassies and consulates might be extended local access, the FEDEC system would otherwise function only within the United States. U.S. currency circulating in foreign countries could continue to be serviced by the U.S. government, particularly in countries where it is the official national currency, as in Liberia and Panama, but also where it plays an important unofficial role, for instance, in Eastern Europe.

Americans traveling to foreign countries lacking compatible electronic money systems would simply follow today's practices of purchasing traveler's checks before departing or acquiring foreign currency either in the United States or abroad and/or using credit cards to make payments overseas. However, if foreign governments adopt electronic money systems compatible with the U.S. system, perhaps their electronic currency could be honored in the United States and vice versa. The exchange rate between the various currencies would be automatically computed. Travelers from such countries would no longer have to exchange currencies, pay exchange fees, or risk carrying cash in unfamiliar surroundings. Of course, this is not new. Forerunners of this arrangement, international credit card and ATM systems, have been operational for years.

To prevent criminals and tax evaders from using foreign FEDEC interchange arrangements as international vehicles for illicit money transactions, it would be essential to implement procedural safeguards. Reciprocal arrangements, many already in place, would have to be conditioned, among other things, on compatible foreign anticrime practices and accessibility of foreign data to U.S. authorities. Conversely, the United States would provide foreign law enforcement authorities domestic data on request. These arrangements are already used by the Financial Crimes Enforcement Network (FinCEN) and other federal agencies to acquire foreign data and to provide justice information to Interpol and foreign law enforcement organizations.

TRADE-OFFS IN CONVENIENCE

Many harbor the view that the simplest payment procedure is the passing of cash from one person to another. It is easy to overlook the necessary preparation, including obtaining a supply of currency and coins to carry about in the first place, as well as making change, counting, and disposing of excess coins, not to mention the security precautions one must take. The time spent waiting while clerks bang out new rolls of coins into cash registers, while ladies pack coins and bills into various purse compartments, and while someone must be sent off to find change must also be taken into account. All things considered, electronic-cash payment is actually simpler.

More than 95 percent of today's cash transactions are between consumers and retailers, and it follows that a like number of FEDEC transactions would also be negotiated at POS. There, paying by FEDEC would hardly be distinguishable from paying by today's bankcards. Thus, all but a few FEDEC transactions would be familiar, at least to bankcard users. Even Americans who still rely on cash as their principal payment medium would have little trouble converting to FEDEC.

It is human to balk at having to do things differently, and until such tasks are accomplished, one tends to exaggerate them. I am often amused after explaining the concept of replacing cash with electronic currency and receiving an initial "This sounds like Star Wars" reaction, to hear ultimately, "Oh, that would be easy. Actually, I use bankcards for just about everything. I carry very little cash."

Admittedly, cash has its merits. One can simply look at it, count it, and know how much one has. It can be given or exchanged for another value immediately and directly, without the use of a terminal or an intermediary bank and without documentation, identification, or delay. Consequently, using a terminal for every "cash" transaction is a comparative nuisance and might seem impractical. Small purchases, say of newspapers and chewing gum, would become more complicated. A terminal/special card of some type would have to be used to give lunch money to a child or to pay off a lost bet.

On the other hand, electronic money would eliminate the nuisance of counting out currency and coins and do away with the common problem of lacking coins needed for telephones, parking meters, pay toilets, and transit tolls. As both the minor and the major benefits of the new electronic money were realized, objections to its procedures would wane. Eventually, payment through a FEDEC terminal would come to be viewed by most Americans as equal to the convenience of using a telephone.

The necessity of using a terminal, even for very small transactions, would be offset by advantages. The child could neither lose the lunch money nor have it stolen. Parking tickets for meter expiration might no longer be given, for one's FEDEC account would simply be charged for the time used.[4] Birmingham, Michigan, equipped over six hundred of its parking meters for payments with debit cards. Increasingly, across the country, one can pay a bridge or highway toll without stopping. Programming offers untold options. With FEDEC, ticket-vending machines might be programmed to give discounts to senior citizens, to frequent users, or to other categories of individuals. Conceivably, cigarette-vending machines might be programmed to refuse purchases by underage cardholders. Clearly, electronic money is quite flexible.

From an individual's point of view some transactions would become more time-consuming and complicated using FEDEC money, without providing offsetting benefits. For instance, one would no longer be able to pay the tab and/or a tip at a restaurant by simply leaving cash on the table and departing; instead, payment would have to be made on a waitress' or cashier's terminal. One would no longer be able to toss coins to a vendor at a ball game or play poker with real money. Nor would one be able to pay a U.S. Forest Service campsite fee by dropping a cash-stuffed envelope into a designated slot. Grandparents and others in the habit of making anonymous cash gifts would have to use money orders, checks, or gift certificates instead. The venerable collection plate and the toss-in

Salvation Army bucket would become relics of the past, although, as pointed out earlier, terminals have even been adapted to these.

While the ease of using cash in certain scenarios might be viewed by some consumers as a lost benefit, ending cash would be eagerly welcomed on the other side of the sales counter. Overseers of cash-handling employees must be constantly concerned with pilferage and embezzlement. Moreover, cash handling burdens businesses with increased security and insurance costs. Of course, these are often passed on to consumers.

Checking the balance in one's FEDEC account might seem a nuisance. However, several possibilities exist for determining it, ranging from a terminal procedure that would access the system's computers to the incorporation of an electronic "check-register" memory-chip embedded in one's FEDEC card. Pressing a key on a terminal to exhibit one's balance would probably take less time than counting the currency in one's wallet or purse. Mondex markets a small "balance reader" for this purpose that is carried as a fob on one's key ring.

This brings up the issue of the types of transaction cards and terminals that might be used. A bare-bones FEDEC card would probably be issued by the government, gratis. However, transaction cards and/or terminals with extra features, ranging from simply keeping a balance to printing out statements listing payments and dates, might be available for a price, either from the government or, more likely, from private-sector vendors. (Transaction cards are discussed in Chapter 9.)

Many seemingly minor, yet important, incidental questions remain to be answered. For example, would there be a charge for replacing a lost FEDEC card? Some such regulation has already been addressed in the federal food stamp program and might be adopted by FEDEC.

Having to carry portable terminals about for personal transactions could be inconvenient, depending on their size and weight. Fortunately, making devices small and light is a thing electronic manufacturers do very well. Amazingly, they never stop producing ever smaller, more functional, and less expensive electronic devices. Members of the Olympic Committee in Nagano at the 1998 Winter Olympics tried out wristwatch mobile phones weighing just a bit over 40 grams. The lightweight wireless, handheld terminal has also arrived. Half-a-dozen manufacturers produce mobile bankcard telephones, and new wireless telephone networks promise largely to replace today's all-wire telephone system. For instance, Omron Systems of America supplies a handheld terminal called POS-50 to U.S. Wireless Service that incorporates cellular-telephone technology, has a PIN pad, and is designed for debit-card transactions. It is used by service retailers such as appliance repair companies, pizza deliverers, towing companies, and taxi companies.[5] Intellect Electronics, Inc., advertises a similar lightweight device that operates wirelessly, accepts mag-stripe and chip cards and processes debit and credit transactions.[6] In 1993, Motorola, Inc., announced a credit-card-size wireless receiver. In October 1995, Siemens Wireless Terminals Division announced that it will produce $40 million in pocket-size handsets that will accommodate credit-card-size smart cards. There are reports of a miniature portable terminal the size of Dick Tracy's wrist-radio.[7]

AT&T Wireless Service and NOVA announced that they

will provide businesses with the capability to handle credit-card transactions easily from virtually any location in less than six seconds, for just pennies per transaction. Mobile businesses such as taxi or towing services, unwired establishments such as stadiums and parking garages, and fixed businesses that need portability during heavy retail periods, can now process credit-card purchases easily with reliability and throughput comparable to conventional landline connections.

Clearly, little if any research would be required to develop basic technologies and products for FEDEC, for they are already on the shelf.

How would one cope if his or her FEDEC card/terminal were lost or stolen? The answers seem fairly obvious. First, one could keep a spare tucked away at home. Second, in most scenarios, one could temporarily use a credit card or other non-FEDEC payment-system device, perhaps a private stored-value card. Beyond that, FEDEC replacement cards and personal terminals could be made available at convenient locations, say, at post offices. Upon proof of identity, such as fingerprint or other biometric ID, a replacement would be immediately issued. Planners may well devise other solutions. If a FEDEC card's disappearance were discovered when post offices were closed, the owner would likely be inconvenienced until the next day. But, is this any worse than predicaments today when one's wallet or purse is suddenly missing?

Americans would have to adjust to a few novel FEDEC procedures, but one would be able to pay bills more easily, never lose money, and not have to store, carry, and count currency and coin. Much more significant would be the freedom from robbery and personal danger that a switch to e-currency would provide.

THE INFORMATIONAL ADVANTAGE

Preventing crime by converting cash to an electronic form works in two ways. The first relies on the transformation of cash from a physical chattel to an intangible system of debits and credits. This alone would eliminate any crime in which possession of money is the criminal's goal. The second component has to do with generating electronic-currency data for use in investigating and prosecuting crime.

Clearly, the second component is certain to draw scrutiny and fire from privacy advocates. Indeed, many writers have expressed enthusiasm for the anonymity offered by some new e-cash systems, such as DigiCash. To some of these people, whose motivations range from paranoia to morality, privacy has become a worthy end in and of itself.

As with any right, transaction privacy has its extremes. You have absolute anonymity at one end and an open public record system at the other. No e-money system, even DigiCash, offers either of these. Moreover, the public has not yet been exposed to the idea of employing cash-transaction data to combat crime. After fairly considering the trade-offs involved, as well as the procedural checks that would block privacy abuses, I believe most Americans would accept as reasonable the uses for transaction data proposed in this book.

If crime prevention matters, America would be better off continuing today's cash than adopting fully anonymous e-currency. Street robbers, knowing that getting personal identification from electronic-money transaction data was impossible, would simply force victims to transfer e-currency into the robbers' accounts. The new money would be even less traceable than today's cash, for gone would be the use of marked currency, currency numbers, and the ability to videotape illicit cash changing hands, methods regularly used in stings and other law enforcement tactics.

Law enforcement officials suspect that drug traffickers already use wire and ATM systems to whisk off hundreds of millions in illicit drug dollars to foreign headquarters, but this is difficult to prove. Anonymous e-currency would extend electronic payments to street deals, so that low-level dealers and their buyers could make secure payments as well. Anonymity would free criminals from the bother of money laundering, render antilaundering laws ineffective, and make identification and prosecution of drug offenders even less successful than it is today. In addition, it would provide secure payment media for bribery, loan sharking, embezzlement, illegal gambling, prostitution, fraud, and other crimes. It would insulate sales of stolen property from prosecution, which in turn would inspire more burglaries. Not to be overlooked, transaction anonymity could also catapult the underground economy to economically destabilizing heights.

As a practical matter, therefore, making FEDEC transaction data available to law enforcement agencies is not an optional condition but an essential feature. Of equal importance would be the placement of limits on such access, controlling the type of data that could be obtained, who should have access, and how it could it be used. Fortunately, many such safeguards are already codified. (See Chapter 7, ''Privacy in an Electronic Currency System.'')

The use of transaction data for investigation would not be limited to crimes in which electronic currency was directly involved. Currency data would provide clues and evidence in solving even nonmonetary crimes, for example, acts of revenge, terrorist acts, and crimes of passion. FEDEC transaction records for a given service station's sales, for instance, might be used to trace and identify a witness to a nearby gang shooting.

Information would come from two sources within the system: (1) account holders' application information and (2) operational data.

Application and File Information

By the time FEDEC had reached its last stage of implementation, nearly everyone in the United States would have completed a FEDEC application, opened an account, and begun using it. To prevent criminals from using aliases and to insure accurate identification of account holders, a FEDEC account application would require more information than a credit-card application. Misidentification of financial records is a major privacy problem in the United States.[8] At the least, the application would require a birth date, sex, a physical description, and Social Security number. Passport numbers, driver's license numbers, and other standard identification data might also be called for.[9] Data commonly needed in emergencies such as next-of-kin, blood types, and medical warnings, for example, might be acquired as well. Biometric PIV devices, if incorporated in FEDEC, would not only bar unauthorized access and secure accounts against theft but also render mistakes in account identities a thing of the past.

Businesses—proprietorships, partnerships, and corporations—would also open FEDEC accounts, and IDs for their responsible signatories would also be acquired. For use in compiling statistics, business accounts might also indicate standard industry codes and other commercial categories.

Operational Data

Operational data would be generated from FEDEC transactions. At minimum, a transaction would necessitate (and record) the account numbers of the parties, a dollar amount, the transaction location, and the time and date. Operational data, in the form of transaction records, has obvious value in accounting, indeed, is enlightening, since they would represent former dealings in cash. Individuals could use their FEDEC records for budget observations, proof of purchases, and the like, while businesses and government would find such records invaluable in cash accounting and various types of analyses.

Data from fixed terminals (e.g., at a merchant's counter) would pinpoint transaction locations. To a lesser degree, even transactions conducted through mobile terminals, if transmitted wirelessly, might indicate location. This is because some wireless systems use ubiquitous "microcells," or shoe-box-size base stations located within buildings, on street posts, and on every block, through which communications are sent and received. Mobile terminals in such systems access the closest microcell; thus, by discovering the location of the base station involved, the general location of a transacting party could be ascertained.

If an individual were sought, his or her account could be monitored for transaction activity to learn his or her whereabouts. Targeted FEDEC accounts might be placed under automatic monitor. In this manner, when a transaction occurred involving that person, a requesting agency could be immediately notified. Such data could lead to the location of either a transferor or transferee—who might be a fugitive, domestic-support-payment evader, witness, or victim. The sought individual might, conceivably, be an Alzheimer's sufferer, a lost relative, a prospective organ or blood donor, a teen runaway, or a person who had mysteriously disappeared. Though some readers might deem this Orwell's prediction come true, the practice of watching account activity would be tightly restricted to circumstances warranting it and used only after legal process—hardly the omnipresent eye of *1984*.

General file information would be updated regularly, for example, to correct address changes or name changes. File data might be kept indefinitely. Transaction data, on the other hand, would probably be erased after a period of time, perhaps after three years, to coincide with IRS requirements.

Money Data as Statistics

Because it remains hidden and unreported in the underground economy, a significant portion of income received in cash fails to be included in the dollar figures used to calculate unemployment, income distribution, the gross domestic product, and other statistics. Some unreported activity is taken into account by means of IRS estimates of misreported income and wholesale figures, but these methods fall short. Edgar Feige, professor of economics at the University of Wisconsin, a leading authority on the underground economy, explains the problem as follows:

As economic activity shifts from the recorded to the unrecorded sector, some basic economic indicators such as real growth rates, employment, and productivity may become understated. As false reporting and non-reporting becomes endemic . . . social indicators become contaminated. . . . Distorted information can radically affect the stability of the economic system as it is presently constituted. When monetary policy is targeted on full employment, the outcome with distorted information is accelerating stagflation. When monetary policy is targeted on price stability while fiscal policy is geared to automatic stabilization of income, the outcome may well be higher deficits and higher interest rates. The root problem, however, does not seem to lie in defective theory or necessarily in defective policy prescriptions, for under both regimes we have described, policy can successfully attain stabilizing results so long as the social thermometer works accurately to

produce correct information. However, a distorted information system can desta-
bilize an otherwise stable economic system, and the predicted consequences of
such distortions are broadly consistent with what we increasingly observe in our
present-day economies.[10]

Replacing cash with a data-generating system would be a boon to stat-
isticians by supplying factors that existed previously only in a twilight zone
of secrecy. A simple grand total of FEDEC account balances would provide
a presently unknown number—the true amount of cash circulating in the
United States. It would help produce reliable statistics and economic indicators, figures that influence government borrowing, interest rates, social action programs, market values, and major investment decisions.

The Census Bureau might also make use of the FEDEC system in acquiring demographic data. As the system would be continually updated
with ages, addresses, notices of death, and so forth, certain census statistics
might be compiled more frequently, more accurately (accounting for virtually everyone residing in the United States), all at a fraction of today's
cost.

The FEDEC system could not, however, be allowed to become an all-
purpose databank. As a source from which to develop general statistics,
the FEDEC system can be distinguished from the type of national databank
recommended to Congress by the Ruggles Report in 1965. That proposal,
considered and rejected by Congress,[11] envisioned a comprehensive databank that would have compiled data from all federal agencies. Several
objections to the proposal, such as that "citizens must have access to their
records" and that there was the "danger of unauthorized access," were
subsequently dealt with in the Privacy Act of 1974 and later legislation.[12]
The principal objection by Congress to a national databank was the seem-
ing inevitability that it would develop all-inclusive files on every American. Proponents of the national databank argued that only statistical data
would be extracted and that it would serve as a "clearinghouse for requests for data." They could not deny that a common identifier or an
individual's name would have been used to tie all the various agencies'
information together in what would have amounted to a personal dossier.
Thus, any bit of data collected by one agency concerning an individual
would have flowed to or been available to all agencies via the databank.
Congress's objection to this arrangement would probably stand today.

Data from various departments of government would likely be referenced to verify new FEDEC account applications. FEDEC would have no
reason to amass such external data or to disseminate it on any request.
Its databank, with minor exception, would contain only FEDEC data,
which it would pass on only as specifically allowed by law.

Extraction of data for statistical puposes could be done without reference to individual names or account numbers. FEDEC software could

compile transaction totals for, say, home-appliance sales in the State of Kansas for a given period or the total of individual-to-individual payments for a given locale for a particular month or could sum up all payments made to a particular service industry.

That said, as under current laws and in accordance with due process already required by statute, law enforcement and other government agencies would have legal access to specific FEDEC accounts to investigate suspected crimes, perhaps to locate missing persons or witnesses, and for other authorized purposes.

COIN

As between coin and paper currency, the latter is the more modern, having come into usage, at least in the West, only during the last several centuries. Yet, despite paper currency's relatively lighter weight and ease of storage, we are so well adapted to coin that it might be the more difficult of the two to abandon. Americans handle $60 billion in coin annually, and volume rises each year.

Coin rarely is the object of serious crime. The sheer weight and bulk of coins limit the sums that can be carried off by thieves. Moreover, the value of coins is not what it once was. Dimes, quarters, and half dollars were originally 90 percent silver, until Congress passed the Coinage Act of 1965, which changed their composition to 75 percent copper and 25 percent nickel. One can see on their edges the copper sandwiched between layers of nickel. Pennies are 95 percent copper and 5 percent zinc.

While $5 rolls of dimes and $10 rolls of quarters can mount up in value, they are not usually found in meaningful quantities outside of safes and banks, the penetration of which is hardly worth a burglar's trouble. There are exceptions, as in July 1991, when a New York subway token clerk was shot and killed during a robbery in which only coins and tokens were taken. Rare and collectable coins are a different matter.

Crimes associated with coins include petty thefts from pay telephones, parking meters, vending machines, and coin-operated laundry machines. The real cost of coin thefts is not from the value of the coins taken nor in shortages due to slugs and foreign coins, but in equipment damage. A survey indicates that 57 percent of all vending-machine operators in the United States are victimized by machine crime. In 1989, the average operator lost $2,453 over a twelve-month period. Damage to equipment broken into, on the average, was over twice the value of stolen cash.[13] Operators lost an additional $2,290 in route truck "incidents," which included robberies and embezzlements of coinage.

Neither does coin play a role in the underground economy. Bartenders, sidewalk vendors, phony beggars, parking valets, and others may fail to report and pay taxes on pocketed coin revenues, but not only is the coin tip becoming something of an insult, but these sums are a insignificant fraction of the underground economy. Besides, the IRS mandates that waiters and other specified workers report a predetermined sum as tip income.

The chief problem with coin is the expense and bother to industry of handling it—counting, packaging, safekeeping, loading, transporting, and recounting. According to one source, all this costs up to 6 percent of face value.[14] Coin is unpopular with the general public as well. According to recent research, people accidentally throw away about $2 million in coins each day. The average home in America contains some $30 in piggy banks, lost in sofas, or stored in jars and boxes.[15] Interestingly, several years back Denmark's banks implemented a government-sponsored debit-card system, Danmont, that replaces certain types of coin transactions, ranging from laundries to public telephones.[16] This system was inspired by Danes' dislike of handling their country's large coins. It may constitute the world's first government-initiated debit-card money system.

Pennies are the worst. Retailers in America, particularly fast-food restaurants and convenience stores, regard them as a public nuisance. The National Association of Convenience Stores estimates that workers spend 5.5 million man-hours annually just counting pennies. Banks charge merchants a service fee averaging 6 cents per 50-penny roll for handling. This mounts up to about $15 million a year.

The New York Transit Authority hires an independent company just to wrap coins. When it raised fares from $1.00 to $1.15, it had to stock up on coins for change. As of 1993, it kept a supply of 2,749,600 quarters, 2,088,000 dimes, and 1,227,000 nickels for its 741 toll booths. This amounts to over $1 million that is not kept in a bank, bears no interest, and is unavailable to the Federal Reserve.

Cash-handling expense is not limited to coin; processing paper currency is an expense as well. The Chicago Transit Authority and the Rapid Transit District of Los Angeles, to mention but two mass transit agencies, spend about 3 cents to count and straighten every piece of currency. Since each system receives more than 300,000 bills daily, the combined cost for these two systems runs over $7 million a year.

As a matter of its fiscal efficiency, the Treasury Department prefers coin over paper currency. This is because coins are durable and last many years, whereas one-dollar bills, for example, last only months before they must be replaced. Proposals to replace the one-dollar bill with a coin have been under consideration in the United States for at least a decade. Proponents often point to the success of such conversions in other countries.

Whether such a change from paper to coin would mean more convenience to the American public is questionable. I recently spent time in Australia, where the smallest paper currency is a $5 denomination. Coins include $1 and $2 denominations (gold colored), as well as 5, 10, 20, and

50 cent denominations (silver colored). No coin less than five cents cir-culates, and all transactions are rounded to five cents. One carries coins of more value, and tenders coins more often than in the United States. I found myself more frequently having to pull up coins from my pocket and making more combination tenders involving both coins and bills, which was a relative nuisance. This is less a problem for women, who tend to keep coins and bills in a single purse. Moreover, my financial loss mounted up from those relatively valuable coins that rolled out of my pocket from time to time and became lost between seat cushions. Yet, being freed of the nearly worthless penny was an offsetting benefit; over-all, the two scenarios are probably a tradeoff in inconvenience between the two tangible money systems. Against a modern background of elec-tronic payment systems, coin contrasts as a primitive payment medium, as well as a nuisance to nearly all who have to use it.

EXISTING FEDERAL EFT APPLICATIONS

Though deferring to the private sector for development of electronic payment systems, the federal government has embraced the medium for its own usage. Most notable is the switching of its check payments to direct deposit. Half of federal payments are made electronically. Furthermore, some 1.6 million transaction cards have been put to use by government workers in fleet management, travel, and purchasing services, and there is movement to integrate these into a single "smart card." The Postal Ser-vice sells "LibertyCash" cards to the public, a reusable stored-value card that can be used to purchase numerous postal products. The Treasury Department is also developing a smart card for use in the army and is testing a new "E-Check" system that could serve as a model for Internet payments. The current administration is very keen to have government take advantage of developments in electronic commerce.

Commencing January 1, 1999, all government payments must be made electronically. In anticipation, the Treasury Department has asked the fi-nancial community to accommodate the unserviced segments of society in opening of bare-bones bank accounts into which government benefit payments can be electronically deposited.

When credit cards first appeared in the 1950s, their users were an af-fluent segment used to charging things, mostly business people. Later, bankcard popularity spread to the younger set, which was not only eager to take advantage of credit but also receptive to new technology. Left behind were many individuals still alien to bankcards, particularly older and/or low-income individuals who tend to regard bankcards as unnec-essary and/or too gadgety. But, it does not follow that this segment is unable to adapt quickly.

When the concept of Food Stamp Electronic Benefits Transfer (EBT) was first conceived in the 1980s, concern was expressed that lower socio-economic groups might not be able to cope with the unfamiliar EFT process. Special instruction classes were arranged, and leaders held their breath. With first usage, however, doubt dissipated, for almost all the recipients caught on as quickly as the rest of the average public.

The Food Stamp EBT program might provide some of the regulatory detail necessary for a FEDEC system. In the early 1980s, the U.S. Department of Agriculture, through its Food and Nutrition Service (FNS), was looking for a medium to replace the issuance and redemption of food stamp coupons. The reason is best stated in a government-sponsored report: "Food stamp coupons and paper issuance documents are vulnerable to counterfeiting, theft, loss, and unauthorized transfers. . . . An EBT system eliminates paper documents and makes it harder for anyone but authorized recipients and retailers to gain access to food stamp benefits."[17] The writer could just as well have been discussing the problems with U.S. currency and the advantages of transforming it to an electronic system.

Electronic funds transfer was a logical choice. In July 1983, the FNS employed a private contractor to design and test an on-line electronic benefits transfer (EBT) system. The company elected to employ magnetic-stripe cards and personal identification numbers (PIN). In October 1984, a small EBT demonstration project was conducted at Reading, Pennsylvania, involving 3,400 recipient families and 125 retailers.

The success of the pilot project, later made permanent, led to Food Stamp EBT systems in several other jurisdictions. The FNS approach in these programs left to local administration whether or not, and how, to employ EFT. Thus, within guidelines set by the FNS, each state or region designed and operated its own "stamp" program. Over the last decade, a variety of individualized procedures and hardware have been put into service. Some seven southern states have allied to form a unified debit-card system. Hearings before the House Banking and Financial Services Committee (March 27, 1996) revealed proposals to utilize existing commercial ATM and POS infrastructure and devices for EBT, as well as adding portability to recipients, thus allowing recipients to use EBT cross-regionally. EBT is also being combined with other government benefit systems. As noted above, the lowest socioeconomic layer is being accommodated with supporting bank accounts. Conceivably, the popularity of EBT might ultimately lead this segment to employ bankcards for general usage and thus reduce its reliance on cash.

The diversity in EBT system designs is useful in comparing the benefits and/or drawbacks of a variety of software, hardware, and communication systems. One system uses an exclusively off-line system, while another offers a choice of paper coupons or EBT to recipients, and yet another jurisdiction uses "smart cards." This groundwork, including input from administrators, data processors, industry representatives, program recipients, and others, might provide valuable insight in designing and implementing a FEDEC system.

Viewed alongside the proposed FEDEC undertaking, however, Food Stamp EBT is an incomparably small program with a limited function. Transaction volume is relatively minuscule, and the program pertains only to a narrow stratum of public beneficiaries. Further, EBT functions only at food-store POS (although the program is being expanded to include other types of transactions). Of significance to designers of e-currency, however, might be the ministerial aspects of Food Stamp EBT—the ways in which it deals with particular procedural matters.

The following excerpts from Food Stamp EBT rules[18] exemplify the type of detail dealt with in the program and identify issues (italics added) that might be significant to FEDEC:

The POS receipt [from a Food Stamp EBT transaction] is required to contain, at a minimum, information such as the transaction type, purchase amount, *remaining balance*, date of transaction, terminal location, and account code or receipt code.

The proposed rule also required that balances be made available without the need to wait in a checkout line.

The Department further proposed that State agencies be capable of *providing a transaction history* of up to two months to households that request it in order to facilitate problem identification and resolution, to impose a *replacement fee on EBT cards* not to exceed the actual cost to replace the card, to replace lost or stolen EBT card, or PINS, when a household has forgotten it, within two business days after the household has reported it. . . .

[W]hen accounts are inactive for a three-month period the agency be permitted to store the remaining benefits off-line. . . . that the household be notified prior to storing the benefits off-line and deactivating the benefit card. The proposed rule would permit the agency to expunge dormant account benefits after one year of inactivity.

State agencies cannot *require food retailers to purchase equipment or incur other costs* as a condition of participation in the EBT system. . . .

98% of all EBT transactions must have a processing *response time* of 10 seconds or less.

Regarding terminal standards, the Department proposed just three *requirements for POS terminals*: non-display of balance information, non-display of the PIN, and data encryption at the POS terminal.

Integration of Food Stamp EBT with conventional EFT networks has obviated some of the problems in earlier regulations. Moreover, many Food Stamp EBT regulations would be irrelevant to FEDEC, such as prohibitions against posting checkout lanes as "welfare only" (to avoid stigma and embarrassment), and requiring enough food stores to be equipped in any given area to allow householders a choice of stores. Clearly, answers to many of the ministerial issues in FEDEC would be developed from scratch, for example, the matter of who would pay for personally owned terminals.

Viewed in a different light, however, the ongoing expansion of Food Stamp EBT makes it a sort of forerunner of electronic currency. The Postmaster General recently commented that he foresees the day when recipients of government benefits will be able to download such benefit payments from machines located in every post office to their individual transaction cards.

In a trial by the State of Ohio, recipients of food stamps and other benefits will transact by using chip-embedded smart cards. This will likely become the largest bloc of smart card usage in the United States. According to Ohio officials, in the year 2000, some 450,000 EBT smart-cards will be in use at 7,000 POS counters in Ohio, purchasing $89 million worth of goods per month. Partly funded by the U.S. Department of Agriculture, Citicorp's EBT Services division was awarded a $78 million contract to implement the program over a seven-year period. Stored Value Systems Corporation is the subcontractor that designed the pilot program. Ohio's smart-card program promises to snowball as other states begin replicating the program. Several states are already seeking contractors for that purpose.

CHAPTER 6

BENEFITS OF A FEDERAL
ELECTRONIC CURRENCY SYSTEM

HOW ELECTRONIC CURRENCY WOULD BLOCK CRIME

To analyze how FEDEC would impact crime, offenses can be divided into three categories: (1) crimes that would no longer exist after the abolition of tangible cash; (2) crimes that by their nature do not involve money; and (3) crimes involving money that can be perpetrated in payment media other than cash.

Crimes of the first category, such as bank robbery, ATM robbery, cash-register holdups, and any other crime in which taking possession of cash is the objective would become impossible to commit. Convenience-store and gas-station holdups would cease. Bus and taxi drivers would not be robbed. Pockets would not be picked. Cash-operated machines would not be broken into. With few exceptions, all of the approximately 300,000 robberies of businesses would come to a halt.

While it is obvious that cash plays a key role in these crimes, proving this statistically is difficult because crime statistics are not generally indexed to cash alone. When mentioned in crime statistics, cash is typically in mixed form such as "currency, notes, etc." However, a special analysis conducted for this author by the Bureau of Justice Statistics (BJS) and based on 1991 victimization data revealed that in 1,938,000 thefts (larceny, robbery, or burglary), only cash was taken; the study identified an additional 902,000 thefts of purses and 1,468,000 thefts of wallets. These total up to some 4.3 million thefts, or 12 percent of the 34.7 million crimes reported via the NCVS that year. (Note that this 12 percent figure is used later in this book as a benchmark from which to calculate various cost savings from making cash electronic.) Unfortunately, statistics were not available for crimes in which both noncash items and cash were taken or in which the motive for the crime was to steal cash, even though only noncash items or no items were ultimately taken.

Adding to the difficulty in making calculations based on cash crimes is that the Justice Department methodology used in compiling crime statistics classifies a crime according to its most serious attribute. Thus, a household burglary that also involved a rape is counted as a rape.[1]

We know empirically that robbery, burglary, and larceny theft are committed in large part to obtain cash. Thus, abolishing cash would probably eliminate a majority of America's 1.5 million robberies,[2] 4.8 million burglaries, and 21.1 million larceny thefts.[3] Yet, nonoccurrence of first-category crimes would cause other types of crime to decline as well. For example, as robbery and larceny-theft rates dropped, so would the murder rate decrease, because some 10 percent of all murders are committed during robberies.[4] A significant number of rapes (perpetrated in 3 percent of robberies) and assaults with serious bodily injuries (inflicted in over 8 percent of robberies) would be prevented as well.

The second category of crimes includes those that may have nothing to do with money. Violent crimes such as murder, rape, and assault and battery may neither involve nor be motivated by money. Terrorist attacks and hate crimes could be included (though these crimes are sometimes carried out by paid "hit men"). Thefts of personal property such as automobiles, securities, and jewelry, if not subsequently sold, might also fit in this category.

The third category refers to crimes that may be conducted in noncash payment media. Theft by check or EFT, embezzlement by check or EFT, fraud, insurance fraud, and arson fraud, are typically perpetrated without the use of cash. This group of crimes, as with the second group, is neither prevented nor directly affected by the disuse of currency and coin. Murder-for-hire, bribery, receiving stolen property, extortion, prostitution, loan sharking, and the sale of narcotics, to name a few, can all be committed by the use of a quid pro quo other than cash, including checks, money orders, jewelry, traveler's and cashier's checks, foreign currency, and now e-cash. Of course, the FEDEC system itself would be available as a payment medium in such crimes, but that medium would be a criminal's last choice.

One can piece together the overall crime scenario as it might exist in the post-cash era. Most robberies and burglaries would have been eliminated because the chief objective in committing such crimes would no longer be in circulation. Some burglaries of homes, offices, and automobiles would continue, as would some shoplifting, but converting stolen goods into a payment medium would leave a discoverable trail. With cash itself no longer in the picture, a thief would be limited to stealing jewelry, silver, tools, office equipment, car stereos, and the like—and would then have the problem of selling these items. But, which payment medium would be safe for a thief to accept?

Even today, buyers of stolen goods know they risk being turned in to the authorities by the people they deal with, should such accomplices get arrested. A savvy buyer of stolen goods would not pay with a traceable medium such as a check for obvious reasons, even if the seller would accept it. Using FEDEC dollars would be even worse, as this payment medium would record the transaction in detail. The buyer could use a money order, traveler's check, or cashier's check ("documented money"). By leaving the payee blank on such instruments, they might be negotiated many times over without revealing the identities of the parties involved. (Unregulated e-cash might be used in like manner.) But if any of these payment instruments were later negotiated in a crime, such as an illegal drug sale, subsequent investigation of the same might lead police to the stolen-goods buyer and ultimately reveal the initial crime. Even today, federal regulations require vendors of documented money to keep logs identifying purchasers and to record instrument numbers. That said, from the criminal's point of view, with cash gone and assuming that traceless e-cash does not become available, money orders issued in blank and traveler's checks would become the next best payment media.

The continued use of money orders and traveler's checks might facilitate a limited amount of crime; and if it became a significant trend, it would require further regulation through currency-type reporting and analysis or perhaps legislation requiring identity endorsements. Moreover, dealing in documented money to a significant degree would tag a person as a possible criminal. However, all paper-based transactions are doomed to obsolescence, and the onset of FEDEC would speed their demise. Virtually everyone would have a FEDEC account at his or her disposal, and the use of documented money and checks would fall by the wayside.

There will always be those willing to buy stolen property; but after cash has been removed from circulation, fencing operations are likely to fall into a severe recession. Sales of stolen goods to fences have already been dampened by highly publicized, successful sting operations across the country. This may account for recent statistics revealing a relative shift from burglaries of goods to burglaries of cash and an increase in street holdups. Incidentally, after the FEDEC system was in place, sting operations would be less costly and even more successful.

Deterrence would surely have a strong effect. Even occasional sales of stolen goods to otherwise honest buyers would diminish, for such buyers would understand their increased chance of getting caught. Incidentally, most people know when goods are stolen; they are put on notice by ridiculously low prices, the appearance of the vendor with goods that do not match his evident lifestyle, and the typical circumstances of the offer— on the sidewalk, in a bar, or at the back door.

The crime-preventing and crime-solving benefits of making cash electronic are not limited to specific classes of crimes. Indeed, the new system would work against all criminals in all types of crimes—sometimes directly, and sometimes indirectly. Criminals, along with the general populace, would use electronic currency because, among other reasons, it would likely become the dominant, if not sole, "small money" for use in transit fares, parking meters, and other miscellaneous payments. FEDEC payment data would be available to law enforcement for various uses, for example, to provide evidence including suspects' whereabouts, to disprove alibis, to find witnesses, and to locate criminals on the run. Whatever alternative payment media criminals might use in an attempt to avoid detection, life for them with electronic currency in operation would never be as free from prosecution as it is nowadays.

Currently, crime detectives find it difficult, and often impossible, to turn up the crucial evidence of cash changing hands. They use marked money, videotape surveillance, and the testimony of undercover agents. Such elaborate and expensive methods are, of necessity, limited to ongoing, serious criminal operations. No police department or district attorney's office has enough staff or money to employ such methods on a broad basis and to tie up officers to testify about such cash transactions in time-consuming criminal trials. Clearly, the use of transaction data and computers to locate and identify witnesses and suspects alike, to retroactively place them at specific locations, and to date events tied to crimes would be a giant step forward in criminal investigation procedure. Electronic currency holds the potential equivalent of millions of hours of police work and promises to give a powerful new investigative dimension to law enforcement.

The following illustrates a few ways FEDEC could be used in crime investigation: A woman has been raped in her New York apartment and accuses a pizza delivery man. Investigators find hair and fiber linking the man to the scene. He denies the accusation, explaining to police, after waiving his rights, that he was with his brother in Chicago the entire week of the alleged incident. His brother corroborates the alibi. A check of the suspect's FEDEC-account activity for the week in question reveals no payments in Chicago, but it does show a transaction by the man in New York, one that occurred at a tavern down the street from the victim's apartment building only an hour before the attack.

A police investigator, using a mobile data terminal (MDT) printer in his car, retrieves a FEDEC-generated picture of the man (from his FEDEC application) and shows it to bartenders at the tavern. One of them identifies the man as having been at the tavern the night of the rape and recalls him muttering something about "getting even with that bitch." This testimony, FEDEC transaction-activity printouts, and physical evidence from the crime scene help bring about the conviction of the man.

In another case Mrs. Jones reports the mysterious disappearance of her husband. She informs police that their car, jewelry, and some other valuables are also missing from the couple's home. Using an MDT, police access Mr. Jones's FEDEC account to see if he has made any purchases during or since the day in question. None are shown. Police question local family members, including the victim's nephew who lived nearby, to find out if they might know Mr. Jones's whereabouts. None has any idea where he might have gone.

The nephew tells the police that he had not seen his uncle for several days and that he himself had been working on his Volkswagen in his apartment-house garage all the day of the disappearance. However, a neighbor of the Joneses says he saw the nephew walking down the street that day.

The police obtain a subpoena and check the nephew's FEDEC account, which reveals that he had made a purchase at a gas station at midday on the day of the disappearance. The gas-station attendant who made the sale identifies the nephew from a computer-generated picture and produces a sales slip revealing a license plate number that matches that of Mr. Jones's car.

A court order is obtained, and the nephew's FEDEC account is placed under computer surveillance. Within a week, police are notified that a FEDEC transaction has taken place in which $2,300 was transferred from ABC Pawn Shop to the nephew. The owner of ABC Pawn Shop shows police the jewelry pawned by the nephew which is subsequently identified by Mrs. Jones as part of the property that disappeared along with her husband. Confronted with this evidence, the nephew confesses and leads the police to a lake where he had submerged the Jones car and his uncle's body.

Suppose a twelve-year-old girl, walking with friends on the sidewalk of a shopping mall, is snatched up by a stranger and thrown into a car that speeds away. She is not heard from again. Her young friends at the scene give only sketchy descriptions of the assailant and cannot identify the car at all (the facts of a California case). Police request and obtain an electronically transmitted subpoena from an on-line standby magistrate, which permits them to review FEDEC transaction data from stores in the mall. Thus, police obtain the names of customers who had made purchases within an hour of the crime. In their interviews several provide detailed descriptions of the abductor. A retired body-and-fender repairman recalls the make and year of the car and describes the dents in the vehicle. Another remembers several numbers and letters on the license plate. These clues, together with Department of Motor Vehicle records and other investigative work, lead to the apprehension of the perpetrator and the discovery of what had happened to the victim.

Credit-card data has already been used in this manner. In one of the first of such cases, New York police were investigating the murder of a fellow officer outside a restaurant, but could find no witnesses. Someone got the bright idea of asking American Express to supply them the names of patrons at the restaurant who charged their meals on Amex bankcards that day. It took a couple of days' worth of calling, but from evidence obtained from the list of 20 people provided to them, the police were able to track down and identify the killer.

The links between crimes and bankcards can be utilized in several ways. Criminals frequently steal bankcards from their victims and use the cards for purchases. Discovery of a link is sometimes initiated by store clerks suspicious of particular bankcard transactions. These clerks typically delay the transaction, often telling the customer that "the lines are busy" while they notify the fraud unit of the bankcard company involved. Fraud units established by MasterCard, Visa, American Express and others cooperate with police. Citicorp's fraud unit employs 175 people. When an ancillary crime may be involved, special teams within these units immediately investigate a case. For example, in a Pennsylvania case in 1997, three individuals using a credit card stolen from Henry Egbo, whose body had been dumped in the Monongahela River, attempted to use the card for purchases at a Pittsburgh sporting goods store. The suspicious clerk notified "Code 10 team" at Citibank Universal Card. The team contacted Mrs. Egbo and learned that permission had not been given to anyone to use the card and that it would be odd for Mr. Egbo to make a sporting goods purchase. The police were called, the individuals ultimately gave statements about their involvement in the slaying, and were charged with murder. One of the individuals died in a fall during an attempted escape from Allegheny County Jail, and the other two now await trial. Citibank's Code 10 team, with 21 members, helped solve five murders in 1997. Since its inception in 1991, it has aided in some 7,050 police arrests. Other bankcard companies have similar teams and track records. These fraud units are sometimes able to track down Alzheimer victims when such victims use their bankcards.

One can easily see the application of such methods to FEDEC. If the FEDEC system were to employ biometric PIV devices, such as fingerprints, retinal scans, or voiceprints, the system would be of even greater utility to law enforcement. For one, it would allow police to cut through the use of multiple aliases.

Considering that the great majority of crime in the United States involves cash, it is plausible that at least 15 percent of crime in general and as much as 40 percent (half the percentage that robbery, burglary, and larceny theft constitute of all crimes) would be prevented—either made impossible or deterred—by switching to electronic currency.

HOW ELECTRONIC CURRENCY WOULD UNDERMINE
DRUG CRIME

Transforming cash to FEDEC has the potential of toppling drug traffickers and slashing related criminal activity. Illegal drug crime dominates
justice systems throughout the United States. Mandatory sentencing of
drug criminals has raised prison populations to the overflow mark. The
fiscal cost is enormous. In 1990, the federal, state, and local budget for
drug control alone was $28 billion.[5] That figure continues to rise each
year. For example, the federal portion, which was about $11 billion in
1990, rose to $15 billion in 1993, and to $17.6 billion in 1995 and is
projected to reach $23.3 billion in 1999.[6] The government reports that
"Drug-abuse and drug-related crime costs the U.S. an estimated $67 bil-
lion a year."[7] As we shall see, the total likely runs even higher. Taking
into account the full list of private-sector losses—for stolen goods, medical
expenses, funeral expenses, lost earnings, lowered property values, increased security expense, and insurance rates, as well as a host of other
damages—the sum is astronomical.

Drug trafficking is not about drug addiction; it is about money and profits. Realizing this, a growing number of Americans have concluded that
the drug plague will be ended only by removing the profit factor. Thus,
not a few advocate legalizing the sale of narcotics. While the logic of the
proposal is clear, it is not a clean solution to the problem, and its proponents remain ambiguous as to how to handle such acknowledged side
effects as increased addiction, the self-destructive and violent acts of drug
users, and sales to children.[8]

Preventing crime by ending cash is a concept that stands apart from,
and is neutral in, the controversy about legalization. Indeed, it would help
in either case. On the one hand, making America's cash electronic might
serve as an acceptable alternative to legalization; while it would not eradicate sales of illegal drugs, it could well shrink the problem to a small
percentage of today's volume. On the other hand, electronic currency
could operate contemporaneously with legalization to obstruct and dis-
courage abuses of newly granted liberties.

Drug crime is not just about any form of money; it is about cash. Virtually every drug sale is conducted in U.S. currency. Eliminating cash
would subject transaction data to tracing, creating big payment problems
for users, dealers, and traffickers. Dealing in electronic currency would be
tantamount to putting evidence of drug crimes directly on DEA, IRS, or
other investigative agencies' computer screens—names, addresses,
amounts, dates, computerized pictures, and probably, by the time FEDEC
would come into being, fingerprints or other biometrics.

Drug criminals might turn to private credit- and debit-card systems, but these are a far cry from the anonymity of cash. Though the process is less efficient for authorities, payment trails in these media can also be accessed to identify parties, to document dates and places, and to provide other details of crimes. Moreover, many addicts cannot qualify for such bankcards.

The common drug dealer would be forced to choose other types of payment media. Since the dealer would not be foolish enough to accept ordinary checks from buyers, that leaves only money orders, cashier's checks, or traveler's checks ("documented money"). By using phony or blank payees on documented money, parties to illicit sales would hope to throw law enforcement off their tracks. The switch to electronic currency might be accompanied by an increase in thefts of money orders and cashier's and traveler's checks. Money-order blanks were a prime target of looters in the 1992 Los Angeles riots, in which over 40,000 were stolen. Counterfeiting of these documents would increase, as well. We are already witnessing this trend. However, the concentration of documented money in the hands of drug dealers and traffickers would highlight drug sales. Laundering today's cash would be child's play by comparison, with the result that drug dealers would suffer far more arrests and convictions.

Money orders and traveler's checks, though they might be negotiated without leaving a trail, would obviously be poor substitutes for drug cash. Their use, to any significant extent, would expose drug dealers, thinning their ranks. As important, this type of money would also be problematic for drug *users*. It would mean that a dealer's customers would have to acquire money orders or cashier's or traveler's checks. Drug customers would need some payment medium with which to buy such documented money. This becomes a stumbling block that could reduce today's big-time illegal drug trade to small-time business.

Some drug users have conventional sources of revenue; others resort to crime for income. The former group is comprised of occasional drug users who use cocaine, marijuana, and "designer" drugs for recreation and who pay for such drugs with legitimately acquired income.[9] Employed or affluent drug users would continue purchasing relatively small amounts of illegal drugs without much risk of detection. For example, it would not be difficult to hide the occasional $250 purchase of high-grade marijuana or a $20 "hit" of Ecstasy via money orders or cashier's or traveler's checks or with bankcards (in the limited cases where they might be accepted). All the same, using these types of payments, which might leave a partial trail, for buying illegal drugs would considerably increase risks of being identified and criminally charged. For middle-and upper-class drug users, the thought of being arrested and jailed, an event that could ruin a career, is a strong deterrent. Ending today's untraceable cash is bound to cause a significant percentage of this group to desist from buying illegal drugs.

Heavier drug users and addicts who support their habit primarily by theft would be doubly affected by a switch to electronic money. For them, the problem is not just greater exposure to prosecution because of a payment media trail, but the very basic problem of how to acquire any type of funds in the first place. Drug-addicted prostitutes would acquire funds from clients paying by money order or from those willing to risk exposure by paying in electronic currency or by private-sector bankcards. Some addicts would be crafty enough to embezzle funds from their employers, partners, spouses, or family businesses—or all of these. Tens of thousands of addicts receiving government benefits would buy money orders or traveler's checks and, to the extent acceptable, hand nearly all of this money to drug dealers within the first two to three days of the month.

This brings us to the typical hard-core addict without any regular source of income who nowadays robs and steals to purchase drugs. Putting aside the matter of the drug sale itself, how would this person acquire any form of money in the first place?

One can imagine a robber in a FEDEC society, no longer able to hold up grocery stores, snatch purses, or rob ATM patrons, coercing a victim to buy a money order or cashier's check. Clearly, an act of that sort greatly extends crime-in-progress time, stands a good chance of complications with third parties, and, runs a high risk of being caught and arrested.

Conceivably, a desperate drug user could force a victim under threat of violence to transfer electronic currency into the thief's FEDEC account, an act that could be accomplished out of sight by using a personal FEDEC terminal. This type of crime also spells arrest and would never become widespread. Transaction data and account records would not only identify the criminal but would also provide evidence of the crime. Furthermore, the thief's subsequent use of his FEDEC account (which the thief would have to use in order to spend the stolen funds) could be monitored to locate him. The dead-end nature of a forced FEDEC transaction should render it an infrequent occurrence.

To deter such crime, it is plausible that a FEDEC system would incorporate a procedure allowing anyone who had been "robbed" (i.e., forced to transfer FEDEC funds against their will) to put a stop, via any terminal, on the FEDEC account into which such funds were transferred—the identity of which would be revealed by reference to the last transfer made from the victim's account.

Depriving criminals of a traceless payment medium raises the troubling concern that threats of and actual violence would increase as some segments of society became more desperate to secure illegal drugs. The above scenarios presume that the victim would report the crime. Intimidation would prevent reporting in some cases. Yet, inasmuch as FEDEC data would be available both as evidence and for locating criminals, victims might not be as reluctant to report crimes in the future. Yet, what if a robber were to murder the victim? The answer is that if a criminal had killed a victim as part of a forced FEDEC transaction, transaction data would lead police directly to the killer, a predictable consequence that would serve as a strong deterrent.

As the public learned the workings of electronic currency, the realization would sink in that the new "cash" was not susceptible to theft, at least not without the high likelihood of being caught and convicted. This fact is sure to curtail a large percentage of crime. Nonetheless, eliminating cash, alone, would not eradicate the drug problem and its negative consequences to society.

Where would this cashless society leave the addict, the dealer, and higher functionaries in the illegal drug trade? Initially, some small-time dealers would probably risk accepting electronic currency from the limited number of customers who could and were willing to tender it. However, FEDEC data would quickly lead police to these dealers. Most important, sales would have dropped heavily because of the deterrent effect on occasional users and the inability of hard-core users to raise money of any type. At the same time, the arrest rate for dealers would have increased dramatically.

Electronic monies of all types tend to establish linkage evidence in illegal-drug structures. Even if user-level sales were to be conducted in electronic currency, higher-ups in the drug trade would not take the chance of accepting payment in that form because it might provide hard evidence connecting them with known street drug dealers. Unusual numbers of transactions and high-volume transfers by persons so connected, that is, at distributor levels, made via the FEDEC system would signal suspicious activity to law enforcement officials. Therefore, lower-level dealers accepting electronic-currency payments would be faced with the inadequate remedy of converting such money by purchasing money orders or cashier's checks with which to pay their distributors. Thus, the problem would ripple through their systems. Any continued drug trade under these conditions would see sales falling, more interdiction by law enforcement, and distributors and importers stuck with bundles of difficult-to-use documented money. With the advent of FEDEC, the general popularity of documented money would likely have declined below today's levels. One can imagine some future bank teller's thoughts, therefore, when approached by someone trying to deposit a stack of money orders all made out for $5, $10, or $20.

With cash no longer in circulation, law enforcement would have different battles to fight. Drug traffickers might use private-sector credit- and debit-card systems and increase usage of wire transfers or even new Internet payment channels. Government would continually be challenged to block these avenues. Yet, no matter how devious criminals' payment schemes might be, they would always involve more parties, require more steps, and be subjected to a greater likelihood of discovery than with the use of currency.

In summary, changing cash to an electronic form would significantly undermine illegal drug trafficking in a number of ways. Sales would dry up from the bottom. Occasional users, deterred by fear of being found out through payment transaction records, would fade away. The street addict, backbone of the trade, deprived of traditional sources of income, would be unable to raise an acceptable form of payment for drugs and would be left stranded. The numbers of burglaries and thefts across the nation would decline sharply. Fencing operations would shrink. Dealers' revenues would fall dramatically. Drug suppliers would find themselves unable to hide their earnings both from the police and from the Internal Revenue Service. The common urban American scene of heavily armed youths selling drugs through car windows, their pockets bulging with cash, would become history. The advent of electronic currency could well mark the end of an ugly era of rampant crime.

HOW ELECTRONIC CURRENCY WOULD GENERATE REVENUE FROM THE UNDERGROUND ECONOMY

If tax evasion is included in the definition, all underground activity is illegal. In terms of being otherwise criminal, some experts estimate that a third of underground dollars are transacted in crimes such as receiving stolen property, fraud, counterfeiting, embezzlement, bribery, illegal drugs, smuggling, prostitution, pornography, illegal gambling, and loan sharking. This would mean that about two-thirds of the dollars that go unreported to authorities are produced in otherwise legitimate enterprises.

An absence of transaction recordation and of voluntary reporting in this arena makes it difficult to gauge the extent of the underground economy. Consequently, indirect methods are used to measure its size. Extrapolations are made from reliable statistics, such as wholesale revenues and production figures. Using these, some economists employ complex mathematics to calculate its size. However, these methods can be obtuse and are typically dependent on many assumptions. The absence of direct and complete figures upon which to base calculations puts accuracy beyond reach.

The IRS puts the proportions of the underground economy as consisting of one-quarter from criminal activity and three-quarters from otherwise legal business.[10] One can reasonably assume that virtually all income from crime goes unreported and that, therefore, the entire criminal component comprises one-quarter of the total underground economy. Although they are a bit hazy and vary widely, some crime dollar estimates have been developed, and it is interesting to pit them against the IRS ratio as a means of estimating the size of the underground economy. This can be done by dividing the estimated size of the illegal segment by the percentage of the whole accorded that segment.

U.S. illegal drug trade is estimated by the Department of Justice at $300 billion a year.[11] Dividing this amount by 25 percent would put the size of the underground economy at $1.2 trillion. This is about 16 percent of the GDP, an incredibly high number. Casting further doubt on this figure, the IRS allocation between illegal and otherwise legal components of the underground economy is not limited to illegal drug activity; including additional types of criminal activity would produce an estimate substantially greater than $1.2 trillion. Clearly, something is wrong here.

The Office of National Drug Control Policy (ONDCP) estimates the size of the illegal drug trade in the U.S. at only $50 billion. Using the 25 percent assumption and based on this figure alone, the size of the underground economy would be at least $200 billion. This seems plausible, yet the amount is meaningless because it is not based on the total dollars generated in all criminal activity. However, the dollar amount of all criminal activity is virtually inestimable.

Most research on the size of the underground economy centers on its otherwise legitimate component, which students of the subject concur is the far greater portion. An early researcher once suggested that the legitimate component of underground economy might be equal to 27 percent of the GNP,[12] but most economists today would estimate its size at around 10 percent, which in 1997 would mean about $750 billion. We can use this generally accepted figure to calculate roughly how much might be produced in new tax revenues as a result of converting cash to an electronic currency system.

Incidentally, the IRS does not use a percentage of GDP approach to determine the tax deficiency of the underground economy. The IRS makes little reference to the "underground economy" or equivalent nomenclature. Rather, it concentrates on "tax gaps." The "gross income tax gap is the amount of true income tax liability that is not voluntarily paid."[13] The approach taken by the IRS in determining the extent of tax noncompliance is first to break the problem down into two categories: income-tax-return filers and nonfilers.

The Taxpayer Compliance Measurement Program (TCMP), for 30 years ending in 1996, was the primary IRS method of gathering information about taxpayer compliance. Under it, about 55,000 tax returns each year were put under scrutiny and examined line by line. These unfortunate filers were required to prove every deduction with solid evidence. Their incomes were cross-checked against informational returns such as W-2s, 1099s, and 1087s. The percentage deficiency in tax compliance detected through this program was projected against the returns for the nation as a whole to produce an estimate of gross noncompliance. The TCMP has been replaced by the "financial status" audit, sometimes referred to as the "reality audit," which has brought numerous complaints about intrusive questions relating to how much one spends on vacations, contents of safe deposit boxes, childrens' education, and the like.

Concurrently, the number and identity of nonfilers was estimated by the use of interagency data to locate "matches." Information from the Census Bureau's Household Surveys, Social Security earnings data, and IRS returns were combined in a three-stage filtering process to locate those who did not file returns and to determine the amount of income taxes that should have been paid. Using the results of these two investigative channels, the IRS formed an estimate of the "gross tax gap"—that is, the amount of taxes that should have been, but were not, voluntarily paid. In 1981, the gross tax gap came to $75.9 billion;[14] in 1992, it had reached $127.1 billion, evidencing an annual growth rate of 6.1 percent. Using this growth rate, the tax gap in 1998 stands at $181.3 billion. The missing revenue in 1992, had it been collected, would have reduced the tax burden on those who complied by 22 percent. (See *Impact*, Americans for Fair Taxation, at website address *http://www.fairtax.org/impact/national retail.htm.*)

The IRS depends on its ability to use audit trails to uncover those who fail to file returns or report all of their income. With the benefit of traceless cash, however, many undergrounders leave no trail for the IRS to follow and escape surveillance. They are too well hidden to be included in the formula. Even the IRS admits "that despite the intensity of the TCMP examinations, some income still goes undetected. . . . Although various examination techniques are used by TCMP examiners to elicit information on other forms of income, it is widely believed that substantial amounts of income were never detected."[15] Thus, IRS estimates of the size of the problem, at best, serve only as a low-water mark. Moreover, the "gross tax gap" and the "underground economy," though they overlap in fact, are not synonymous.

A portion of underground transactions are conducted by the use of checks or with documented money, but the great majority are conducted in cash. Some experts suggest that almost all hidden labor income is in the form of currency, while underground income from rents and royalties, capital gains, and other income represents mixed cases, perhaps half checks and half cash.[16]

Studies conducted in the 1970s and 1980s by Peter M. Gutmann, an economics professor at Baruch College at the City College of New York, concluded that practically all unreported underground activity was in cash; his approach to measuring the size of the underground economy was based on this assumption. By observing that the nation's currency holdings had increased at an abnormal rate over several decades, Gutmann estimated the size of the underground economy to have been equal in 1977 to nearly 10 percent of the GNP, and in 1981, to 14 percent.

Other studies have also indicated a relationship between the amount of cash in circulation and underground activity. In 1984, the Board of Governors of the Federal Reserve System commissioned the Survey of Currency and Transaction Account Usage to establish data on the methods by which Americans make their payments: for instance, with cash, checks, money orders, or credit cards. An article prepared by the Board's Division of Research and Statistics discusses the survey, stating that "Although cash is a highly suitable means of payment for many transactions, little information on how it is acquired and used in the United States is available." It reveals that 88 percent of the cash held outside banks is unaccounted for. Under a paragraph labeled "The 'Missing' Cash," the article continues, "Thus, in 1986 as in 1984, a large percentage of the U.S. currency was apparently held in unreported hoards, 'underground' for illegitimate purposes, or offshore" (*Federal Reserve Bulletin*, vol. 73, no. 3, March 1987).

Professor Feige reports that "the available evidence is insufficient to determine the exact proportion of unreported income that is transacted with currency, but it is reasonable to assume that 25 to 35% of such payments are, in fact, made with checks."[17] This assumption would seem to mean, conversely, that 65 percent to 75 percent is in cash. Multiplying the lowest figure, 65 percent, by $750 billion (approximately 10 percent of the GDP) would indicate that $488 billion of the underground economy is conducted in cash. Calculating how much tax revenue might be raised from this $488 billion as a result of making cash electronic involves several steps. First, the gross figure developed above, $488 billion, must be discounted to allow for business expense, for even underground merchants must pay expenses. Thus, assuming a 50 percent overall business expense (which is conservative, considering that many undergrounders are in service businesses where expenses are low), the net taxable income would be $244 billion. (Figures are rounded to billions.)

Second, we must estimate the effectiveness of switching to electronic currency in deterring tax cheating. It is plausible that fear of audit and tax-fraud prosecution would inspire most former tax evaders to begin reporting all of their income. As likely, some undergrounders would remain undeterred. The IRS could not chase down every tax dollar. Moreover, some former cash users would switch their covert transactions to checks, money orders, or other media, taking their chances on traceability and thus sidestepping the direct effects of making cash electronic. Because of these considerations, let's arbitrarily assume that 20 percent of the cash underground would continue even after the new e-money system had replaced cash. This reduces our target net income from $244 billion to $195 billion.

The final step in developing a crude estimate of the amount of income tax revenues that might be generated by abolishing cash is to figure the tax. To remain on the conservative side, and rather than attempting to establish some average adjusted income, let's simply use the lowest federal income tax bracket, which is 15 percent. This tax rate, multiplied by the target net income figure above, $195 billion, produces $29 billion—which is an estimate of the annual amount of previously unrealized federal income tax revenues that would be generated by transforming cash to electronic currency.

Cash transformation would generate tax revenues at the state level as well. Consider state sales taxes. Assuming that 20 percent of the cash underground economy involves sales of taxable goods (allowing for services and other nontaxable items) and using a 4 percent sales-tax rate (which takes into consideration that some states have higher rates and that some impose no sales taxes), this would indicate that another $3.9 billion in sales-tax revenues would be generated across the states ($488 billion × 20 % × 4 % sales tax = $3.9 billion).

State income taxes would be generated as well. At a recent California State Senate hearing, testimony was given that a $60 billion underground economy exists in the state by reason of which the state is cheated out of $3 billion in taxes annually. Without analyzing the underground figures for each of the states with income taxes and taking into consideration that California is a relatively affluent state with high income tax rates, it seems plausible that a minimum of $10 billion in combined state income taxes for the nation would be raised by implementation of a FEDEC system.

Some discount should be made for noncollectibility of taxes. However, this requires analysis of the effectiveness of the FEDEC informational system and would become so abstruse and hypothetical that it would lose all probative value. The overly conservative approach taken herein should offset the noncollectibility factor.

Roughly, new revenues from federal income taxes, state income taxes, and sales taxes, together with additional regulatory fees, local licenses, and permit fees, would likely exceed $40 billion annually (see Table 6.1).

Those who study the underground economy offer little hope of bringing it under control. Yet, despite disagreement as to the size of the underground economy, all the experts seem to agree that it operates predominantly in cash. Transforming cash, then, emerges as an effective method of reducing its size.

ABOUT DETERRENCE

The vast majority of Americans obey the law from moral imperative. Unfortunately, what keeps another segment of the populace within the law is simply the fear of being caught. For every tax cheater, there are

Table 6.1
Projected Tax Benefits of Transforming Cash (in billions)

A.	Gross Domestic Product (GDP)	$7,500.0
B.	Size of Underground Economy @ 10% of A	750.0
C.	Underground Economy Conducted in Cash @ 65% of B	488.0
D.	Discounted 50% for Business Expenses	244.0
E.	Discount 20% for Undetected Underground Activity (80% of D)	195.0
Increased Federal Income Taxes @ 15% of E		**29.0**
plus—State Sales Taxes @ 4% × C × 20%		**3.9**
plus—Revenues from State Income Taxes, Fees, Permits, etc.		**10.0**
TOTAL INCREASED TAX REVENUES		**$42.9**

many more who would do the same, except that they do not believe they could get away with it.

Yet, the new threat that auditable electronic currency would pose to tax evaders and other criminals would have a greater impact than government's ability to follow through. Even after the FEDEC system was in operation, there would be just so many police officers, investigators, prosecutors, and judges and a finite number of dollars available in the criminal justice system. Nevertheless, crime statistics would fall at a rate disproportionately greater than the government's law enforcement capacity. The discrepancy would be attributable to deterrence.

The causal relationship between deterrence and law compliance is statistically demonstrated by a 1973 tax compliance analysis revealing that income reporting profiles are strongly influenced by whether incomes are (1) subject to withholding (W-2s), where income underreporting was less than 0.5 percent, or (2) subject to information document filing (e.g., 1099s, but not W-2s), where income underreporting was about 6.5 percent. Where neither withholding nor information document filing was involved, underreporting was 22 percent.[18] This entire survey was repeated in 1996, with similar findings.

The mere inauguration of electronic currency would transform America into a more law-abiding country. The greatest effect of transforming cash into an auditable payment medium lies far less in catching and convicting criminals than in preventing crimes.

HOW ELECTRONIC CURRENCY WOULD REDUCE GOVERNMENT BENEFITS FRAUD

Cash facilitates government program benefit fraud in a several ways. In some, cash is used to hide income that would disqualify individuals from receiving benefits. In others, it is used to divert program benefits from their intended purposes. Converting cash to an electronic money system would impede these frauds, as well as a type of fraud that does not involve cash directly, namely, the use of alias accounts.

Experts estimate that about 40 percent of welfare fraud involves misrepresentation of recipients' total income. Between 1 percent and 5 percent of general assistance recipients commit fraud by filing under multiple names and/or collecting benefits from more than one county or state.[19] A federal study indicates that overpayments in AFDC alone came to $1 billion in 1991, or some 5 percent of the total paid that year.[20]

This type of fraud is being uncovered in a number of jurisdictions by matching fingerprints to recipients' names. The goal is to spot several names and/or payments being made to the same fingerprint ID. This method, which has proven quite successful, is being used with AFDC, general assistance, and other types of benefits.

Because FEDEC account applicants would likely undergo thorough identification verification, involving fingerprint or other biometric ID, it should be virtually impossible for anyone to secure an alias account. Cross-matching would be automatic and accurate. Most recipients of government benefits would likely opt to have the payments made directly into their FEDEC accounts (probably replacing much of today's EBT systems). If so, alias-account welfare fraud would become a rare occurrence.

The most common government program fraud, however, is for a prospective recipient to conceal income to appear means qualified for benefits. The simplest method is to hide income in cash. Clearly, transforming cash to a recorded system that would be available to authorities is certain to make this type of fraud more risky and reduce perpetration.

Aside from alias-type fraud, hard data on government program fraud is difficult to find. Indeed, it was necessary to use dated studies in researching the subject. On the other hand, little has changed over the years that would lead one to believe that fraud statistics have changed much.

In 1984, the IRS contracted with Abt Associates, Inc., to research the extent of government benefits fraud. The following is excerpted from their report:

In this section we estimate fraudulent income obtained from six government benefit programs: AFDC, SSI, UI, Medicaid, Medicare and Food Stamps. . . . Most of the literature on the subject focuses on ways to prevent it, rather than to estimate its extent . . . conversation with personnel at both state and federal levels indicated that enforcement personnel have little idea of the extent of fraud not referred to them for investigation.[21]

The Abt Associates report indicates that the following percentages of total benefits paid under each of the following programs (in 1982) were fraudulent:

AFDC	2.5 %
Food Stamp	4.5 %
SSI	0.5 %
UI	2.5 %[22]

Because of the difficulty in detecting fraud, these figures likely under-state the extent of the problem. Abt Associates, Inc., indicates the same:

[L]osses to fraud, unlike theft, are only noticed if the fraud is discovered. In the case of government benefits, it is relatively easy to tell how much money has been paid, but very difficult to tell how much of these payments constitutes losses to fraud. To the extent that they are based on discovered cases, our estimates will tend to underestimate the true loss to fraud.[23]

It is even more difficult to discover how much welfare fraud in-volves the use of cash. Empirical evidence suggests that government benefit program fraud is typically perpetrated by omitting to declare cash income. My own interviews with scores of low-income-housing residents indicate that at least every fourth welfare recipient hides on-the-side income at least occasionally. In almost every instance the income is received in cash.

Some fraud involves diversion of government benefits from their in-tended purposes. Such is the case with food stamp fraud. Food stamp recipients often sell their food coupons for cash, typically at a 30 percent discount, to crooked grocers. The latter, in turn, present them to the gov-ernment for 100 percent payment. As recently as mid-1995, investigators estimated that $2 billion is embezzled annually from the food stamp pro-gram in this manner, with much of it being used to buy alcoholic bever-ages and illegal drugs.

The Department of Agriculture thought it had this problem solved in jurisdictions that had switched from food coupons to EBT. However, it was subsequently discovered that fraudulent recipients continued to col-lude with crooked merchants to perpetrate the same old fraud, albeit in an EBT system. The merchants processed the transactions using the recip-ients' EBT cards; just as before EBT came into being, instead of handing over food, they would give discounted sums of cash to the recipients. One might jump to the erroneous conclusion that the EBT system offers no more protection against food stamp fraud than cash. However, the EBT systems replaced only food coupons. Cash, not EBT, was the culprit.

Some welfare cheaters are caught and prosecuted, but most are never even challenged. Investigation of any meaningful portion of welfare fraud poses a dilemma because of the prohibitive costs involved and the shortage of funds needed for benefit disbursements. In California, which may or may not be representative of the nation as a whole, only about 10 percent of welfare cases are audited. In some California counties, Alameda County, for example, only 4 percent of welfare cases are audited.

Liberal observers make the argument that greater moral good is achieved by disregarding minor amounts of disqualifying income and assets of welfare recipients because relief for the near-destitute sector is more important than distinctions in degrees of poverty. Some view program benefits such as for welfare, unemployment, and disability as far too stringent and coldly conditioned on desperation. The problem with this argument is that it is not just the destitute and near-destitute who draw governmental humanitarian aid. Some program recipients enjoy relatively substantial hidden incomes.

Overall, transformation of cash to an electronic medium would improve government benefit programs in several ways: First, it would eliminate currency as an avenue for benefit program fraud. Second, data processing in the new system would aid in verifying the income qualifications of applicants. Third, new computer programs would generate accurate data for use by government planners and administrators in meeting the needs of the truly needy. Fourth, the monetary changeover would help put American taxpayers at ease in knowing that government benefits were not being siphoned off by individuals receiving undeclared cash income or drawing multiple disbursements under alias accounts.

It would be conservative, in estimating the fiscal effect of switching to electronic currency on government benefit program fraud, to assume that only 1 in 20, or 5 percent, of recipients commits fraud by failing to disclose cash income. As indicated in Table 6.2, this should result in an annual cost savings of at least $17.2 billion.

HOW ELECTRONIC CURRENCY WOULD REDUCE CRIMINAL JUSTICE EXPENSE

In 1990, the combined cost of federal, state, and local police, criminal courts, prosecution, publicly funded legal defense, prisons, and jails in the United States amounted to $74 billion dollars.[24] In 1998, it runs about $100 billion a year.[25]

To calculate the justice expenditures that could be saved by making currency electronic, one might multiply the percentage of crime that would be eliminated by the amount of current outlays. One of the problems in this approach is developing an appropriate percentage. Particular crimes, such as bank robbery, would be prevented totally, and it is predictable that a great deal of other criminal activity would be prevented as well—but how much?

Only the Bureau of Justice Statistics analysis described earlier, indicating

Table 6.2
Federal, State, and Local Social Benefit Programs That Would Be Impacted by Electronic Money (based on 1994 statistics)[26]

Program	Total Expenditures (in billions)
Medical Care	161.1
Cash Aid	83.8
Food Benefits	38.1
Housing Benefits	26.1
Educational Aid	15.7
Services	12.0
Jobs and Training	5.5
Energy Assistance	1.9
TOTAL	$344.2
FRAUD (ASSUME 5%)	$17.2

that 12 percent of all reported crimes are cash-wallet-purse thefts, provides the type of statistical basis needed. Virtually all such crimes would be prevented by conversion to electronic currency. Thus, it is reasonable to assume that at least 12 percent of justice expense would be prevented by eliminating cash. Yet, among other failings, this approach does not describe the crimes in which those items were taken or fully address crimes known to have a significant relationship to cash, including robbery and burglary. Therefore, this approach can only provide a minimal observation.

Another approach rests on the fact that robberies, burglaries, and larceny thefts collectively comprise about 75 percent of all reported crimes (see Table 1.1). The probability of a major impact on this group of crimes is high. Assuming that half of all robberies, burglaries, and larceny thefts (excluding auto thefts) would be prevented as a result of converting cash to electronic currency, then roughly 38 percent of all reported crimes would be eliminated. Would this mean a concomitant 38 percent reduction in justice expenditures?

Clearly, a number of factors must be figured in. For example, justice expenditure is far greater for some crimes than others—for example, murder (in the course of robbery) versus petty theft. Many crimes do not even result in formal prosecutions, and thefts of wallets and purses may fall into this category.

As many law enforcement agencies are presently understaffed, a reduction in the number of crimes committed might not be accompanied by a concomitant downsizing of personnel. Of course, the benefit of this consequence would be in kind, rather than in dollar savings. That is, communities would probably experience quicker police response time, lower court caseloads, less-crowded jails, and more parole supervision. Moreover, the general deterrent effect on crime might have such a positive result as to skew estimates.

A further consideration is the usage of electronic currency as an investigative and evidence-providing tool. For example, FEDEC would serve as an efficient device for locating subjects and witnesses, thus substantially reducing the time and costs currently spent by law enforcement. As well, the use of e-currency transaction records as evidence would make cases easier to prove and inspire more guilty pleas.

The cost savings of e-currency would extend beyond the crimes of robbery, burglary, and larceny theft. For instance, cash is the common payment medium used in bribery, extortion, loan sharking, and sales of stolen property. Thus, the 35 percent reduction in justice expenditures developed above, though merely a thumbnail estimate, begins to appear plausible, if not conservative. At a minimum, it would seem that conversion to electronic money would result in a savings of $12 billion in reduced criminal justice expenditures (12% × $100 billion). Yet, the true percentage of resultant crime prevention would very likely be much higher, producing a justice savings at least as much as $38 billion per year. In Table 6.4, "Cost Benefit Summary of a Cashless Society," the average of these two figures, $25 billion, is used.

HOW ELECTRONIC CURRENCY WOULD REDUCE CRIME-VICTIM COSTS

Were crime prevented to any degree as a result of ending cash, it follows that a concomitant percentage of victim cost would be prevented with it. To figure this, one has to know the amount of current victim costs resulting from cash-related crime. This is difficult. First, the absence of a practical and/or standard definition of "victim cost" and, therefore, the subjective discretion in setting its parameters make any reliable projection impossible. Second is the difficulty of figuring the causal impact of ending cash. The dearth of specific cash-crime statistics does not help. Yet, the obviously enormous cost of crime to victims in the United States warrants at least an attempt to place a dollar figure on victim costs that would be eliminated by transforming cash to e-currency. The following rough estimates of prospective savings, more speculation than prediction, provide no reliable numeric conclusion. Yet, as most would agree, even the lowest dollar figures one encounters are so strikingly high as to make any effort in developing accurate cost estimates a pointless exercise.

The NCVS provides estimates of crime-victim costs. On the low side as victim-cost estimates go, they might serve in calculating a minimum in personal loss that would be saved by switching to electronic currency. The NCVS estimate for gross crime losses to victims and households in 1991 is $19.4 billion. Gross loss, in its survey, "was derived by summing up the amount of stolen cash, the value of stolen property, estimated or actual costs of replacing damaged property, medical expenses, lost pay from employment because of injuries, police-related activities, court-related activities, or time spent repairing or replacing property."[27] In 1992, the figure had dropped to $17.6 billion.[28] Such victim costs may have declined even further because crime rates have fallen; on the other hand, the value of goods stolen has increased, and medical and other costs have risen. Applying the 12 percent figure developed above to the $17.4 billion estimate of victim costs, indicates that $2.1 billion would be saved in such victim costs by transforming cash into e-currency. Again, however, this approach does not take into account that individuals suffer losses from cash crimes other than those in which cash, wallets, and purses are taken.

Another approach rests on the assumption that half of all robbery, burglary, and larceny theft would be eliminated by changing to the electronic money system. As these crimes comprise roughly 75 percent of all crimes, switching from cash to electronic currency should prevent about 38 percent (half of 75 percent) of all crime—and, therefore, 38 percent of victim costs as well. Thirty-eight percent of the "gross loss" as developed by NCVS, that is, 38 percent of $17.4 billion, would mean a loss savings to victims of $6.6 billion a year. But, this method, crude at best, serves only as a low-water mark.

A recent in-depth report prepared for the National Institute of Justice (NIJ) by Ted Miller and Mark A. Cohen gives a better picture of just how expensive crime is to its victims. The two-year multidisciplinary study concludes that tangible losses from personal crime cost Americans around $105 billion annually. If pain, suffering, and reduced quality of life are also taken into account, the figure soars to $405 billion.[29]

Though general data has been developed on the cost of crime, existing studies are of limited value here because their scope and purpose are not pertinent to a cash-related inquiry. No study isolates the cost of cash-related crime. The NIJ study referenced above includes crimes with little relevance to cash—such as domestic violence, rape, child abuse, and drunk driving—and excludes many crimes involving cash—such as crimes against business (theft, fraud, embezzlement), crimes against government (including tax evasion), and "victimless" crimes (illegal-drug possession, gambling, loan sharking, and prostitution). The purpose of the NIJ study is to serve as "an important tool in formulating criminal justice policy" and "to help guide resource allocations across crimes."

An in-depth study on the costs of crime to victims published in *Health Affairs*[30] criticizes the NCVS "gross loss" as being seriously understated because it fails to include data on children under twelve years of age, as well as data on military personnel, the institutionalized, and the homeless.

Consequently, cost-of-crime figures developed in the *Health Affairs* study are substantially higher than those of the NCVS.

According to the *Health Affairs* report:

The quality of the injury costs from the NCS [same as NCVS] victim self-reports is suspect for several reasons. The survey asks victims to recall details of crimes that occurred up to six months earlier. Victims who suffered minor injuries at the start of this time period may forget small costs, while those who suffered serious injury may be unaware of the cumulative costs. For example, hospital bills may go directly to the insurer, so that the insured never learns of the amount. Also, the NCS includes only costs through the interview date, on average only three months after victimization.

Victim of crime losses in the *Health Affairs* report include the following outlays: medical, medical mental health, emergency response services, and insurance administration. Also included are losses from reduced direct productivity, losses in the form of wages, fringe benefits, and housework, and nonmonetary losses such as pain, suffering, and lost quality of life.

The research team for this extensive study were quite resourceful. They secured direct data from some 21 hospital emergency rooms. They also utilized factors from the International Classification of Diseases and based long-term crime-caused medical costs, in part, on the Detailed Claims Information database of the National Council on Compensation Insurance. "This database longitudinally tracks the medical care costs of 450,000 randomly sampled victims of disabling work place injuries suffered between 1979 and 1987."[31]

Unfortunately, the *Health Affairs* report addresses victim costs for only four crimes: rape, robbery, assault, and arson. Since cashlessness would have an unpredictable effect on rape (although 3 percent of robbery victims are raped[32]) and an inestimable effect on arson and assault, the *Health Affairs* report is of limited use. Therefore, I have used only its data relating to robbery, a crime known from common knowledge as well as from courtroom evidence to be perpetrated in a high percentage of cases with the motive of taking cash.

The *Health Affairs* report states that there were an average of 1,482,000 robbery victimizations each year between 1987 and 1990, which includes both completed offenses and attempts.[33] It indicates that 36 percent of robbery victims were injured. "More than 4% of injured victims sustained gunshot or stab wounds, and almost 7% had bones broken or teeth knocked out."[34] Its statement that 2,600 murders were perpetrated in the course of robberies is supported by FBI statistics indicating that about 10 percent of all homicides are committed with robbery as the circumstance.

Cost factors in the *Health Affairs* report are divided into three groups:

monetary, mental health, and quality of life. Monetary costs include medical expenses, the cost of emergency services, lost productivity, and administrative costs. Mental health costs include mental health medical expenses, mental health productivity losses, and mental health productivity lost because of psychological injury. Quality of life is not broken down into components.

All factors included, costs to an injured robbery victim run about $25,000, and a robbery-caused death represents a $2.4 million loss. In the United States, the latter is often the figure placed on a single life. It is quoted by attorneys in wrongful death cases, for example, in comparing the cost of vehicle safety devices to the value of the lives that would be saved.

By multiplying the $25,000 figure (total cost per injured robbery victim) by the number of victims injured in robberies, some 534,000 (36 percent of 1,482,000 robberies), shows that robbery-injury costs run at some $13.4 billion annually. Add to this 2,500 robbery deaths at $2.4 million each, or $6 billion, and total robbery victim costs rise to $19.4 billion. Including the value of property stolen in robberies, $6.6 million,[35] the total exceeds $20 billion.

Before determining how much of this cost would be prevented by abolishing cash, one has to qualify and downsize the figures developed in the *Health Affairs* report, for as one goes down its list of cost factors, they decrease dramatically in objective quantification. For example, it is difficult to employ any logical method in assessing dollar values for the last factor, "quality of life."

Thus, omitting the mental-health and quality-of-life factors, but retaining the $6 billion cost of robbery deaths and the $600 million cost of stolen property produces a plausible total robbery victim cost of $8.2 billion.

Figuring how much of this cost could be saved by making cash electronic turns on what percentage of robbery would be prevented. In other sections of this book I have postulated that "half of all robberies, burglaries, and larceny thefts would be eliminated" by ending cash. The percentage for robbery alone, however, should be higher, for empirical evidence indicates that robbery, more than any other crime, targets cash. Lacking any statistics on this particular point, it seems appropriate to assume a robbery-to-cash ratio of at least 75 percent. Thus, it can be fairly estimated that by switching from cash to electronic money, the public would save 75 percent of $8.2 billion, or $6 billion, every year. Note, however, that this figure represents only victim costs from the crime of robbery.

DRUG-CRIME COSTS

Drug crime is treated separately in crime statistics, as though it were a different genre. It is sometimes referred to as victimless, yet drug crime is inextricably related to general categories of crime. Indeed, many victim costs of crime can be calculated, in part, by analyzing statistics related to the cost of property stolen to support illegal drug purchases.

The Office of National Drug Control Policy (ONDCP) estimated that in 1990 there were between 1.7 and 1.8 million heavy cocaine users, 0.7 million heroin users, and 5.5 million "users who are clearly in need of treatment."[36] On the other hand, there are experts who would put the number of heavy drug users at substantially less than one million and who challenge the numbers given by the government.[37] Whatever the true numbers, it is doubtful they have decreased over the last eight years. Indeed, indications point the other way. Cocaine-and heroin-related hospital emergencies increased sharply in 1992, causing the then Chief of Staff of the White House Office of National Drug Control Policy, Terence Pell, to acknowledge that these hospital statistics "show the hard-core [drug] problem is as bad as ever. It is very disappointing."[38] In 1995, Lee Brown, another former director of ONDCP, announced that drug use is up again, with 11.7 million Americans using drugs on a regular basis and with new strains of drugs sweeping across the nation.

The amount of crime committed by a core group of drug users is believed to be quite high. Some experts contend that serious drug addicts may each be responsible for as many as 90 robberies and burglaries a year.[39] Other estimates put the figure much higher, at 22 crimes a month, or 264 crimes a year, on the average. Presentencing investigation data from bank robberies reveals that one-quarter of all bank robbers intended to use the stolen cash to support drug use. "Drug use appears to be common among bank robbers, according to two different data sources. . . . Twenty-eight percent of all bank robbers were considered addicted [to opiates]. . . . The FBI has estimated that as many as 42% of all bank robbers used drugs. . . . Pre-sentence investigation reports revealed that 8% of the offenders were intoxicated with some drug (excluding alcohol) at the time of their offense."[40]

The causal relationship between robberies and burglaries, on the one hand, and cash, on the other, is exemplified by police experience. When Operation Pressure Point was put into effect in Manhattan in 1983 by the NYPD, which targeted street drug sales (conducted exclusively in cash), burglaries in the area fell by one-third and robberies dropped by one-half.[41]

The true number of heavy drug users lies somewhere between the government's figures and those of other experts. Let's assume that there are 1.25 million heavy drug addicts. It seems plausible that these addicts, who typically spend between $100 and $250 a day for drugs and who have little or no legitimate income, would commit at least one robbery or burglary a month. (Until the recent cutoff, approximately 80 thousand addicts received SSI payments, but that usually lasted only a day or two.) This

Table 6.3
Property Losses from Crime—1996

Number of Offenses		Average Property Loss	Totals
Robbery	1,134,000	$929	$1,053,486,000
Burglary	5,471,000	$1,332	$7,287,372,000
(Includes residential and commercial burglaries)			
Larceny-Theft	21,438,000	$532	$11,405,016,000
(Includes personal theft, excludes auto theft)			
Total Losses			$19,745,874,000

Source: U.S. Department of Justice, Bureau of Justice Statistics, "Sourcebook of Criminal Justice Statistics Online," *http://www.albany.edu/sourcebook*.

would mean that heavy addicts commit 15 million crimes a year (1.25 million addicts × 12 months).

The rough average value of property stolen in robberies and burglaries is around $1,066.[42] Multiplying this against the estimated number of robberies and burglaries committed by hard-core drug users, some 15 million crimes, indicates some $16 billion in annual victims' costs from robberies and burglaries committed by hard-core drug addicts.[43]

The effect of cashlessness turns on the percentage of crime that would be reduced by cashlessness. For robbery, we used a 75 percent figure. Burglary rates a lower percentage because it includes theft of noncash items that are sometimes fenced for noncash payments such as drugs. Let's assume an average 60 percent reduction of both robbery and burglary by ending cash. Thus, victims would likely save $9.6 billion in losses from robberies and burglaries committed by hard-core drug users (60% × $16 billion = $9.6 billion).

Yet another approach would rely on figures developed by the Justice Department indicating property losses in crime categories highly associated with theft of cash or with theft of items to sell for cash: the assumption can be made, plausibly I believe, that at least half of the overall losses from these crimes would be prevented either because a criminal's direct theft objective, cash, no longer existed, or because stolen property could no longer be sold for today's traceless cash and this would act as a deterrent. The figures in table 6.3 are compiled from the source indicated.

Lack of data specific to cash's involvement in crimes, ranging from how much is actually stolen to how much property is fenced for cash, renders the task of projecting the full cost savings that can be achieved by ending cash difficult, if not impossible. Perhaps the most that can be concluded from the limited data is a minimum victim-loss savings. One can reasonably surmise that *at least* one half of the $19,745,874,000 figure developed above, approximately $10 billion, would be saved by making cash electronic. This figure is used in Table 6.4 "Cost Benefit Summary of a Cashless society."

If the reader suspects this $10 billion figure is too high, bear in mind that it does not include losses from other crimes that are certain to decline in the changeover to a FEDEC system, including embezzlement, fraud, kidnapping, bribery and loan sharking, to name but a few. The necessary data for these crimes is even more wanting. Moreover, the $10 billion figure represents only direct cash and property losses and fails to include indirect proximate victim losses such as medical expense, lost wages, and so on.

Although psychological damages were deleted from our cost-of-crime calculations because they are too vague to quantify and while it is convenient to discuss the benefits of cashlessness in pecuniary terms, the psychological impact of violence—even that experienced vicariously through news media—is real and must not be dismissed without comment.

The daily news stream about brutal murders and other violent crimes makes victims of us all. Having to endure constant crime horrors is a reminder of our vulnerability and the dangers around us. Although unmeasurable in dollars, it is another cost of crime—in large part, of *cash* crime.

Americans are victims of crime in many ways. In addition to direct costs of crime, such as for stolen goods, medical expenses, and lost earnings, one is forced to pay increased costs for insurance and higher prices for other consumer goods and services. Likewise, one must pay for personal security in the form of locks, burglar alarms, iron bars, and firearms.

Personal security products and services comprise an $18 billion per year industry. U.S. companies spend another $64.4 billion for guards, alarms, video systems, investigators, and other security measures; this figure is expected to rise to $103 billion by the year 2000.[44]

The matter of fixing the scope of victimization came up recently in a congressional hearing on a bill that would require those convicted of federal crimes to make restitution to their victims. The issue arose as to who would be included in the definition of "victim." This is relatively easy to define in a theft of money, but more difficult where someone is injured, prevented from earning a living, or killed. In such cases does the term include the surviving spouse? The children? Those who witnessed a shocking crime? Those who had to testify? The medical insurer that paid the bills? These are all possibilities, of course. The issue illuminates the reason that criminal cases are filed as "The People vs. So-and-So." Everyone is a victim of crime.

Replacing cash with electronic currency promises to cut victims' costs in a wholesale manner. Robberies and burglaries would decline steeply, stolen goods would become difficult to fence, and a large portion of the nation's enormous security expense could be cut. A reduction in robbery-

Table 6.4
Cost Benefit Summary of a Cashless Society (in billions)

A.	Victims' Cost Savings	$10.0
B.	Reduced Criminal Justice Costs	25.0
C.	Increased Tax Revenues	42.9
D.	Reduced Government Fraud	17.2
E.	Reduced Cash-handling Expense	60.0
	TOTAL SAVINGS	$155.1

murders, robbery-injuries, and property thefts would result in turn in lower premiums for worker's compensation, liability, and theft insurance. The collective crime-related savings to business and industry would mean reduced costs of doing business, more jobs, and lower costs for goods and services to Americans for practically everything.

The grand total of pecuniary benefits that Americans would realize by switching to electronic currency is proportionate to the economic aspects included within the calculation. Communities and neighborhoods would benefit. Freed from the constant threat of cash robberies, retail businesses would very likely reestablish themselves in inner cities. Not only would this fill the shopping needs of local residents, but in a chain reaction, it would result in the creation of inner-city jobs, increase the desirability of local housing, and thus raise property values, bring in more local real property taxes, and so on.

Low-income Americans would reap greater benefits than any other segment of society, for they are the victims of most crime. But, they would benefit in other ways, as well. Consider check cashing. About 25 percent of all U.S. families, mostly poor, do not have bank accounts; most receive their income by check. Because of a lack of local bank branches near them and/or the common requirement that one have a bank account in order to get a check cashed at a bank, such families commonly resort to check-cashing services.

Check cashing is one of America's fastest-growing industries. It cashed some $60 billion in checks in 1995 and earns fees averaging between 2 percent and 3 percent of the amount of the check. Some fees run to as much as 20 percent. At an average fee of 2.5 percent, this means that customers of check-cashing services—predominantly the poor—pay out over $1.5 billion a year just to have their checks converted to cash—an expense that would be obviated by electronic currency.

It becomes clear that Americans would benefit immensely from ending the use of cash. It would likely prevent victims' cost of crime by over $10 billion. (Table 6.4). Whatever the true numbers, they are so convincingly high that we may forego the need to calculate them precisely.

CHAPTER 7

PRIVACY IN AN ELECTRONIC CURRENCY SYSTEM

HOW MUCH LESS PRIVACY?

The idea of recording all transactions in cash-replacing federal electronic currency and compiling a database heightens concern about data privacy, confidentiality, and dissemination and warrants scrutiny. One might naively ask, what money data would one hide and keep private except evidence of some wrong? Why the high degree of concern for privacy in an e-currency system?

Unrestricted exposure of FEDEC data could make an account holder's life an open book that could be abused by commercial interests and government alike. Information supplied on a FEDEC account application would provide an eavesdropper with a verified name, address, description, picture, Social Security number, birth date, marital status, and more. Transaction data from most Americans' FEDEC accounts would provide a financial profile as well.

The debit side would reveal where one shops, which restaurants one frequents, how much one spends at each, how much one spends on jewelry and other luxuries, to which friends or relatives or institutions one gives money, one's medical and/or legal payments, whether one gambles, buys lotto tickets, spends money at bars, or rents X-rated movies, how much one tips waiters, and where one travels. Such information, especially if augmented by data from private-sector databanks, could result in inequitable denials of government benefits, employment, insurance coverage, and business, social, or political opportunities and undoubtedly would bring barrages of unwelcome telephone sales pitches and junk mail.

The credit side of one's account could reveal sources of income such as wages, worker's compensation payments, unemployment insurance benefits, dividend and investment income, and gifts and, perhaps, connections to political contributors, defendants being prosecuted, known drug users, criminals, and others.

Unrestricted access to a person's financial data conjures images of Big Brother and the fear that cash data in the hands of government might lead to some sort of *1984* society. But, though this aspect is often bundled up with rights of privacy, "Big Brother" speaks to the matter of totalitarianism, technological empowerment, and the morality of governance and therefore is discussed in a following section.

Before delving into the constitutionality or philosophy of privacy, several realities should be taken into account about privacy and money. As long as cash remains freely negotiable without any sort of recording, it is possible for individuals to keep their monetary affairs fairly secret, and this amount to a broad de facto privacy.

Cash is legitimately used for the privacy it affords by many who feel their transactions are nobody else's business. Some regard the cash transaction as a last bastion of freedom in an increasingly complex financial world. Others use it as an escape route from accountability or as an emergency refuge from creditors. Some individuals use cash because it leaves no trail in crimes. Irrespective of the particular advantages of privacy through cash, some such privacy is protected by law, and some is not.

While many would have psychological misgivings about losing the de facto privacy that cash affords, making cash transaction data accessible to those already entitled to it would not result in any loss of legal rights of privacy. Rights of privacy in federal electronic currency should parallel present law, which provides no sanctuary for deals done in cash. In child support or bankruptcy proceedings, for example, examination of one's cash transactions is not precluded by any right of privacy. Thus, after implementation of the new money system, where it might be relevant in court proceedings, FEDEC data would have to be made available in discovery and as evidence. Moreover, FEDEC data would have to be made accessible to legitimate creditors to a degree sufficient to allow them to enforce judgments; otherwise, the new money system would become a safe harbor for deadbeats.

Though a switch to FEDEC would eliminate some privacy that cash affords, FEDEC data would enjoy far greater privacy than data kept in commercial checking and savings accounts. Investigators listed in telephone books across the country will supply anyone, for a fee, with balances and other personal information from private checking and savings accounts. Though confidential personal data occasionally leaks from government databanks, such breaches of privacy are infrequent, and that type of personal exposure would not exist in the proposed money system.

The FEDEC transaction could not prevent all commercial observation: Even if one were to transact exclusively in FEDEC, industry has other methods of extracting private data from the transaction environment. Whenever one makes a telephone call, subscribes to a magazine, buys through a mail-order catalog, signs up for cable TV, or pays taxes, the information taken verbally or from application cards, receipts, and other papers generated in such transactions goes into some databank, irrespective of the payment medium used. Even data from today's cash sales generate personal data that ends up in commercial databanks—via service contracts, mail-in warranty cards, and the like. There is little reason to believe such exposure to commercial exploitation would come to a halt after FEDEC was in operation.

CURRENT PRIVACY LAW

One wonders why the framers failed to mention privacy in the Constitution. Apparently, in their minds and in those times, it was not threatened. Or, perhaps they found that the subject resisted clear wording. Arthur R. Miller points out, "The concept of privacy is difficult to define because it is exasperatingly vague and evanescent, often meaning strikingly different things to different people."[1]

Curiously, no court cases involving privacy appeared until the end of the nineteenth century. Personal data cases began to emerge only after the Industrial Revolution, along with the rise of yellow journalism, trade lists, and the development of snooping devices. Privacy law evolved in the United States by judicial interpretation of various constitutional articles and amendments and later, by Congress, through legislation. States have developed parallel privacy law.

Today's battle between privacy advocates and law enforcement began in a 1928 landmark criminal case, *Olmstead v. United States*,[2] in which the legality of government surveillance was constitutionally challenged. In an appeal from a conviction of conspiracy to violate the National Prohibition Act, defendants in this case argued that the police acquisition of wiretap evidence through defendant's telephone lines was an act in violation of the Fourth Amendment's "search and seizure" clause. The prosecution argued, successfully, that since the wiretap was conducted in the basement of an office building on a public street and since no entry was made into the defendant's premises, no search had been conducted as proscribed by the Fourth Amendment.

For several decades, this and similar types of surveillance, like listening through walls with special microphones, were upheld by federal courts as constitutional and not in violation of the Fourth Amendment. The key in such cases was that no physical intrusion was made into the defendant's private chambers.

Not until relatively recently, in 1967, in the *Katz v. United States* case,[3] was Olmstead overturned and a new rule established. In *Katz*, investigators attached an electronic listening device to the outside of a telephone booth that the defendant was known to use. The Supreme Court, in this case, threw out the physical intrusion test and, on the grounds that there was no probable cause for the surveillance, reversed the defendant's conviction. The new rule established in this case had two parts: "first that a person have exhibited an actual (subjective) expectation of privacy, and second, that the expectation be one that society is prepared to recognize as 'reasonable' " (Justice Harlan, concurring).

The "reasonable expectation" test was refined in subsequent cases, for example in *United States v. Hall*,[4] where the court made the distinction that transmissions between mobile telephones are not protected but that transmissions between a mobile telephone and a land line are protected. At the same time, the Supreme Court continued the requirement that any criminal surveillance be based upon probable cause.

The balancing test first announced in *Katz* was subsequently extended by the Court to noncriminal cases. Thus, on a case-by-case basis, particular human settings were delineated wherein personal expectations of privacy were weighed against society's interest in the subject matter. Through such reasoning, the NAACP was freed from an order to hand over the names of its membership to the state.[5] Other social areas ruled upon include the privacy of one's bedroom, homosexuality, pornography, and the abortion issue adjudicated in *Roe v. Wade*.[6]

In the early 1960s, the United States government began acquiring electronic data-processing equipment. By 1972, it had almost 7,000 central processing units in place, and the number was rising exponentially. The amount of personal information being accumulated by government about Americans was growing at a staggering rate, and its use went virtually unchecked by the courts. This was cause for alarm, and as a result Congress passed the Privacy Act of 1974.[7]

The Privacy Act of 1974, designed to regulate the federal government's acquisition, use, dissemination, and maintenance of personal data, controls the bulk of the raw material flowing into the government's growing electronic databanks. For example, the act allows federal agencies to maintain only those records and information that are "relevant and necessary" to the accomplishment of that agency's legitimate tasks; it requires that such records be maintained with a high degree of accuracy and completeness in order to ensure fairness to the individual.[8] Provision is made for internal procedural security safeguards to protect against "substantial harm, embarrassment, inconvenience, or unfairness to an individual on whom information is maintained."[9] Provision is made for individual access to records concerning such individuals for the purpose of correcting inaccuracies or incompletions. The act authorizes awards of civil remedies against agencies in violation of the act, including court orders to agencies to make corrections in records, to disclose records withheld, to pay damages to individuals, and to pay costs of prosecution against agencies.[10] The act also makes it a crime for agency officials and others to violate the act. Moreover, the act established the Privacy Protection Study Commission, charged with the responsibility of analyzing the act's effectiveness in preserving personal privacy.[11]

Under the Privacy Act of 1974, agencies are conditionally allowed to exchange data on individuals. Thus, information can be transferred between the Bureau of the Census, the Comptroller General, Congress, the courts, and others. However, what is criticized by privacy advocates as a loophole in the act that has seen a free flow of information between agencies, sometimes to the detriment of individuals, is the provision that data can be exchanged for any "routine use"; "routine use" is defined as "with respect to the disclosure of a record, the use of such record for a purpose which is compatible with the purpose for which it was collected."[12]

Another problematic exposure of private data was pointed out in a report by the Privacy Protection Study Commission in 1977,[13] to the effect that the Privacy Act of 1974 failed to protect the right to financial privacy as regards personal data in private-sector financial institutions. A series of court cases, (especially *United States v. Miller*)[14] illuminated how the 1974 act failed to prevent the government from using privately acquired financial data in criminal prosecution. *Miller* involved criminal charges from operating an unregistered still. The defendant's bank records were subpoenaed by a federal grand jury and used as evidence to convict him. On appeal, the Supreme Court disagreed with the defendant's argument that bank records are within the purview of a legitimate "expectation of privacy" and therefore, inadmissible as prosecutorial evidence.

Miller sparked a reaction in Congress that resulted in enactment of the Right to Financial Privacy Act of 1978.[15] This act regulates government acquisition and use of financial data held in private financial institutions. It prohibits such acquisition except where the individual consents, where the government has a search warrant or subpoena, or where the government uses a special formal written request that is limited to law enforcement, requires bank customer notification, and is allowed only if no other legal process is available.

Consequently, whenever government attempts to obtain private data from financial institutions, it must notify the individual affected by means of a prescribed form that sets out the nature of the request and explain the individual's rights to challenge the request, including his or her right of appeal. Even after the government has properly obtained such data, it must subsequently so notify the individual if the data is to be transferred to another government agency.

However, if immediate notice could result in physical danger to individuals, intimidation of witnesses, tampering with evidence, or flight from prosecution or could hamper an ongoing criminal investigation, then a court-ordered delay in notification to the account holder is allowed. Special rules apply to use of data by the Justice Department involving violations of federal law, especially that relating to money laundering.

As with the Privacy Act of 1974, the Financial Privacy Act provides civil penalties, damages, costs, and attorney's fees for successful litigants. Wronged bank customers can get punitive damages if they can prove that violations were willful or intentional.

Other relevant legislation includes the Freedom of Information Act (5 U.S.C. 552), which, in contrast to the Privacy Act, establishes a presumption that records in the possession of Executive Branch agencies and departments are accessible to the public; the Electronic Communications Privacy Act of 1986 (18 U.S.C. 2510), which protects the content of private communications, regardless of how they are transmitted; the Computer Security Act of 1987, which provides methods for improving security and privacy of sensitive information in federal computer systems; the Federal Managers' Financial Integrity Act of 1982 (31 U.S.C. 3512), which requires an ongoing evaluation of the internal control and accounting systems that protect federal programs against fraud, waste, and abuse; and the Computer Matching and Privacy Protection Act of 1988 (5 U.S.C. 552A), hereafter "Computer Matching Act."

The Computer Matching Act is of particular interest. In 1974, when the Privacy Act was passed, computers were used only to store and retrieve data. The ability of computers to share and manipulate and reassemble data, especially at nearly instantaneous speeds, was unforeseen. By the mid-1980s federal agencies were able to electronically analyze two or more sets of records at one time. Thus, a "matching" procedure was developed "to compare (1) two or more automated federal systems of records, or (2) federal systems of records with non-federal records to identify similarities or dissimilarities in the data."[16] Databases from different government programs are commonly "matched" for purposes such as uncovering unreported income, discovering errors in tax information, and illuminating duplicate benefit payments.

The Computer Matching Act set procedural safeguards in performance of certain types of computerized matching programs. It requires agencies to formalize agreements specifying the terms under which matches can be performed and grants due-process rights for record subjects. For instance, it might require agencies to verify independently any matching results before taking adverse actions against subjects and then to do so only after giving 30 days' notice. This act authorizes matches for several purposes: to establish eligibility for federal benefits programs, to verify compliance with such programs, and to recoup payments under such programs. Matches may be between federal, state, or even private enterprises. In 1989, the effective year of the act, computer matching resulted in nearly seven million cases of further action by federal agencies and the IRS. In 1990, the GAO reported that 46 federal agencies were involved in computer matching; 78 percent was conducted for law enforcement, while 18 percent was for tax purposes.

The Computer Matching Act and its safeguards do not apply to the gathering of statistical data (without personal identifiers) or where personal rights, benefits, and privileges are not involved, to background investigations, to tax return information, or where matches are for law enforcement purposes.

Privacy advocates assert that computer matching makes control by individuals over personal information more difficult and that the lack of probable cause in conducting many computer matches violates the Fourth Amendment right against unreasonable search and seizure.

Two other types of computer-file comparison techniques must be distinguished from basic matching. The first is "front-end verification," which "involves certifying the accuracy and authenticity of information supplied by an applicant by comparing it with similar information held in a [third-party database]."[17] This method is typically used in processing applications for program benefits. The second is "computer profiling," which employs inductive logic by searching databanks for certain characteristics deemed indicative of targeted behavior, such as drug crime. These two computer procedures contrast with each another in that the first begins with a known individual and deals only with his or her files, whereas the second, profiling, searches for the names of persons on the basis of a computer data formula. Privacy advocates are particularly critical of the latter procedure.

A current battle over financial data privacy centers on the Financial Crimes Enforcement Network. FinCEN has developed its own unique brand of computer matching. The background of this agency goes to 1970 when, in an attempt to prevent money laundering, the Bank Secrecy Act (BSA)[18] was enacted (touched on earlier under "money laundering"); it requires financial institutions to file a Currency Transaction Report[19] on each deposit, withdrawal, exchange of currency, or other payment or transfer, by or to such institution that involves a currency transaction of more than $10,000 in cash. Subsequent legislation extended cash transaction reporting requirements to business and foreign banks, attached criminal penalties for willful failure to report or evade reporting, and lowered the threshold to $3,000.

In April 1990, to coordinate multi-agency efforts in the use of CTRs and other financial data in investigating and prosecuting money laundering, the Treasury Department established FinCEN. With a budget of about $20 million and a staff of 200, FinCEN's purpose is to assist other agencies in:

- identifying suspected offenders and reporting on trend and patterns in money laundering by analyzing various databases maintained by other agencies;
- developing and disseminating research on money laundering enforcement;
- supporting government-wide law enforcement by providing tactical support for ongoing investigations; and
- supporting other law enforcement agencies by using database queries to answer requests for information received at a communications center.[20]

Although not a law enforcement agency itself, FinCEN acts as an analytical networking unit that aids virtually any law enforcement agency, domestic or foreign, in combating money laundering. The primary source of intelligence information accessed and disseminated by FinCEN is from BSA-required reports, 95 percent of which consist of CTRs. These and other data are compiled in the FinCEN database officially known as "Treasury/DO .200."

FinCen does not initiate or carry out any investigations on its own. Rather, it provides other agencies with tactical and strategic intelligence analyses that identify emerging trends and geographical patterns of money laundering as well as suspected offenders. Additionally, when requested, it provides specially trained investigators experienced in analyzing financial records and data to document money laundering violations and to trace the proceeds of criminal activity. FinCEN also operates a communications center for answering requests from law enforcement agencies for specific data information. . . . [FinCEN] is also in a unique position to coordinate the efforts of other law enforcement agencies investigating money laundering cases and therefore to prevent duplication of effort.

While it is generally recognized that narcotics traffickers create the greatest demand for money laundering schemes, numerous other types of activities typical of organized crime also create an appreciable demand for such schemes. Violation of tax laws are an inevitable by-product of laundering schemes that conceal the existence of or an illegal source of income. Estimates of the amount of money annually laundered range from $100 billion to $300 billion.[21]

FinCEN developed and uses a type of BSA data analysis designed to identify suspicious transactions. Known as Artificial Intelligence Targeting System, it has been in use since March 1993 and is modified and enhanced from time to time. Employing a number of factors, rules, and conditions, it screens, evaluates, and groups BSA reports and other data to link individuals, businesses, or accounts. The end product is a list of suspected criminals. The procedure is attacked on its face by privacy advocates for several reasons. What has exacerbated the issue are legislative and administrative efforts at overriding the privacy protections incorporated in the Privacy Act of 1974 and the Financial Privacy Act of 1978, all of which are aimed at exempting FinCEN from them.

Since 1990, members of Congress have submitted at least eight bills that would, with some variation, amend section 3412 of the Financial Privacy Act by reducing or doing away with the limits it imposes on the use and dissemination of financial data acquired by government, as well as its requirement of notice to individuals. Moreover, in 1991, the Treasury Department, through a Final Rule,[22] exempted FinCEN from the provisions of the Privacy Act that give individuals (1) the right to copies of records relating to themselves; (2) the right to request corrections of records; and (3) the ability to discover what disclosures to third parties have been made. The rule also does away with the requirements that only "relevant and necessary" records can be accessed by FinCEN and that it first request data from individuals if feasible.

Principles of privacy, espoused by privacy advocates and differing from privacy laws, were enumerated in the preamble to the Privacy Act of 1974. They are, briefly, (1) openness, (2) individual access, (3) individual participation, (4) collection limitation, (5) use limitation, (6) disclosure limitation, (7) information management, and (8) accountability. In applying these principles to FinCEN's operations, in light of its exemptions from provisions of the Privacy Act of 1974, privacy advocates contend that all but the first principle (which has to do with the government's openness as to the existence of a given databank) are violated. Thus, they argue, an individual is given no opportunity to correct a mistaken record, to require that data be relevant to an inquiry, or to insist that it not be disseminated freely.

FinCEN advocates point out that if given notice, financial criminals would have the opportunity to alter their course of conduct, destroy evidence, and flee arrest, thus thwarting investigative efforts. They also argue that it is impossible to pre-limit source data, for its relevance cannot be known until it is compared with other data. Unrestricted dissemination of data to other agencies is essential in allowing law enforcement to employ it in the manner best suited to achieve its goals.

To resolve this polarized impasse, some have proposed that the United States follow European models by establishing a privacy protection board or agency that would act as a neutral party to make sure that rights of privacy are adhered to by the government. Government would be allowed, where necessary—as in criminal investigations—to process private data without notice to affected individuals. Such a board would act as a trustee of individuals' rights of privacy to ensure the accuracy and relevance of data and to uphold other protective aspects of the principles of privacy. Proponents of such an agency point to privacy protection systems in Sweden, Germany, and France as proof that such systems work.

TRADE-OFFS BETWEEN PRIVACY AND CRIME SUPPRESSION

A federal electronic currency system can be operated within the principles set forth in the Privacy Act of 1974 and yet be highly effective in preventing a great deal of crime. Some, favoring strong law enforcement, might resist abiding by those principles. Any tender of a FEDEC proposal in government would surely fuel the ongoing struggle between guardians of privacy and warriors against crime.

Privacy advocates tend to view any new government databank as a privacy threat and a net loss to society. Thus, on first learning of the FEDEC proposal, many react with a reference to "Big Brother" and are reluctant, at best, to consider the benefits. A first problem in discussing FEDEC privacy issues is getting a fair hearing. The second problem is getting people to believe that crime can be prevented.

A general perception prevails that crime has a life of its own and that crime rates have far more to do with job availability and education than direct anticrime programs. The liberal wing in the United States is particularly loathe to acknowledge that expanded law enforcement and stiffer penalties for crimes have anything to do with recent decreases in crime rates. Yet, the idea of focusing on the cash-crime nexus as a means of preventing crime is novel and deserves an unbiased review.

Assessing the trade-offs between privacy rights and the need for financial data access by government necessitates fair and equal focus on the competing factors. Well-founded concern and sometimes justified outrage are expressed at government intrusions on privacy. It would be a mistake however, in considering FEDEC, for officials to presume that crime, though its statistics fluctuate, is an unstoppable fact of society on which legislation has very limited effect. Such cynical attitudes toward crime prevention too easily ignore the relationship between cash and crime in America and the opportunity this presents.

The legal battle over financial-data privacy is reflective of other underlying substantive problems in society where crime, particularly violent crime, has become so rampant as to exceed the capacity of civilized government to contain it. The question in the minds of many citizens is, what good are lofty-sounding rights and freedoms when one cannot walk the street without fear of physical attack? Some scholars have warned that our democratic system of government is simply not geared to handle today's widespread disobedience of the law.

Indeed, one social observer predicts that the decreasing ability of governments across the globe to control crime will gradually undermine the nation-state structure, citing West Africa, with its crumbling governmental structures, horrors, and bedlam, as an example of things to come: "West Africa is becoming the symbol of worldwide demographic, environmental and societal stress, in which criminal anarchy emerges as the real 'strategic' danger. . . . West Africa provides an appropriate introduction to the issues, often extremely unpleasant to discuss, that will soon confront our civilization."[23]

Arguments about privacy are often between intellectuals, and the adversarial nature of the privacy debate imputes a certain equanimity between the two sides that is not commensurate with public attitudes. At the layman's level, law enforcement easily has the vote. While most Americans express some concern that their privacy is being violated by government and private organizations,[24] many regard the warnings and demands of privacy advocates as overblown, pedantic, sometimes irresponsible, and even paranoid. Americans have already revealed their shallow concern for financial-data privacy by switching, over the last quarter century, from the use of traceless cash to recorded bankcard transactions.

Numerous polls taken lately indicate that crime predominates as a leading public issue and that it overshadows most concerns with privacy. In polls and actual circumstances, it has been shown that most Americans readily forego their Fourth Amendment rights against unreasonable searches and seizures by voluntarily submitting to automobile searches at roadblock checks and, as well, to gun sweeps through public housing projects. The public's quick downgrading of rights of privacy under such circumstances is a natural response to its experience with crime. In contrast, Americans have suffered relatively little from invasions of privacy. Thus, the threat of privacy incursions, especially by government, holds a much lower priority.

The most egregious examples that privacy advocates can muster of computer-based governmental violations of rights of privacy, including a case of mistaken identity that resulted in an innocent man's being held in jail five months,[25] are simply not in the same league with the widespread loss of life, family grief, disabling permanent injuries, major pecuniary losses, and social degeneration caused by crime. Nor do the few privacy violations by government begin even to approach the millions of serious crimes committed in the United States.

In weighing privacy trade-offs one must realize the vast social damage that ending cash can prevent. The impact on robbery alone (almost always perpetrated to get cash) outweighs any rational privacy concerns. Every year in the United States 125,000 robbery victims suffer serious injuries, including gunshot wounds, knifings, rapes, broken bones, or beatings so severe that they require hospitalization. Some 10 percent of robbery victims are killed. Clearly, no parity exists between the harm that might ensue by misuse of electronic money data leakage and the injury from crimes that would be averted by changing over to such a system.

This is not to deny the fundamental danger in granting authorities extraordinary powers to combat crime. What has developed from the government's "crackdown mentality" toward drug offenders, for example, is a "drug exception" to the Bill of Rights that threatens everyone. Seizures and forfeitures without fault and irreconcilably harsh mandatory prison sentences are actions that most thinking citizens would label as basically wrong and "un-American"; yet they have become standard in the United States. Mandatory sentences of life imprisonment without the possibility of parole for first offenses of possession of illegal substances—while murderers go free after only as little as six years in prison—are patently unjust.[26] What all this has accomplished, however, has been merely to expend horrendous amounts of money and to reduce important personal freedoms.

Many privacy advocates tend to use the term "privacy" without clear definition and to include loose interpolations of the Bill of Rights, as well as portions of the preamble to the Constitution, under its mantle. Unfortunately, such vague usage of the term is in keeping with court decisions. In the landmark case of *Griswald v. Connecticut*, 381 U.S. 347 (1967), the Supreme Court, referring to the First, Third, Fourth, and Fifth Amendments and pointing out that the Constitution does not mention "privacy," said: "specific guarantees in the Bill of Rights have *penumbras*, formed by *emanations* from those guarantees that help give them life and substance. . . . [These] create *zones* of privacy" (italics added).

Privacy can be given even broader definition than privacy advocates typically attach to it. In its most fundamental sense, privacy is invaded not only when one's telephone is tapped or one's private finances are pried into but as well when a victim's home is burglarized or when one is physically attacked by a robber, kidnapped, or raped. If we include such base violations within the term "invasion of privacy," then the debate between the two factions is reduced to mere disagreement about the method of achieving a common goal. If privacy advocates agree that adoption of an electronic money system would substantially reduce the incidence of such serious crimes, which is hard to deny, they should also agree that giving up a degree of informational privacy inherent in such an undertaking would achieve privacy of a more important and fundamental order.

In their own minds, each camp appreciates the other's point of emphasis. Privacy advocates hardly oppose reducing crime. They comprehend clearly how financial data can be employed to achieve that end, though they often pay only lip service to this. Law enforcement officials understand the right to and value of individual privacy, but their compulsion to catch criminals sometimes exceeds their respect for privacy laws.

American financial privacy law, beset by polarization of the two factions and cross-purpose goals (the conflict of which is codified in the Freedom of Information Act and the Privacy Act of 1974), has developed erratically in the courts and the legislature over the last half century and has failed to arrive at a common meeting ground.

SURVEILLANCE OF ELECTRONIC CURRENCY TRANSACTIONS

No doubt, some privacy-minded individuals will shake their heads at this chapter heading, thinking it belongs in *1984* or *Mein Kampf*. The question arises as to whether a FEDEC database might be subjected to the same investigative procedures used by FinCEN today, including random profiling without notice to affected individuals. The answer points in the other direction. Times change, and one must keep an open mind. A switch from cash to electronic currency would alter the information landscape somewhat and requires analysis.

First, the sheer volume of FEDEC data would render such investigations unfeasible on any meaningful scale. Consider that since FinCEN cannot process its current database of some 50 million CTRs, then, even allowing for the development of incredibly faster computers, it is highly unlikely that it could survey an anticipated 550 billion or more annual transactions. True, such random investigative techniques might be applied on a sample basis in limited geographical areas or on a selected number of businesses, for example, but such methodology would not seem to have much investigative value.

Second, with currency transactions being recorded and their data available to law enforcement agencies, most of the police work formerly aimed at "underlying" crime could be accomplished directly. There would no longer be a need for the bulk of FinCEN's obtuse, indirect methods of investigation.

A change to electronic currency is virtually certain to be accompanied by a sharp drop in the incidence of crimes. This does not beg the question, for as a matter of logic, many crimes would be rendered impossible. Lowered crime statistics should ease public pressure on legislators and justice officials to convict and imprison. The decrease might reduce the perceived need and justification by law enforcement for using methods that encroach on privacy and would allow government to back away from questionably extraconstitutional tactics such as random profiling of financial data, seizures, and excessive mandatory sentencing.

A portion of today's cash crime would shift to other payment media, including, at least initially, "documented money" such as money orders. In our earlier discussion of the underground economy it was estimated that up to 35 percent of today's underground transactions are conducted in noncash media. After the switch to FEDEC this figure might increase. Current law requires issuers of money orders and cashier's checks to keep logs showing purchasers' identifications. This is limited to issuances of large denominations, and the required record keeping is relatively informal. Depending on the extent of criminal activity that might be conducted in documented money, it might prove necessary to expand such federal reporting requirements. Furthermore, the usage of "profiling," particularly on a group dominated by criminals, might prove essential to "plug the hole" in the overall plan of reducing crime by eliminating cash and therefore justify encroachment on the principles of financial-data privacy.

As for using FEDEC data in direct investigations of suspected criminals, procedures could be carried out within the principles of privacy. Thus, in most cases, suspects would have to be given notice of such action by law enforcement. This would not undermine effectiveness, for the principles provide that such notice to affected parties may be dispensed with in cases where the use of notice might lead to flight from prosecution, destruction of evidence, violence against a witness, and the like.

Automatic monitoring of FEDEC accounts would break new ground. In this procedure, an account number would be flagged so that whenever a transaction occurred, the system's computers would notify a given agency or investigator. In one sense, the use of account monitoring can be viewed as a high-tech version of age-old methodology: Instead of a detective passing out business cards to various individuals and asking them to "call me at this number if you see so-and-so," the FEDEC system's computers would do the job automatically.

This procedure would hardly emulate Big Brother's ubiquitous eye. The actual number of surveillances would be minuscule. In view of the over one billion electronic currency transactions that would be processed each day, they would have to be. The number of personal data retrievals by investigators, for both criminal investigative and private humanitarian purposes, would be quite small. Add to this the periodic information requested by account holders, occasional IRS verifications, and rare miscellaneous incursions. Several years later, they would be destroyed. In general, the records of all but a tiny fraction of FEDEC would go unread, undisclosed, and remain secure and private.

This scenario might create an opportunity for privacy advocates to press Congress for the establishment of a data protection board. If abolishment of cash proves successful in substantially reducing crime, the subsequent legislative environment for enacting proper privacy regulation will have been much improved. However, FEDEC's implementation should not be conditioned on setting up the board. The studies, reports, hearings, arguments, and political settlements necessary for an implementation of such a board might span years—time during which the profound benefits of electronic currency could already have been realized. It is in the public interest to end cash sooner than later, though this may require temporary indulgence of less-than-desirable current privacy law.

Even if the number of data-privacy violations were to match the number of crimes that were prevented by abolishing cash, which is preposterous, adoption of FEDEC would still amount to a lopsided bargain for Americans. This is because the possible harm resulting from misuse of FEDEC data, including wrongful denials of employment and of government benefits, groundless arrests, or even incarcerations of innocent citizens—as reprehensible as all this might be—does not approach the profound damages suffered daily and hourly by Americans through cash-inspired and cash-facilitated crime.

BIG BROTHER

The mere suggestion that cash be transformed into federal electronic currency, to many on the left and right alike, raises the nebulous "threat" of a Big Brother police state—the Great Mother of today's politically correct dogma. To an amazingly large number of people, mere mention of recording cash-payment data brings to mind the personal dossiers used under Stalinism and Nazism. Extremists see this as supplying the one thing officials lack to control the populace totally, a device that demagogic forces would seize upon to spy on a citizen's every move. Ridiculous.

Big Brother was born in the aftermath of World War II, when the world was still reflecting on the horrors of that epoch and asking itself how such terror, aggression, and mass suffering could possibly have come about in a civilized Europe. Orwell's hypothesis of how it could happen again in England and America was a warning to all. Western society has been troubled by his vision ever since. Its experience with fascist regimes during the first half of this century, coupled with Orwell's strong suggestion, has sensitized modern society to the symptoms of totalitarianism and made it wary of the slightest encroachment by government on personal privacy.

Contrary to *1984*'s warning, totalitarianism has not developed in the West, and the United States is hardly teetering on the brink. One wonders, after 50 years, how many more will pass before the fearful discover that totalitarianism in America is extremely improbable and that Orwell was simply wrong.

This does not mean that it cannot happen in the United States or that it never occurred here. Robert Nisbet points out that:

Few Americans have any genuine awareness of the sheer totalitarianism of the American war venture in 1917–18. Industry-labor councils with absolute powers

over wages and prices, 175,000 Four-Minute Men with orders to invade any as-
semblage whatever for propagandist purposes, sedition laws, systematic mobili-
zation of teachers, clergy, artists, writers, actors, and the like, arrests, with heavy
fines or imprisonments, in the name of "Pro-Germanism," and above all the in-
fectious spirit of a centralized collectivism fighting for a great moral objective—all
of this and more offered a preview to what would become grim reality in Russia,
Italy, and Germany. It is a tribute to the native conservatism of the American
people of 1918 that virtually all of the machinery of totalitarianism was dismantled
once the war was ended.[27]

Some observers stress that most government programs, such as the IRS
and Social Security, by their nature necessarily compromise privacy; in
combination, a multiplicity of programs delegate too much power to government.

Orwell's book can serve us today as a warning . . . that the further we travel along
the road to "perfect technology," . . . the closer we are to his horrible vision. The
menace is all the greater because it is presented with all the marks of well-
intentioned reason. . . . Each step taken is the logical answer to a given problem.
It may well be that here too the devil is in the details, but he only becomes visible
when one regards the whole.[28]

Orwell's description of two-way television and other spying devices in
1984 suggests that development of information-gathering technology can
lead to oppressive, if not totalitarian, regimes. Yet, there is a dearth of
evidence to support this contention, and much to contradict it.

Totalitarianism has only been achieved the old-fashioned way—with
messianic propaganda, a secret police, an army of informants, and an ex-
ecutioner's pistol. Obviously, information technology played no role in
the French Revolution, Europe's first experience with totalitarianism.
Even in our modern age it lent little or no support in establishing repres-
sive regimes such as those in Albania, Cambodia, Cuba, and the Middle
East, not to mention African states. The totalitarian community in Jones-
town, Guiana, before its tragic end, came into being in nearly primitive
conditions. It is difficult to identify any totalitarian regime that has come
into or maintained power by means of technological information devices.

The most erratic or absolute dictators elsewhere in the world—be it Idi Amin,
Muammar Khadafi, or "Papa Doc" Duvalier—have typically lacked the technology, the ideology, or the sophistication to move significantly in the direction of
Big Brother. Modern technology has had an ambiguous impact. If television can
present American presidential candidates—and winners—as invariably attractive
and informed, modern communications also make it impossible for public figures
to maintain the privacy and safety that earlier would-be leaders had. . . . If we
know very little of the private lives of Fidel Castro, Yuri Andropov, or Deng Xiao-

ping, they nonetheless can scarcely conceal their infirmities as kings and despots could in earlier times.[29]

This raises the contrary point that information technology has increasingly acted as force against excessive government. The defunct Soviet Union restricted access to computers, reportedly because such activity would have exposed knowledge and truth and was therefore considered a threat to the state. Computerized financial records played a role in the Iran-Contra investigation, the Whitewater matter, political contribution investigations, and other probes of government. Computer-stored data serves citizens around the world in detecting and deterring fraud and bribery involving government officials. Recall that it was through facsimile technology that foreign support found its way to dissidents in the Tiananmen revolt. Clearly, information technology is a two-edged sword.

It is not for lack of means that the United States has not developed into a police state. Even the low-tech telephone system has long been available as a spying device: Government agents could surreptitiously listen in on every citizen's confidential telephone conversations and compile information about one's political correctness, attitude towards certain officials, private associations, personal plans and intentions, and whereabouts. But government wiretaps have been severely limited by law, and their proper use is scrutinized by the courts—just as the monitoring of FEDEC accounts would be. Moreover, the nation's usage of wiretaps is overseen by Congress on a regular basis. Each federal and state judge is required to file a written report with the Administrative Office of the U.S. Courts (AO) on each application for an order authorizing the interception of a wire, oral or electronic communication. Prosecutors are also required to file similar reports. The director of the AO compiles the information and submits a comprehensive report to Congress annually.[30]

For the year 1997, 1,186 such interceptions were authorized, including 569 by federal judges and 617 by state judges. Seventy-three percent of these were for narcotics investigations. Gambling and racketeering accounted for another eight percent. This resulted in 3,086 arrests, and 542 convictions. The total number of overall wiretaps rose three percent from 1996 to 1997, with federal number decreasing two percent while the state number rose by nine percent. See table 7.1 for a summary from the 1997 AO report to Congress, covering years 1987 to 1997.

One might distinguish the FEDEC system from labor-intensive telephone taps in that the former would employ efficient computers to record financial data automatically in a file on every American. This argument disregards the existence of over 2,000 government databanks storing names, addresses, financial and occupational information, and much more on tens of millions of Americans.[31] As far back as 1982, some 3,530 million personal files were held in all federal agencies on Americans; this

Table 7.1
Summary Report on Authorized Intercepts Granted Pursuant to 18 U.S.C. 2519 for Calendar Years 1987–1997

Summary Item	1987	1988	1989	1990	1991	1992	1993	1994	1995	1996	1997
Intercept applications requested	673	740	763	872	856	919	976	1,154	1,058	1,150	1,186
Intercept applications denied	-	2	-	-	-	-	-	-	-	1	-
Intercept applications authorized	673	738	763	872	856	919	976	1,154	1,058	1,149	1,186
Federal	236	293	310	324	356	340	450	554	532	581	569
State	437	445	453	548	500	579	526	600	526	568	617
Avg. days of original authorization	25	27	27	28	28	28	28	29	29	28	28
Number of extensions	402	556	519	581	601	646	825	861	834	887	1,028
Average length of extensions (days)	26	28	28	29	29	30	29	29	29	28	28
Location of authorized intercepts:											
Single-Family Dwelling	285	272	304	341	327	303	267	319	322	281	273
Apartment	134	146	132	145	112	135	139	131	101	150	108
Multiple Dwelling	7	6	2	7	-	3	4	1	5	3	1
Business	124	120	133	156	144	119	124	118	101	101	78
Business and living quarters and multiple locations	51	70	75	66	89	70	92	97	115	149	197
Not indicated or other	72	124	117	157	184	289	350	488	414	465	529
Major offense specified:											
Arson, explosives, and weapons	3	3	-	-	-	-	-	-	4	-	3
Bribery	13	32	10	11	16	8	1	6	4	10	13
Extortion (includes usury and loan-sharking)	22	21	18	17	2	7	9	8	18	9	24

Gambling	135	126	111	116	98	66	96	86	95	114	98
Homicide and assault	18	14	20	21	21	35	28	19	30	41	31
Larceny and theft	14	9	8	51	17	16	13	18	12	7	22
Narcotics	379	435	471	520	536	634	679	876	732	821	870
Robbery and burglary	12	-	-	6	2	-	-	6	5	4	5
Other or unspecified	16	18	33	40	50	63	48	47	60	38	27
Racketeering	61	80	89	90	114	90	101	88	98	105	93
Intercept applications installed*	**634**	**678**	**720**	**812**	**802**	**846**	**938**	**1,100**	**1,024**	**1,035**	**1,094**
Federal	233	266	305	321	349	332	444	549	527	574	563
State	401	392	415	491	453	514	494	551	497	461	531
For intercepts installed:											
Total days in operation	19,752	26,380	27,766	28,782	30,002	32,430	39,819	44,500	43,179	43,635	48,871
Avg. number of persons intercepted	104	129	178	131	121	117	100	84	140	192	197
Average number of intercepted communications	1,299	1,251	1,656	1,487	1,584	1,861	1,801	2,139	2,028	1,969	2,081
Average number of incriminating intercepted communications	230	316	337	321	290	347	364	373	459	422	418
Authorizations for which costs reported	611	652	691	794	775	829	912	1,042	983	1,007	1,029
Average cost of intercepts for which costs reported	36,904	49,284	53,108	45,125	45,033	46,492	57,256	49,478	56,454	61,436	61,176

*Installed intercepts include only those intercepts for which reports were received from prosecuting officials.

Source: From the *1997 Wiretap Report, A Report of the Director of the Administrative Office of the United States Courts on Applications for Orders Authorizing or Approving the Interception of Wire, Oral, or Electronic Communications*, Administrative Office of the U.S. Courts.

143

averaged out to fifteen files for every man, woman, and child in America. Three-quarters of such data were held by the following five departments: Health and Human Services, Treasury, Education, Defense, and Commerce.[32] An extensive databank is already being compiled by the U.S. Post Office that will identify by number every addressee in the country. The FBI is assembling a DNA-based genetic databank. Moreover, many states electronically fingerprint all licensed drivers, and efforts are underway to integrate this into a nationwide system.

As part of an $8 billion computer upgrade, scheduled to be completed in 2008, the IRS is vastly expanding the database it keeps on virtually every American. Included will be news stories, tips from informants, credit reports, and real estate and motor vehicle records. Taxpayers will not be allowed to see this raw material, even during audits. The mixed public reaction to the plan reflects society's competing forces: Citizens for Tax Justice, trying to reduce the tax burden on middle- and low-income taxpayers, likes it, while privacy advocates are appalled. FEDEC might render it unnecessary.

If an autocratic regime in Washington were to get serious about compiling private transaction data for use in controlling the masses, it could simply siphon confidential information from the flow of private checking data, 35 percent of which passes through government computers as it is cleared and settled in the federally administered Automated Clearinghouse (ACH). Checking payments represent a far greater dollar value (10 percent of all payments) than cash transactions (which represent only .3 percent),[33] and ACH data would reveal matters of far greater import than cash data, where consumer payments today average about $4. The Fed processed 15 billion checks in 1995.

This is hardly meant to elevate apprehension about the government's ability to gather intelligence about individuals but rather to demonstrate that, notwithstanding imperfections in maintaining the integrity of financial privacy, there is no indication that the United States is headed toward becoming a police state. This is true despite its abundant technological facility to do so and the extensive personal data within its computers. Indeed, all of these government files, with reasonable exceptions, are available "to any person" under the Freedom of Information Act.

Americans who adamantly oppose any form of electronic currency simply because of some Orwellian distrust do themselves a disservice; they ignore a criminal-court system near collapse, overflowing prisons, and the highest crime rates in the industrialized world. They are still fighting Hitler and Stalin. Their guard is down to a real and current enemy, while they stand vigilant against an empty threat of totalitarianism.

Having the means to intrude upon privacy does not entice or cause the government to do so. Moreover, opposing constitutional forces tend to prevent it. It is the success of America's institutions—including its courts, the fiber of those who govern, and the participation of those who are governed—that keeps privacy violations in check and personal freedoms alive in the United States. Indeed, the stated purpose of the Freedom of Information Act (FOIA) is to insure that the public has access to governmental information to enable the public to scrutinize federal administration and to uncover possible abuses.

Even today, recent court decisions are correcting law enforcement excesses in the "War against Drugs" by disallowing certain government seizures. This demonstrates, albeit sometimes at a snail's pace, that, overall, systemic forces within the American government uphold individual rights of privacy. Implementation of an electronic currency system would not lessen this.

CHAPTER 8

PRACTICAL CONSIDERATIONS ABOUT FEDERAL ELECTRONIC CURRENCY

SECURITY OF ELECTRONIC CURRENCY FROM THEFT

A frequent question about federal electronic currency is, "How safe would that be?" Such concern is understandable. Credit-card and wire-transfer frauds are in the news, though they typically fail to reveal the nearly insignificant fraction of volume that such frauds represent. When large credit-card write-offs are reported, which run about 4 percent of volume, the media often fail to distinguish fraud and theft from simple delinquencies. News media also tell of hackers penetrating secret industrial and government computer files.

Public concern is not just the result of the news stories. Bankcard companies advise users to destroy expired bankcards, warning of the great amount of debt that criminals can run up. It is no wonder, then, that upon hearing of electronic currency, many declare, "Criminals will just begin stealing electronic currency."

The most reassuring point to be made to prospective FEDEC account holders is that exposure to losses from unauthorized transfers from FEDEC accounts would either be very limited by the Electronic Fund Transfer Act or virtually eliminated by more specific federal law defining the government's guarantee of the electronic currency.

No type of money is absolutely free of risk. It is a relative matter as to which is safer and which is riskier. In comparing the security of various forms of money, cash deserves a failing mark. At least $1.2 billion in cash is reported stolen every year, and no one knows how much stolen cash goes unreported. This figure is derived from an (unpublished) analysis of the National Crime Victimization Survey for 1991 conducted by the Bureau of Justice Statistics at the request of this author; it indicates that in 8 percent of all crimes in which something is stolen, the "something" consists of cash only. An FBI report indicates that the total value of property stolen in 1991 was $14,972,819,000.[1] Eight percent of this comes to $1.2 billion, a figure that, if anything, is too low, for it fails to include cash stolen along with other property.

No matter how small the amount, cash is pursued by thieves, robbers, burglars, muggers, and pickpockets, who all too often employ force and violence. Unguarded cash finds a new owner quickly in America. I recently read an article describing nursing-home workers who regularly pilfered small amounts of cash and other items from Alzheimer's sufferers and other helpless patients.

Cash also plays a role in and supports frauds conducted in other types of payment media, for example, in the passing of bad checks for cash. Fraudulent checks cost U.S. retailers some $15 billion a year. In many costly cases the cash is not received in exchange for the check. "The main reason for fraudulent conversion [by means of bad checks] is the ability to take the merchandise and convert it into cash," says Joseph Cabrelli, senior vice president at NPC Check Services of Riverdale, New Jersey. He notes that small, expensive merchandise—electronics, jewelry, cameras, fine leather, handbags, watches—is the easiest to convert to cash and the most likely target of a bad-check artist.[2]

World-class credit-card fraud rings, some headquartered in the Far East, seem to have the same modus operandi. That is, they purchase expensive, easily resold items with stolen or bogus credit cards and then convert the merchandise to currency. In parallel, most wire-transfer thieves break the audit trail at some point by converting stolen electronic funds into currency.

Apprehension about making cash electronic not only places far more trust in cash than it deserves but also reveals a lack of awareness that virtually all liquid assets, except for cash, are held and/or transferred electronically. The general public worries little that its checking accounts are kept electronically or that mutual funds, futures, options, and other assets are held and transferred electronically—and why should it worry? One seldom if ever hears of bank accounts being electronically plundered (although, as discussed later, forged checks cost nearly $1 billion a year). Nor, after FEDEC implementation, would one hear of FEDEC accounts being robbed.

The bankcard industry's caution to cardholders to protect themselves by avoiding practices conducive to fraud is not intended so much to create public apprehension about security of electronic funds as it is to reduce industry losses. By law, the cost of fraud is borne almost entirely by industry. Thus, such warnings are self-serving and made for the purpose of saving issuers such expense.

In 1992, credit-card losses in the United States due to fraud ran about $864 million a year, less than two-tenths of 1 percent of credit-card gross volume that year.[3] Between 1989 and 1993, these losses tripled. Beginning in 1994, industry began its high-tech counterattack. Devices including "Card Verification Value Program" and "Neutral Networks" had made an impact. By the end of 1994, fraud rates had fallen by 6 percent. Clearly, means exist to fight fraud.

Some aspects of credit-card security are not as tight as they might be. For example, the use of photo IDs on bankcards, a seemingly rudimentary security measure used for decades in electronic access systems, is not required on most bankcards. Bankcard issuers did not even offer photo ID as an option until the early 1990s. There are reasons for this, of course. While photo ID on bankcards may make sense from a security point of view, photographic and printing costs must be taken into account. Moreover, in a fiercely competitive bankcard market, a bothersome requirement that potential credit-card holders have their photos taken might impede a bank's acquisition of new accounts.

Credit-card security could be improved at the sales counter, where clerks more often than not fail to demand separate identification. Card issuers have not taken a hard stance here, perhaps because they are fearful that enforcing such security checks might alienate some retailers and cause them to take their business to less stringent issuers.

As with all costs of business, most bankcard issuers pass fraud losses on to consumers. Thus, until fraud losses become exorbitant in relation to sales volume and until the public rebels at the practice, the industry will likely continue to defray credit-card fraud losses by simply charging higher credit-card interest rates.

Comparing prospective FEDEC security to that of credit-card systems is comparing apples and oranges and is not fair to the FEDEC system. FEDEC, by reason of its proposed debit-system structure and operation, would suffer an insignificant amount of fraud. A FEDEC account holder would either have or not have sufficient money in an account to cover a transaction. Neither credit nor grace periods would be involved. If one lacked sufficient FEDEC funds, the transaction would not go through. Even if a thief were to somehow access another's debit-system account, the most that could be stolen would be the account balance. This contrasts with credit-card systems, where the amounts that can be charged are equal to unused lines of credit, often in the thousands of dollars. This is the prime factor keeping today's debit-card fraud losses extremely low.

There is also checking-account security to consider. The American Bankers Association estimates that 500 million fraudulent checks are passed in the nation's banks each year, amounting to at least $2.8 billion. In contrast, bank robbers take only $50 million.[4] A substantial and growing portion of check fraud is accomplished by impersonation. Criminals print valid account names and account numbers on bogus check blanks. This sort of check fraud was perpetrated 537,000 times in 1993 for a total loss of $568 million.[5]

Undermining the security of all paper instruments of value today, including personal, business, and cashier's checks, money orders, and traveler's checks—even gift certificates and theater and sporting-event tickets—is the alarming rise in counterfeiting. According to *American Banker*:

Modern printing technology is causing a flood of counterfeit personal and cashier's checks, money orders, and gift certificates to flow through banking and retailing industries at a cost estimated in the billions of dollars, according to security experts. Emergence in the last three years of sophisticated laser printers, scanning devices and desktop publishing systems have been a boon to counterfeiters.[6]

The insidious rise of counterfeit frauds is supported by the availability of inexpensive printing equipment that can produce nearly perfect fakes of bank emblems and stationery, payroll checks, traveler's checks, and even concert tickets. In light of this development, it is unsettling to realize how readily cashier's checks are accepted, often without bank verification, in exchange for valuable real estate, expensive jewelry, stocks, bonds, automobiles, and boats.

Some types of check fraud are quite low-tech. In 1991, the U.S. Postal Service suffered fraud losses of $1.7 million from its money-order operations. Almost all was caused by prison inmates who modified $1 postal money orders to read $700. A prisoner would typically obtain the small-denomination money order from an accomplice outside the prison and, after altering the document, would dupe a romantic pen pal into depositing the bogus money order into the pen pal's bank account. The pen pal was then instructed to draw a check to the prisoner's "friend" on the outside to help the prisoner with his legal defense. Of course, by the time the fraud is discovered, the check has cleared, and the pen pal is called to make up the $699. The Postal Service has since added to their paper a watermark image of Benjamin Franklin, aluminized polyester thread, and multicolored fibers that are visible under fluorescent light. It also has modernized its old Paymaster imprinters to make altering money orders extremely difficult, and it posts warnings of this "Prison Pen Pal" money order scam.

Another check fraud scheme is called "check washing," and in these cases crooks steal outbound mail from mailboxes. Using special fluids, they remove the payees's names from any checks they find, substitute names for which the crooks have identification, and cash them.

This author, unfortunately, learned a hard lesson about check counterfeiting. Several years ago, in reply to a telephone order, my firm shipped a piece of electronic equipment, COD, to a purchaser in Boston via United Parcel Service. A week later payment was received in the form of a $5,000 cashier's check written on a New England bank. Although the check appeared quite official, with a neat logo and double signatures, the bank was nonexistent. I learned subsequently that the order had been placed from a cellular phone. The delivery address turned out to be a vacant house. The Treasury Department now publishes a warning list of phony banks and related scams.

FEDEC SECURITY FEATURES

Any thief penetrating FEDEC security would face the problem of where to safely transfer "stolen" funds. Recall that FEDEC is a closed system in which debits and credits are made between FEDEC accounts; no method exists by which to transfer funds directly out of the system. As the identity of each account holder would be known, verified, and kept current, police would summarily identify a thief who "stole" money by transferring it into his or her own FEDEC account.

Using an accomplice would not help the thief much. Any unauthorized transfer of funds to a conspirator's FEDEC account would merely mean that the accomplice would be identified and called upon to explain how and why the funds were transferred. As accomplices would be responsible for repayments, they might prove difficult to recruit.

Couldn't a thief simply use a stolen FEDEC card to make purchases of goods from merchants, so that the stolen funds, instead of going into the thief's account, would go into the merchant's account? Perhaps. However, several factors render this more difficult than perpetrating today's similar check and credit-card frauds.

First, except for transactions below a very low threshold, FEDEC security would require some form of PIV, for example, a PIN or biometric entry. The use of PINs has been effective in keeping ATM fraud down, which in large part underlies its contrast with credit-card fraud, the latter of which does not generally require PINs. The Department of Agriculture, replying to a suggestion from a retailers' organization that food stamp EBT cards bear the cardholder's photo for better security, replied by saying that photo ID was unnecessary "because EBT systems can adequately safeguard against fraudulent and/or duplicate issuances by use of the PIN."[7]

ATM/debit fraud would be even lower but for the fact that cardholders, as a matter of convenience, too often write their PIN numbers directly on their ATM/debit cards. Twenty-three percent of the sample reviewed in one survey had PINs written on their cards.[8] Likewise, a variety of other PIV technologies might be incorporated in the FEDEC system, including fingerprint, voiceprint, and signature devices, any one of which would render a stolen FEDEC card virtually useless to a thief. (See "Personal Identification Verification Devices" in Chapter 9.)

As with today's bankcards, if a FEDEC account holder knew or suspected his or her card was stolen, that person could notify authorities immediately, have the card number deactivated, and obtain a new card/ number. Indeed, it might be incumbent to do so: Under today's Electronic Funds Transfer Act[9], failure to instigate such measures subjects an account holder to losses from subsequent unauthorized use of a stolen card.

Though the EFT Act, including its consumer protections from unauthorized use of bankcards, would be adapted to FEDEC, these provisions would likely be revamped. For example, Regulation E leaves the cardholder responsible for the first $50 of unauthorized fund transfers.[10] If the bulk of FEDEC's payments were comparable to today's cash, which average around $5, the Regulation E protection, as it pertained to FEDEC, would be rather meaningless. Thus, it would seem, government, as issuer and operator of FEDEC, would have to be responsible for perhaps all funds taken without authorization from one's account. Thus, if one's funds had mysteriously disappeared from FEDEC computers—for example, because transferred or deleted by a hacker—and the account holder could establish, by means of monthly statements, for example, that a certain sum should be in the account, FEDEC would then replace the missing funds.

Such FEDEC guarantees would exceed those of today's currency, for today government does not replace mysteriously absent cash. Yet, some personal liability should attach to negligent handling of one's FEDEC account, such as openly displaying one's PIN (though better PIV methods, such as fingerprints, can be expected to supersede PIN). With guarantees too broad, one can imagine how many individuals would conspire to defraud the system. Therefore, the guarantee might have to be narrowed. One possibility would be to apply a relatively short statute of limitations to FEDEC claims. This would not only limit government liability but also force users to pay attention to their account activity.

Government would guarantee FEDEC money both as a keeper of funds and as a warrantor of their genuineness. Warranty of genuiness is exemplified as follows: If one had deposited illicitly obtained money in a FEDEC and subsequently transferred it to an innocent transferee, that is, to a bona fide purchaser without knowledge of the taint, government would guarantee the money in the transferee's account against any prior claims.

FEDEC could employ a variety of systemic security measures, ranging from new cryptological methods to practical devices in current usage. For example, employee embezzlers commonly make out payments to fictitious payees: The FEDEC system might provide businesses computer-programmed security barriers, such as time locks permitting payment only between given hours on given days, required multiple digital signatures (computer-identifiable authorizations), and restrictions of payments to predesignated payees, such as named suppliers. Inexpensive software would be effective here.

The FEDEC system would also employ sophisticated technology that is increasingly beyond penetration by crooks. For example, FEDEC communication would be digital and likely transmitted via optic cable, which is extremely difficult to intercept. Using advanced encryption and high-speed computer chips, data encoding has been raised to such high levels that the best code busters in the National Security Agency and the FBI, until recently, could not intercept or decipher such private-sector communication. As a consequence, the FBI sought legislation requiring industry to provide government access. This resulted in enactment of the Communications Assistance for Law Enforcement Act, signed by the president in October 1995, ensuring government's ability to conduct court-authorized wiretaps. The act requires industry to install and supply government with hidden "keys." It also provides $100 million to reimburse telecommunication carriers for modifying their equipment and providing these services. Clearly, a FEDEC system using such technology would not be breached very easily or often, if ever.

Fraud-detection devices would be available for additional security in the FEDEC system. "Neural Networks" and the "Card Verification Value Program" were mentioned earlier as methods of detecting credit-card fraud. Several other security devices are also available or are under development, one of which is based on a discovery that each mag-stripe on a bankcard has a unique magnetic formation; this serves as the card's "fingerprint" and can be read to determine whether it is counterfeit or genuine. This is but one of the many fraud-detection methods constantly being researched in industry. Furthermore, if necessary, government could set its own R&D forces in motion to develop even better fraud and theft prevention methods.

That said, FEDEC would never be absolutely impenetrable. Technical vulnerabilities would be discovered from time to time, both by thieves and by system analysts. There are always insiders who know how to override security barriers. Occasionally, before such breaches were closed off, thefts would occur. One can speculate as to who would predominate in future battles between high-tech thieves and their high-tech government counterparts. Yet, this would focus on a relatively minor aspect and tends to obscure a more significant point—that EFT criminals would comprise only a tiny group. The bulk of today's thieves, uneducated and with no criminal skills other than force, guile, and adeptness at taking advantage of opportunity, would be stymied at EFT security barriers and would not even attempt to breach them.

Whatever losses might occur, it seems unlikely that they would approach the estimated $10 billion in cash that is stolen each year. And, even if they did, this sum, as detailed in following chapters, is a small fraction of the overall savings anticipated by ending cash.

It can hardly be overemphasized that even if a few technically proficient thieves might penetrate FEDEC security from time to time, for example, by means of simulated FEDEC cards or by somehow intercepting identification data, their crimes would be perpetrated surreptitiously and non-violently. Losses in such cases would only be monetary (which government would likely cover anyway). Ending cash would still have put a stop to losses measured in lives and bodily injuries—especially to shopkeepers, bank tellers, taxi drivers, gas-station attendants, and others who must deal with cash.

The key question one should ask about FEDEC security is: Would it be better or worse than that of tangible cash—the currency and coin in one's wallet or purse, the cash register, and safe? The answer is clear. The lack of security in cash—worse yet, the danger inherent in possessing it— constitutes the very impetus for abolishing it. Any form of money is more secure than cash.

RELIABILITY AND SYSTEM BREAKDOWN

On March 13, 1993, eighteen inches of snow fell on the EDS data center in Clifton, New Jersey. It collapsed the roof and knocked out service to 5,200 ATMs and several networks. Yet, service was restored to 98 percent of cardholders within 48 hours. If this accident happened today, there would probably be no service loss at all, and if there were, service could be restored faster. Not only have bankcard and other EFT systems proven themselves extremely dependable, but their reliability is being constantly improved.

Beginning at about three o'clock P.M. eastern time on April 13, 1998, an AT&T frame-relay switch failed, causing a data network outage that spread across the United States and disabled tens of thousands of POS terminals. The bulk of the nation's banks, grocery chains, and other retailers had to use alternatives for on-line bankcard transactions, such as getting telephone authorizations (voice and wireless transmissions were unaffected), using paper charge slips, or simply accepting checks and cash. Full service was restored in 20 hours.

Not every retailer suffered this fate. K-Mart Corporation, for example, was prepared, and as soon as AT&T's frame-relay connection went down, K-Mart's data systems automatically began communicating via a satellite network. Although on-line bankcard processing was then a bit slower, the impact was minimal. Surely, other organizations that process data on-line have learned from such breakdowns and are equipping themselves with backup systems.

Overall, however, these events are rare and short lived. EFT systems have proven themselves extremely dependable, and their reliability is being constantly improved with redundant communication systems and other contingency safeguards. NationsBank Corporation, one of the country's largest banks, for example, estimating it could lose up to $50 million per day of down time in a disaster, sends transaction data to an IBM disaster recovery unit that uses Remote Dual Copy™ software, a procedure that backs up data almost instantaneously and restores lost data in 12 to 24 hours. Newly developed compression technology halves the number of high-speed transmission lines required to transfer data and therefore helps cut the costs of such recovery safeguards.

FEDEC would, of course, take advantage of the latest such disaster recovery systems. FEDEC records would not be lost in disasters, for they would be constantly backed up and stored in unaffected locales. Moreover, any regional disaster that had disabled FEDEC temporarily would not necessarily mean that no one in the region could make a payment during that period, for FEDEC would coexist with other payment media. Thus, if the system were to go down, one could still write a check, write an IOU, or possibly use a bankcard.

One tends to harbor the false notion that if all other payment media were to somehow fail, one could at least buy essentials of life using currency and coin. In fact, cash fails even as a temporary substitute. Although cash is not subject to computer viruses, equipment sabotage, or power outages, it has become integrated with systems that are. When power is off, as during storms and natural disasters, ATM cash-dispensing machines and cash registers will not operate. When bank computers are down, tellers cannot dispense cash or even accept deposits. During power outages, because their lights are out and their security systems are down, most retailers and banks simply close their doors. Under such circumstances, the cash in wallets and purses, the typical amounts of which would not keep Americans going very long anyway, cannot be spent. Moreover, with law enforcement officials typically preoccupied during disasters, the danger inherent in possessing sums of cash rises manyfold.

Fortunately, electronic payment and communication systems have proven themselves quite stable. The United States endures debilitating hurricanes, vast flooding, deep sub-zero winters, ruinous fires, and earthquakes, yet the nation's electronic payment systems have kept humming along with only insignificant interruptions.

Unfolding technology continues to increase EFT reliability. For example, Sprint and other communication systems have developed SONET (synchronous optical network), which reduces network breakdowns from matters of hours to only milliseconds. This device works by integrating existing fiber optic lines in rings around service areas. The idea is that when a break occurs, the system automatically reroutes the communication stream to the unaffected side of the ring.[11]

OPERATIONAL COSTS

Automatic computer entries of FEDEC debits and credits would cost virtually nothing. Data communication, in fraction-of-a-second blips, would cost next to nothing. FEDEC can operate with extreme efficiency.

That said, defenders of today's paper currency system point out that it too is efficient and that it costs less than half a cent to circulate a dollar bill for a year. The overall cost of manufacturing, delivering, and replacing today's currency runs only $254 million a year, or less than $1 per American per year. However, this represents only government's operational costs. This is like judging a polluting car by its gas mileage. First, accounting must be added for government expense in monitoring cash for counterfeiting, laundering, and other illegal activities. If we add in criminal justice costs attributable to cash, the sum rises sharply. The greatest contrast in costs between tangible and electronic currency lies in the externalities. Government merely makes cash available. All but a small percentage of the overall cash-processing cost is borne by the private sector, this from endless counting, packaging, and transporting, not to mention necessary security outlays.

The idea of fully replacing a nation's currency with electronic money has never been tried anywhere, and cost statistics are nonexistent. One can look to bankcard processors such as Visa and MasterCard for comparable costs of EFT operations; however, such companies are reluctant to reveal proprietary figures, and their operations vary substantially from the proposed FEDEC debit-system structure. Complicating the picture, their processing is staged and linked between card issuers and/or financial institutions, on the one hand, and data processors and/or networks on the other, with diverse fees and charges billed and collected among them.

Credit-card transactions are little help in estimating what FEDEC payments might cost to process. A typical credit-card transaction involves at least five entities: the customer, the card issuer, the merchant, its bank, the bankcard network, and possibly intervening processors. Up to nine steps are involved in the transaction, including switching, processing through multiple computers, and follow-up paperwork and accounting for the various fees levied between the parties.

The basic FEDEC transaction, a debit-card type, would involve only three entities: The payer, the payee, and the FEDEC system. A FEDEC payment would entail only a fraction of the communication and accounting involved in any of today's bankcard transactions, thus allowing lower overall operating costs. As well, the number of FEDEC transactions, which would run six times those of all other payment systems combined, would benefit from economies of scale. Absence of a profit factor promises to reduce operational costs even further. These factors would give FEDEC substantial cost advantages over any private-sector payment system.

Experts long ago, before high-speed chips and optic cable existed, believed that a $0.05 processing cost for commercial debit card transactions was achievable.[12] It costs the federal government only $.02 to make an EFT payment.[13] Certain types of payment, such as by smart card off-line, may cost substantially less. A senior official at AT&T Universal Card recently commented that the Mondex system is commercially viable for selling goods valued as low as five cents.[14] Its operational cost could not run more than a small fraction of five cents, say, one cent. If this is true for private-sector systems, then the less complicated, high-volume FEDEC transaction might cost half again as much, or around $.005.

Assuming 550 billion FEDEC payments per year at a cost of one U.S. cent each, FEDEC processing costs would run $5.5 billion annually. True, this is some five and a half times as much as the government's current cost (about $1 billion) of producing and distributing cash. Yet, it would amount to only one-eleventh of industry's current annual cost (about $60 billion) of handling cash. Furthermore, government would more than recoup the $5.5 billion by means of reduced law enforcement costs and increased tax revenues.

The Federal Reserve, which might run FEDEC, operates a fully computerized automated clearinghouse (ACH). The federal ACH began in the early 1970s as a "paperless check clearing system." It now clears and settles about 35 percent of the nation's bank checks. In 1991, it processed over 1.6 billion transactions.[15] It also performs a number of other services, including the processing of direct electronic deposits for over 40 million Americans receiving Social Security benefits, Civil Service retirement, Veterans Administration compensation, welfare, and federal salaries. This has saved taxpayers millions of dollars in paperwork and mail costs and has averted a great deal of forgery, theft, and other crime associated with payments made by government checks. The federal ACH also processes direct deposit for private-sector payrolls and corporate dividend payments.

The Fed seems the logical choice of government bodies to operate a FEDEC system. However, it is not without its critics, who sometimes accuse it of being more interested in self-preservation than progress. Specifically, bankers point to its failure to take steps that would make check processing more efficient, for example, by accepting checks for processing in electronic rather than paper form, which would eliminate the national expense of transporting paper checks to the Fed's processing centers.

Food Stamp EBT operating costs bear limited relevance and value in estimating FEDEC's operational costs. The various Food Stamp EBT programs are locally designed and operated and suffer from small size and other inefficiencies. Food Stamp EBT relies on private-sector contractors for processing, so that a profit factor is included in overall costs. It is difficult to compare operational costs, for Food Stamp EBT statistics are kept on a cost-per-case-per-month basis.

What this boils down to, according to Jeffrey N. Cohen, a supervisor in the Program Development Division at the Department of Agriculture, is an approximate cost (in 1996) of 10 to 15 cents per transaction. He believes this cost will fall as the various states' operating procedures are streamlined, particularly if a nationwide standard is adopted for Food Stamp EBT.

Several factors in the FEDEC system's ultimate design would bear heavily on transaction cost. The first is whether the system incorporates the use of prepayment cards or "smart cards"; the second is whether off-line communication is used; and the third turns on the modes of communication employed.

An advantage of both prepayment cards and off-line communication lies in the fact that FEDEC payments could be made without calling up a remote processing center for each transaction and could thereby save costs. Off-line procedure is distinct from, and may or may not be used in conjunction with, prepayment cards. As its name implies, an off-line transaction is conducted without contacting the system's remote processing computers. Transaction data is sent to a processor later. The advantages of off-line payment procedure are (1) a quicker transaction procedure, (2) transmittal of multiple transactions in batch form with a single call, and (3) allowing off-line transactions in conditions where communication is impractical or impossible. In off-line operations, the cardholder's account is unaffected at the time of the transaction and is debited only after the data is transmitted to a central processing unit. Thus, a time lapse (float) occurs between the transaction and the time one's account is debited— just the reverse of the prepayment card arrangement, in which one pays first and transacts later.

Both on-line and off-line transaction procedures might be incorporated in the FEDEC system, the particular usage depending on various factors such as the dollar amount of the sale, the frequency of payments experienced by a particular payee, and communication availability. FEDEC might emulate private-sector procedures. In fast-food operations, for instance, off-line bankcard payments are typically stored in the restaurant's on-site computer until the end of the day, when they are forwarded in batch form to bankcard processing centers.

Transaction communication is undergoing fundamental changes. Today's modes include standard phone line, digital phone line, coaxial cable, fiber optic cable, and satellite. Moreover, both cellular and wireless local links feed into these modes. Communication technology is unfolding at such a fast clip that by the time the FEDEC system's designers touched pen to paper newer communication devices and schemes might vary significantly from those now available. Some foresee a sharp decline in telecommunication rates in coming years.

With these and other ponderables and until more of the system's basic design were known, it seems pointless to attempt to compile operational costs. One can roughly estimate, however, that they would run somewhere between $1 and $5 billion a year. If so, considering the ancillary benefits, this would be quite a good deal for the American public.

PUTTING THE NEW MONEY SYSTEM INTO OPERATION

By rule of thumb, federal programs require some ten years from inception to implementation. Given the enormity of the task, FEDEC could easily prove the rule. Yet, if due weight is given to the crime-prevention attributes of ending cash, not to mention its economic benefits, the process warrants acceleration. A murder takes place every 27 minutes in the United States, a robbery every 59 seconds, a burglary every 13 seconds, and a larceny theft every 4 seconds.[16] Illegal drug sales occur nonstop around the clock. FEDEC offers to slash these crime rates.

An initial barrier to changing the currency system has already been breached: Government has stirred from its dormant position regarding e-money. Some officials, alarmed over deployment of private e-cash systems, are at least pondering the possibility of an active role for government in consumer EFT. A few years ago, the Director of the Mint suggested a commission to study the possibility of a smart-card currency. As noted earlier, the Treasury Department and other divisions of government are involved with limited diverse applications of consumer EFT, for example, in military smart cards, direct deposit, and so on. The success and advantages of such programs might influence attitudes in Washington to investigate the concept of issuing a general-usage federal e-currency.

Initial rounds of informal inquiry, with input from a wide field of advisors, would narrow the concept and see it jell into a rough design, thus providing a basis for review by both government and the private sector. Potential problems would be exposed and solutions be developed, all of which would culminate in rough projections of the inherent tasks, outlays, and benefits.

Any suggestion for issuance of an e-currency would undergo the scrutiny of congressional banking and other committees. This process might involve a review a variety of e-currency schemes. If favorably impressed with its feasibility, security, and advantages, Congress might call for a FEDEC pilot project that would be conducted in a defined manner for a given period. Conditioned on positive feedback from such trials, it might call for issuance of a permanent e-currency—perhaps one that would at first circulate along with tangible cash. Having gained experience in this test period, subsequent legislation and regulation could then be more focused and comprehensive, not only to include technical matters, rules of usage, and the legal rights and duties of transacting parties but also to cover rights of privacy, to define new crimes, and to address many other areas that would be impacted.

Ultimately, whether in a singular bill or in multiple bills and by whatever congressional route, the proposal for transformation of all cash to an electronic currency system would travel through both houses, be signed by the president, and become law. This would set a timetable for implementation.

Fully transforming America's cash to an electronic currency system promises to be a monumental project—not only for governments (at several levels) but for industry and the public in general. The job of processing and verifying some 200 million account applications is, alone, daunting. On the material side, the heart of the system—high-speed, high-volume computers—would be designed, assembled, tested, and put through trials before being put into operation. A similar process would ensue for personal terminals and transaction cards, which, at full implementation, would have been manufactured in the hundreds of millions. A national communications network would have to be designed and established, which would involve links with diverse private-sector systems. Clearly, this will take years to accomplish.

Federal, state, and local governments would be faced with conversion of cash-operated transit-fare collection devices, postage-stamp dispensing machines, parking meters, and so on. Industry would also have to retrofit or replace all its coin-operated equipment—including telephones, food- and drink-dispensing machines, and numerous other devices. Even the smallest retailer would have to equip itself with one or more terminals.

Fortunately, devices and equipment for the new e-currency would not have to be designed from scratch. Computers handling tremendous volume have long been employed in securities markets, telecommunications, and other industries. Conversion of coin devices to card readers began years ago. We see them in transit systems and service stations and on copying machines, telephones, and food-vending machines. Contactless readers are used on an increasing number of toll roads and bridges in the United States and around the world. Virtually all the technology and much of the equipment are available "off the shelf."

Transition would be eased by the fact that, until the very last day of the implementation period, currency and coin would remain in circulation. Indeed, even after paper currency was discontinued, coin might be left in circulation for an extended time; stripped of its legal-tender status, it could be used only as token money in coin-operated devices.

FEDEC's pilot projects would be confined to geographical areas where system equipment and technical procedures could be tested. The process would not only iron out technical and equipment wrinkles but also address informational, educational, financial, and other miscellaneous services. It would afford an opportunity to discover unforeseen problems, make modifications, and develop statistics. In its mature state, it would serve as a model for replication and expansion. Subsequently, additional areas of the country would be brought into the growing infrastructure.

With the entire nation finally on board, the legal tender status of cash could then be removed. One can expect that even before the ink was dry, virtually every retailer in the United States would immediately post a sign reading, "CASH NOT ACCEPTED HERE." Reluctant segments of the public might be nudged into the new system by the government's partial withdrawal of currency and coin from circulation.

The final act of transformation might occur in one of two ways: Conceivably, it might be marked by the arrival of a date beyond which it would be against the law to transact in currency and coin within the United States. This would hardly be necessary, because businesses and consumers alike would have already enthusiastically switched to FEDEC. Some Americans would probably keep a slip of currency or two and some coins as memorabilia, as was done with Continental and Confederate money. U.S. currency could remain in usage in foreign countries; it might have some use to Americans for travel abroad.

A generation hence, future historians would remark with wonderment how odd it was that physical cash remained in circulation so long into the electronic age. At that point in time, the common meaning of "cash" would no longer denote physical money; the term would be used only to distinguish between an immediate payment as opposed to one made on credit.

CHAPTER 9

THE TECHNICAL COMPONENTS

TRANSACTION CARDS

First-generation transaction cards are distinguished from following generations by their lack of electronics. Western Union's first cards, typical of the nonelectronic cards commonly issued during the first half of the twentieth century, simply bore the account holder's name and account number. First-generation "charge cards," as they became known, typically employed raised (or embossed) lettering. Included in this category were department-store stamped-metal charge plates that were used at POS by inserting the card, together with paper invoices, into hand-operated inked-ribbon imprinters. The metal plates were subsequently replaced with thermally embossed plastic cards. Nonelectronic cards are still used around the world. Indeed, such cards have an advantage over all other classes of transaction cards, except optical cards, in that the data on them are not affected by proximity to strong magnetic and electric fields.

First-generation cards are manufactured in materials ranging from paper to plastic. Most are quite simple, cheap to produce, and commonly used in prepayment mode, like tickets or tokens. More sophisticated models are coupled with enhancements such as bar codes, holographs, and machine-readable type like that printed on checks. Holographic first-generation cards have been used in some telephone systems in Europe since 1983. However, the cheaply produced, simple versions of these cards are more common. Several reasons, besides being unaffected by magnetism and electric fields, support their continued usage. For one, they are more secure than currency or coin because they are limited to particular types of transactions. Though cheaply produced, many are quite durable. They often serve as advertising vehicles, bearing, for example, company names and logos.

The majority of transaction cards used worldwide are second-generation cards. These have electromagnetic stripes running across their backs—a technique for storing and transferring data developed during World War II. The simplest of these "mag-stripe" cards uses a single stripe and is made of thin, stiff paper. Consumers obtain the cards from special cash- or bankcard-operated machines. The same can be accomplished at some ATMs, in which case the funds come from the cardholder's bank account. They are commonly used in transit-system turnstiles. Station-to-station fares are automatically calculated and electronically deducted from the cards' memories.

The mag-stripe card most familiar to Americans, however, is the plastic variety used as credit and ATM/debit cards. These usually employ three magnetic stripes. Even proponents of competing smart cards concede that magnetic-stripe usage will serve as the basic form for credit and debit cards at least until the end of the century and probably beyond. Mag-stripe cards are popular because they are inexpensive, with production costing as little as 5 cents each. Their card readers are also relatively cheap. The card's stripes hold considerable memory (1.6K+), and these cards provide adequate protection against fraud (although some consumer advocates challenge this). Security enhancements on today's mag-stripe bankcards include holograms, signature panels, and fine-line printing.

Some experts feel that the full potential of this class of card has yet to be reached. Features continue to be added to give it wider usage, more security, and longer life. Harder, more durable stripe material has been developed to prevent wear and scraping. Additional stripes are easily added to increase the card's memory capacity. Bar codes and account holders' pictures (engraved, laminated, or electronically encoded) have been added for security and/or for particular card applications. CardLogix, a transaction-card manufacturer, offers a new mag-stripe card that can be turned on manually via a keypad PIN entry; the card turns itself off automatically after a set number of seconds, in which state it is unusable.

Beyond first- and second-generation card groups lies another genre of transaction card altogether, called the "smart card." Also referred to as an "IC card" (for integrated circuit), in industry it has been dubbed a "chip card." The term "smart card" is the subject of much confusion. Because it sounds like something on the leading edge of technology, marketing strategists cannot resist applying the appellation to any sort of card. Genuine smart cards incorporate a data microprocessor and memory storage device, a "chip," within the smart card itself. While smart cards can store much more memory than magnetic-stripe cards, it is their ability to calculate and to perform other significant functions—such as comparing data, searching for data, and actuating electronic switches—that distinguishes them from simple data-storage cards like magnetic-stripe cards.

In France, Roland Moreno is looked upon as the inventor of the smart card. In Japan, in 1970, Kumitake Arimura filed a smart-card patent that led him to be regarded there as the inventor. Since that time, many millions of dollars have been invested in developing variations of this type of card. An array of smart cards has emerged, with newer models in constant development. They are the heart of e-cash.

First-generation smart cards (some experts categorize these simply as third-generation cards) employ physical contacts that engage a terminal. They usually have eight gold contacts located on their edges. This type of smart card shares a mechanical aspect of magnetic-stripe cards in that both make contact with terminals. Significantly, this type of card requires the use of a terminal in order to access the card's memory and to employ its IC functions.

Second-generation smart cards, or "proximity cards," eliminate the contact feature. Communication between card and terminal is conducted by very-close-distance radio transmission. The user simply approximates the card, held at any angle, with a terminal. The terminal does not need or have an opening or slot on its face. This obviates some of the problems experienced with swipe or pass-through terminals, such as dirty electronic contacts and vandalism. Additionally, it eliminates the need for prescribed card dimensions. Smart cards themselves can be of any shape and will work in nearly any position. Thus, both the smart card and its reader can be made in irregular and/or smaller sizes. Some cards use infrared light transmission instead of radio communication. A number of transit authorities, including the Washington, D.C., Metro, are trying out proximity cards.

Freedom from size restriction has seen the development of "data tags" that are used for various purposes. Some are produced similar in size to military "dog tags" and can be worn alongside or in lieu of them. One type of smart card has been made in the shape of a key. Similar devices are used for medical patients' charts. Still another type of smart card is attached to machinery to store maintenance records and troubleshooting instructions.

Third-generation smart cards, in addition to second-generation features, have numeric keypads and read-out display panels. Some are battery or solar powered. It was a natural progression for companies already making electronic calculators, like Toshiba and Casio, to get involved in the development of this type of smart card. Several French companies, however, dominate in the manufacture of smart cards.

Smart cards are capable of performing a number of electronic functions beyond simply adding and decreasing stored-value data. Because they are programmable, they can be tailored to specific tasks. Of significance in providing security is the ability of third-generation cards to self-authorize.

Self-authorization uses data hidden in a chip card's firmware. Most self-authorizing cards allow their owners to select their own confidential PINs. Once entered by the user (via the card's keypad), the PIN becomes permanent chip data. It cannot be accessed or altered, and the data cannot be brought up on the card's readout panel. In order to use the card, one has to enter the same PIN via the card's keypad, which switches on a circuit in the card, and the card's possessor can then proceed with a transaction. Without a match, the path is blocked. Some self-authorizing cards use a less secure alternative whereby the PIN is placed in the card's memory at the issuing facility and is confidentially revealed to the card's owner.

Hidden data is not limited to PINs; it can consist of biometrics or imaged photos, for example. Thus, hidden data might consist of the electronic equivalent of one's signature, voiceprint, or palm geography. However, the use of certain types of biometric data requires peripheral equipment to read and display the verification, such as an electronic signature pad and/or a video screen. Cards containing biometric data are commonly used in industry to restrict access to secure areas, computer data, equipment, and file cabinets. Some types of verification devices automatically control locks, gates, or other physical barriers.

With the use of a PIN, comparison verification can be accomplished on the smart card itself, for all that is required is a matching of numbers. If an external reader is required, the card is probably being used only as a memory-storage device. For example, employees in some workplaces carry cards containing their electronic pictures; in order to enter restricted areas, the cards are inserted into readers wired to video screens. A guard visually verifies that the employee is the same person as in the video picture. Newer systems have the ability to scan one's face and compare it with that stored on the card, thus making the comparison automatically and perhaps eliminating the need for a guard.

Until recently, the size of biometric readers limited true self-verification somewhat to the use of PINs. Laser scanners that read fingerprints, for example, would hardly fit on a card. Newly developed smart cards, however, permit some types of biometric verification within the card itself. One such product has a built-in fingerprint verification device. Some advanced cards, Xanadu's E-pass, for example, provide picture and illustration displays.

Transaction-card IC chips can be programmed to keep journals and records, a feature that makes e-cash possible. Some have the capacity to store data from multiple systems—such as credit and debit systems, VISA, MasterCard, and FEDEC—all in one card. Thus, the E-pass card is dubbed by some as the next generation of card, in that it can supplant the need to carry credit cards, checkbooks, driver's licenses, passports, and more.

Interestingly, the card is both solar and battery powered, the latter of which is recharged when the card is engaged in a transaction, as at a cash register.

A decade ago, Visa developed an experimental "Super Smart Card," a hybrid smart card that combined a number of features including embossing and a magnetic-stripe simulator that allowed it to be used in most magnetic-stripe terminals. The card had a sixteen-character liquid-crystal display, a twelve-key numeric keypad, eight functional keys, 64K bits of memory storage, and a built-in battery power supply. Moreover, it was programmed with a PIN-based self-authorizer.

Enthusiasts have long proclaimed that smart cards are the cards of the future. Judging by their growing usage around the world, they may be right. When smart cards were first introduced in the 1980s, some experts denigrated them a bit, stressing their greater cost over magnetic-stripe cards and asserting that smart cards do not speed transaction time or prove more effective against fraud.[1] Some pointed out that when they were used merely as numeric storage devices their cost was unjustified, for this function is more cheaply served by mag-stripe cards, and that smart cards are more easily damaged than mag-stripe cards. In those days, smart cards cost from $3 to $8 dollars each. Today, the cost vis-à-vis that of a mag-stripe is falling, and some believe that in high-volume production it will drop to around $1, or perhaps even less. Today's embedded chips are smaller and more secure from damage, and the cards are more flexible. Moreover, they have proven very effective in preventing fraud. For example, in the early 1980s, French bankcards were mag stripe, and fraud was rampant. With the introduction of smart cards such fraud all but disappeared. When smart cards were first employed in the French telephone system, years ago, it experienced a 30 percent rise in sales, a halving of vandalism, and a doubling of card usage.

Smart-card integration with other devices, as with telephones and automatic toll collectors, offers overall applications not currently possible with mag-stripe cards. Several firms, including Visa, joined in a consortium to develop a smart card dubbed the "Electronic Purse," which was designed to replace many types of coin transactions, including bridge and highway toll payments. A number of major players are active in this sort of thing. Motorola has developed a highly secure "contactless" smartcard microchip that has particular application in commuter transactions. VeriFone, Inc., recently unveiled several new mobile transaction-card terminals, including the OMNI 1250, "a robust, battery-powered smart-card solution designed to accept multiple electronic payment in one terminal, anytime, anywhere." These latter two companies have formed an alliance in marketing wireless payment systems worldwide.

When electronic credit cards were first introduced, authorizations were by telephone and transaction delay was a serious inconvenience. Early on-line authorization procedure improved the situation. Today, bankcard transaction speed has been reduced to or below that of cash transactions (at least, where change must be returned). Off-line transactions do not require remote communication; thus a transaction can be authorized within a second or two of swiping one's bankcard. However, that isn't fast enough for toll payments, where it would likely cause traffic snarls. This is where the fourth-generation smart cards come into play. These cards have the ability to communicate remotely by means of built-in antennae loops or "transponders" (from "transmission responders"). This allows longer-range transmissions than second-generation proximity cards. Typically placed on dashboards, the cards work even in poor weather conditions. As cars speed through toll stations, antenna readers receive signals and record vehicle/account data, times, dates, and lane numbers. These systems use either a prepaid account system, whereby the cardholder's account is debited for each toll, or prepaid cards, which decremate with each toll payment. Cameras are coordinated with toll payments (or lack thereof) to record the license-plate numbers of cars passing through.

The roll-through toll payment technique has been adapted to the gas pump. Although many Americans already swipe their bankcards at pump-mounted terminals and no longer pay a human attendant, newer systems, such as Mobile^R Speedpass™, allow customers to pay by merely waving a bankcard close to the pump. In others, the card on the dash suffices. On approval, a pump light flashes, notifying the customer to commence fueling. (Fueling is being automated, as well.)

Adding to the growing array of transaction cards are newly developed smart cards containing "combi" chips that communicate both via traditional land-line networks and by wireless radio. With this type of card, one could pay a bridge toll in the wireless mode without stopping the car and use the same card to pay for a restaurant dinner by swiping it through a standard terminal. (See *Electronic Engineering Times*, May 3, 1996.) Visa, working with Australia's Commonwealth Bank, is testing such a "contact/contactless" card. It contains two chips, one chip for physical terminal usage and a Motorola chip that works by radio signals.

Smart-card features continue to develop and expand in amazing ways. Motorola Semiconductor Products Sector recently announced a miniature display device called "SmartVue (TM)." This unique pocket smart-card reader, when held to the eye, gives an image equivalent to that of a 17-inch monitor, thus allowing crisp presentation of a tremendous amount of data.

Until recently, optical cards were not a contender for consumer payments. Despite their tremendous storage capacity, they were considered too expensive to encode. However, Sandia Imaging recently unveiled its VIVID 2000 (TM), a card printer allowing optical-card encoding during the printing process, a major breakthrough. Used in high-speed printers, this might reduce costs, thus opening the door for possible usage in payment transactions.

Many experts deem it inevitable that America will ultimately convert to chip-embedded smart cards. The technology and product are ready to use, the result of twenty years of (mostly European) investment; and smart cards offer incomparable security and applications. However, a lot of enthusiasm over smart cards centers on their value-stored application, and for several reasons some question whether the value-stored feature will become widely popular in the United States. They doubt that individuals will pay float simply for convenience. It is true that prepaid cards have made more sense in areas of the world lacking the relatively efficient communication systems enjoyed in the United States. Prepaid cards circumvent on-line communication. When on-line transaction processing time becomes fast enough and when payment devices become portable and cheap enough, the utility of most prepayment cards falls. This may be happening in the United States.

An application for which smart cards seem well suited is the all-in-one card, that is, a card containing multiple credit and/or debit cards, thus eliminating the necessity of carrying a wallet full of cards. A few years back, this idea was widely touted. Some smart cards have been used to store money access and medical and other diverse data. But, when it comes to multiple credit and/or debit cards, there's a problem: How do you get competing card issuers to cooperate in storing data on common cards? What's in it for them? Moreover, how would this be physically accomplished? Would the cards have to be sent from issuer to issuer? So far, we have not seen many multiple-issuer cards.

DATA COMMUNICATION SYSTEMS

Radio could well form an indispensable link in future bankcard data transmission. The cost of using airwaves is little or nothing, whereas ground lines are expensive to install, limited physically, and require maintenance.

Referring to "radio" is not as clear as it once was, for the term now includes analog and digital cellular, wireless, personal communication networks (PCNs), local area networks (LANs), wide area networks (WANs), packet radio, various satellite radio systems, and combinations of these. Techniques have been developed that integrate various radio systems with optic cable and that, further, automatically select the most efficient communication path for each call.

Nearly a quarter of Americans regularly communicate via cell phones. Some 42 million use wireless pagers. Both systems are organized in regional cells in which central radio towers receive and retransmit calls, areas usually several miles in diameter. Newer systems use zones dubbed "microcells" that are only a few blocks in diameter. In lieu of towers, shoe-box-size mini-base stations are installed at frequent intervals, every-where—in building hallways, in underground transit stations, on sidewalk light poles, and in factories. The idea is that wherever one is located, a line-of-sight station will exist nearby linking the user to the larger communication system. In addition to eliminating broadcast ob-structions, such as buildings, this system also requires less transmission energy, a significant factor when using battery-powered portable termin-als.

Short-distance radio transmission provides another advantage—fre-quency reusage. By keeping the radio link down to short distances, as between a radio-phone and a nearby transceiver, and by using optic cable or satellite for the long distances, the same radio frequencies can be used in separate locales.

An ongoing trend in communications is the combining of functions in a single hardware device. Housing a payment terminal with a radio-operated telephone has obvious utility. Thus, Pacific Bell Mobile Services, of Pleasanton, California, is trying out a system that integrates a smart-card reader with a mobile phone to allow the user to buy goods and serv-ices from any location. A host of other companies are developing similar products.

A new technology providing greater communication efficiency is called ATM, which refers not to an automatic teller machine, but rather to "asynchronous transfer mode." It integrates diverse data into a continu-ous communications stream, thereby taking advantage of otherwise wasted gaps and spaces. With ATM, single communication lines can carry up to six signals contemporaneously. By fully utilizing a line's capacity in this manner, transmission time is greatly reduced. Uses for this technology range from banking to telephone and from cable TV to in-flight enter-tainment.

Communication satellites were first placed in orbit at the beginning of the 1960s. What began with the launching of "Echo 1," a plasticized 100-foot diameter balloon that passively reflected signals to and from earth, has advanced dramatically. Passive satellites were soon replaced by active ones that drew energy from solar panels, which enabled them to generate their own radio signals. These high-altitude satellite systems required powerful ground transmitters and relatively huge ground antennas. They provided limited channels, territorial coverage, and time slots. In turn, they have been supplanted by fleets of new low-orbit active satellites sup-plying continuous universal links for everything from television to the Internet. These new "unwired" communication systems can be accessed by low-power handsets. Over the next ten years, some 1,300 satellites will have been put in orbit.

Frequency reuse, analogous to that in cellular communication systems, is accomplished from satellites by use of concentrating beams to small regions on earth. Moreover, by using a technique labeled TDMA, in which communication times are parceled out, even greater satellite efficiency is effected. These and other unfolding methods, such as "hopping spot beam," continue to render satellite communication cheaper, more reliable, and universally available for payment communications.

Wireless communication has yet to reach its apex. Thirty years' worth of satellite technology, invention, ingenuity, and discovery has only recently leveled off at a point where industry has begun investing capital in fixed systems. In half a dozen projects, multiple satellite systems are now being placed in service. The Iridium project, led by Motorola, Inc., having been spun off as a separate company in 1997, has launched a number of its planned 66 satellites. (This project originally envisioned a total of 77 satellites—hence reference to the element iridium, which has that many electrons). GlobeStar (a joint venture of Qualcomm, Inc., and Loral Space and Communication, Inc.) is launching another 48 satellites. Odyssey, Inc. (a partnership of Teleglobe, Inc., and TRW, Inc.) plan to launch twelve satellites, and Hughes Electronics Corporation another eight. Bill Gates and Craig McCaw have teamed up to launch a network of some 228 low-orbit satellites. Overall, about two satellites per week are being sent up.

This intense competition in satellite communication promises not only instant communication access but lower user costs. It is reported that subscriber costs for the Iridium system will run $3 per minute. This is still some ten times higher than many of today's digital cellular phone rates, a good indication that such satellite rates will fall. Yet, even at $3 a minute, when scaled down to fractional-second data bursts, a payment made via wireless satellite might cost, say, half a cent. Assuming that other system costs run about the same amount per payment, the overall cost of a FEDEC payment might be around $.01.

PERSONAL IDENTIFICATION VERIFICATION (PIV) DEVICES

Highly publicized incidents of "identity theft," whereby an individual is mysteriously deluged with bills and credit-card charges run up by an impersonator who, having acquired the individual's personal data, has fabricated bogus bankcards and drivers licenses and other identification documents, underlines the need for better identity verification. These cases are often treated by the press as simply invasion-of-privacy perils inherent in an electronic world, and news stories are typically followed with advice to:

- Guard your card as you would the cash equivalent.
- Use a tiered, see-through container in your wallet for credit cards, so you will notice if one is missing.

- Destroy an expired card to prevent anyone from altering it for use.

- Keep your card out of the view of others in a store or at a public telephone so they cannot read the name and account number. (*Source*: New York Times, July 11, 1994)

This inept response to "identity theft," certain to inflame paranoia, does little to check the problem, for it is practically impossible to keep personal identification numbers from ever being seen by strangers, and fakes of today's cards are quickly made. On the other hand, such impersonation can be halted by use of newer PIV methods. These are proving highly effective in scenarios ranging from thumb-printing in check cashing, to iris-scanning at ATMs. "Identity theft" is proving to be more of a technical security issue than an inherent privacy problem.

Huge sums have been expended over the last 25 years developing biometric personal identification verification (PIV) devices. Many were originally designed to control access to military equipment, computers, safes, and sensitive areas. The methods include fingerprints, palm-geography, signature-dynamics, retina patterns, iris patterns, voiceprints, and photo imaging. Just a few years ago, prices for such PIV devices were far too high for use in ordinary POS EFT transactions. As they became smaller, faster, and more accurate, their prices also began dropping dramatically. Some are already being employed at POS, and they might be appropriate for use in FEDEC.

For example, Sensar, Inc., manufactures its patented "IrisIdent" system, which verifies identity using a camera placed several feet away that zooms in on one's unique iris pattern. Its estimated $5,000 price may be too high for today's market, but the company predicts it will ultimately cost only several hundred dollars, in which case it might replace, or be used in addition to, PIN verification in ATM machines. Indeed, in England the Nationwide Building Society has already put them in service. "The customer simply puts in their ATM card and a camera mounted in the machine photographs the colored portion of the eye, the iris. If the iris staring back matches the record on the databank, the ATM will allow instant access to your bank account without the need for a PIN number."[2] Fingerprint PIV, which works by comparing prints, is also becoming affordable. Some industry observers predict that fingerprint technology will be more likely to replace PIN verification.

Most types of PIV devices work by seeking a match between data proffered to gain authorization, access, or entry and prestored data. The types of data subjected to such matching schemes may consist of account numbers, including PINs, or biometrics, all of which are personal to users. Other EFT security measures scrutinize nonpersonal data, such as electronic aberrations in mag-stripes or peculiarities in electronic equipment.

Still other security schemes analyze and compare spending patterns, as with a particular purchase for which one seeks on-line authorization.

PIV data against which subsequently presented data is to be compared may be prestored in any of several places, depending on system design; this might be in a transaction card, in a local POS computer, or in a remote central computer.

Any matching-type security device can be defeated if an unauthorized person obtains the prestored data and replicates it for presentation. Thus, protecting prestored PIV data is as important as protecting the thing being secured, such as money in bank accounts. Prestored data may consist of something as low-tech as PIN numbers, and the thief may acquire this in as nontechnical a method as looking over a victim's shoulder during a transaction. Surprisingly, PINs have kept fraud low. However, the trend in security devices is towards the use of data that cannot be seen or memorized, data that can be acquired only by electronic means.

Radio communication, as compared with ground-line communication, has greater vulnerability to interception. Cellular telephone systems are sometimes abused by crooks who acquire access codes and telephone numbers over the air and use them in subsequent unauthorized calls. To combat the use of hijacked telephone numbers and access codes, California-based PacTel Cellular and ESL, Inc., have been testing a system that determines if a call is legitimate by comparing the unique frequency pattern of the telephone itself to a pattern on file. Telephone companies use software that highlights calls that do not fit into a customer's calling profile.

Interception of telephone communication has mainly been a problem associated with analog, as opposed to digital communication (coded strings of 1s and 0s). Noted earlier, even the FBI cannot seem to tap some digital codes. Wireless, advanced cellular, and satellite communication are increasingly sent in encrypted digital form, making interception extremely difficult.

Password data can be prestored in a card. Thus, it might consist of a hidden PIN in a smart card, to be matched internally with a PIN entry on the card's keypad. Or, it might consist of facial-picture data stored in a card and displayed on a video monitor. Or, it might comprise signature data to be electronically compared with the cardholder's signature as it is inscribed on a signature-reading device. All such methods are in use.

PIV data can be prestored in a local computer. For example, a cardholder's picture might be prestored in a company computer located on premises and referenced by the cardholder's account number, so that at a physical barrier a security guard would swipe a proffered card through a computer terminal, bring up the cardholder's picture on the monitor screen, and visually compare it with the person seeking entry. The Miros company produces a system called TrueFace Access™ that works somewhat in this manner. Products that match data work on a variety of biometrics. In some, use of a human guard is rendered unnecessary. For example, in another scheme, hand-geography data is kept in a security checkpoint computer, so that when the person seeking access (or entry or authorization) swipes or proximates his or her card and places a hand in a hand scanner, a comparison is automatically made by the computer.

However, storing data locally has application where the targeted population and area involved are limited and may not be usable in FEDEC. It is suited for usage, for example, with employees at an airport, in a secured office building, or in a factory. The population involved in a FEDEC system would include virtually everyone in the nation, whose data would hardly compress into a local computer.

One way around the problem of storing massive data in local computers is to concentrate on the system's abusers. Thus, only data on "bad" accounts is stored. The use of "blacklists" in France in the 1980s was responsible for cutting bankcard fraud dramatically. This approach is used in the United States as well, for example, with fast-food bankcard transactions. This method employs an on-site computer that keeps a blacklist of "bad" account numbers; these are accounts that are over their authorization limits, have been reported lost or stolen, or are being used fraudulently. Such lists are updated each night by an on-line batch-feed communication sent from a central computer. Thus, in a transaction procedure, a customer's bankcard number is run through the local POS computer for a match with any of the "bad" numbers in local memory; if there is a match, the transaction is declined; otherwise, it is allowed to proceed.

PIV data might also be kept at a system's remote central processing unit (CPU). In this scenario, the cardholder presents his account number, PIN, or biometric data, and the corresponding data is obtained in an on-line direct communication with the system's CPU.

Each of these storage methods has advantages, limitations, and particular requirements. Electronic fingerprint PIV (which has nothing to do with ink) is finding numerous applications. One is in state motor-vehicle departments, which are jointly developing a nationwide DMV fingerprint system. Various county welfare departments are using this system to their advantage as well. As early as 1990, the Los Angeles County Department of Social Services installed an automated fingerprint-image reporting and match system, called "Affirm," that compares fingerprints of individuals receiving General Assistance benefits and exposes those receiving benefits under multiple names. By the end of 1991, the first full year in which Affirm was used, the program had saved Los Angeles County over $5.4 million. This program has been adopted by several other counties in California and has been expanded to cover other benefit programs, including AFDC.

Fingerprint readers work in a variety of ways. Most fingerprint optical readers operate by spotting minutiae, "constellations" of data points that denote unique patterns in fingerprints, including skips or convolutions that occur in each print. This is a particularly useful technique where only partial prints are available, as for example from crime scenes. But some systems, like Comparator System, compare a full print. Moreover, other systems work on a touch screen, thus allowing verification in a remote scenario, say, for TV home shopping.

Voiceprint PIV converts sound waves into digital data and automatically compares it with previously stored data. By applying sophisticated software to such data, computers can recognize spoken numbers and words (speech recognition). One of the earliest applications of this technology was a voice-operated device for blind or other disabled persons. Thus, it has been used for alphanumerical procedures in elevator command consoles.

Sprint Corporation's Voice Foncard uses voice recognition both for PIV and telephone procedure. Here, the caller speaks an access code, and the system's computer verifies the voiceprint for a match with that on file. Then, the caller speaks the telephone number desired. AT&T and other companies are testing voice PIV in bankcard transactions. This technology employs relatively inexpensive equipment and could conceivably be put to use in FEDEC. Thus, instead of pressing terminal keys for dollar amounts, one might speak the amount instead. The same voice command might efficiently serve both as a security clearance and to actuate the transaction.

Signature-dynamics PIV involves more than just the appearance and linear flow of one's signature. In modern systems, both the speed and stroke pressures of one's signature are measured and matched electronically. Both signature and voice PIV comprise a unique type of hidden data, for they share the fact that the subject is not conscious of the dynamics involved in his or her own act. Thus, both seem quite foolproof against direct forgery. A practical problem with signature PIV, however, is that it requires a signature pad. In some POS settings, as at a toll crossing, this clearly would not work.

Palm geography involves measurements of the length, width, and thickness of one's fingers as well as the unique contours of one's hand. The Immigration and Naturalization Service tried out this PIV in a year-long program called "Inspass." The program was aimed at speeding up repeat entries of travelers from abroad. Initially, a traveler inserts his or her hand into an electronic measuring device that records the data both in a central databank and in a wallet-size smart card. When reentering the United States, the traveler avoids long lines at immigration checkpoints, proceeding instead to an Inspass kiosk where the entrant inserts the smart card into a slot. At the same time, the entrant places a hand alongside in an electronic measuring device. The machine compares the two data for a match, then dispenses a pass that allows the traveler to proceed. This takes about 35 seconds.

Retina-scan PIV measures the pattern in one's retina, which, like a fingerprint, is unique. Despite its potential, however, retina scan has remained unpopular because of the common fear that its laser scanner will zap one's eyes. A newer type of eye biometrics that measures and matches the over-400 identifying features of one's iris averts this problem. Originally designed for smart-bomb aiming, measurement can be accomplished several feet away from the eye. Moreover, it is even more accurate. Sensar, Inc., offering the patented system called IrisIdent, claims by company spokesman that the error rate is only one in 131,578, and the cost of a system should soon fall to several hundred dollars.

Imaging technology was not developed specifically for security matching, but rather for the efficiency of capturing documents in picture form into computer memory. It has flowered into an industry of its own and is employed in a wide range of applications. This is another off-the-shelf technology.

Imaging is used by the banking industry to capture, transmit, and store checks and as a way to cut down on the account holder's float time, as well as to reduce fraud. It also allows banks to retrieve canceled checks quickly and at a fraction of the former cost. By miniaturizing the check size (by "compressing" the data), banks save computer memory. File-and-paper-intensive organizations ranging from insurance companies to justice systems utilize imaging to save space and to take advantage of software that automatically files, sorts, and retrieves data.

In like manner, an imaged facial picture can be stored in a transaction card and projected on a video monitor for visual verification by a guard, teller, or other attendant. This type of device has been around for several years. With newer technology, first used by the military, data from a live camera is electronically compared with the stored image for a match. A similar recognition system was recently developed that is based on unique infrared-detected heat patterns in human heads.

While advanced technology abounds, any attempt to employ cutting-edge PIV devices in FEDEC could bring delay, for this might become mired in years of refinement, testing, and adaptation. PIV requirements could be amply met using today's technologies and products. Ending cash should take priority over perfecting security by use of state-of-the-art devices.

A CARDLESS SYSTEM

Looking to the biometric future, it appears that it might be possible to transact electronically without the use of transaction cards. Clearly, if biometric devices can verify identities, they can also recognize account holders. The convenience and advantages of not having to carry and use a transaction card speaks for itself. This would have particular significance for children and others prone to losing things.

In a cardless system, one would merely press a fingerprint, speak, or pen a signature in order to access one's account. The system would find a match with the account holder's pre-stored biometric data and allow the rest of the transaction to proceed, perhaps by pressing terminal keys or by voicing commands.

A cardless national payment system would probably be limited to on-line transactions, for as we have considered, it is impractical to store massive data locally, in this case biometric PIV. Moreover, until portable (i.e., pocket-sized) terminals with biometric capabilities have been fully developed, cardless payments would be limited to fixed-terminal transactions, as at POS. Yet this would not mean that cardless procedure would be put on hold until such products were deployed; cardless and card-type transactions might function contemporaneously. Thus, one transacting on the grocer's fixed terminal, which is biometric-enabled, might do so without using a transaction card, for example, by impressing a finger. Yet, when transferring funds to a friend via a personal mobile terminal that was not biometric-enabled, one would have to swipe one's card.

CHAPTER 10

HOW FEDERAL ELECTRONIC CURRENCY MIGHT IMPACT THE BANKING AND BANKCARD INDUSTRIES

The post-cash era will alter banking and bankcard operations in several ways. The all-electronic environment will slash fixed and operational costs by eliminating both vulnerability to robbery and cash handling. Cash flows could change, and certain e-money operations would be impacted.

Gone will be the archaic necessity of counting, recounting, and packaging the approximately $135 billion worth of coin and currency, circulating in the United States.[1] Eliminated as well will be cash-handling equipment and currency transaction reports (CTRs), the latter costing banks some nine dollars each to prepare. Absent the threat of bank robbery, which rose 42 percent between 1989 and 1993, elaborate safes, armed guards, armored car services, alarms, and surveillance systems could almost entirely be eliminated. Associated costs of cash, including compensation for employees injured or killed in bank robberies, will go as well.

Indeed, absent today's heavy capital investments in bank security, a new operations scenario would likely emerge. In-person services could be conducted at smaller, less expensive branches, consisting of office suites. A community benefit that might ensue would be the opening of branches in depressed neighborhoods. Overall, however, disuse of cash would mark the end of a major bank operation and therefore significantly reduce the need for in-person services.

Over the last decade, banks have successfully shifted a high percentage of former in-person cash transactions from both banks and merchants to automatic teller machines (ATMs). This brings up the question of what role these machines and networks would play in the post-cash era. Whether the end of ATM cash transactions would amount to a net loss to bankers or a blessing, depends on one's source of information. Today's continuing expansion of ATM networks, largely by banks, gives credence to assertions by some, especially consumer advocates, that banks earn huge profits from them. Yet, crime at ATM sites has made them increasingly expensive to operate. A sort of dual connection has developed between ATMs and the drug underworld. The convenience of the cash-dispensing machines for nighttime drug users has won them the slang name "coke machines." Ordinary ATM customers, particularly at isolated locations, are easy robbery targets who, in the act of withdrawing cash, are easily overpowered by addicts in need of cash.

ATM robberies have become common enough to have resulted in lawsuits against banks alleging insufficient security. Several states have imposed ATM security standards, and a number of cities have enacted stringent building-code requirements for ATMs. Banks have responded by providing better lighting and patrol services and, recently, by installing "911" functions at ATM panels.[2] Bankers assert that transaction fees do not offset ATM operational costs and that banks actually lose money. In the bigger picture, however, this loss is still far less than if all those ATM transactions had to be conducted by live tellers.

Though ATM cash disbursements would become history, ATM machines are finding noncash uses. For example, at an increasing number of ATMs, one can purchase transit and theater tickets, pay bills, and transfer funds from one account to another. These are fee-generating functions, and firms invested in ATM machines and networks, including some of America's biggest banks, are diligently looking for even further uses. During the years that would pass before cash fell from circulation, these and emerging uses for the ATM could eclipse the cash disbursement function, and thus the ATM might well survive.

Much will depend on the development and popularity of competing ways to accomplish these new ATM functions. For example, expansion of Internet access to the public might provide more convenient methods of shifting funds or paying bills. It would seem, however, that a low-end segment of consumers will always resist investing in the necessary equipment, such as computers, as well as learning procedures involved for such alternative methods. Given these factors and absent the cash-crime ATM costs, the ATM might be around for a long time.

At first impression, it would seem that transforming tangible cash to FEDEC would result in a wholesale shift of bank money stock to the new system, with negative ramifications. However, a number of variables would govern such results, for example, whether or not interest were paid on FEDEC accounts. Analysis of the interrelationship of FEDEC and banking systems is a study in and of itself and lies beyond the purview of this book, if not the ken of this author. Some observations can be made.

It would hardly be the purpose of government to establish a monetary system to compete with the private sector or to undermine financial commerce. Yet, transformation of cash to federal electronic currency would necessarily change money flows, to some degree, between financial institutions, merchants, the FEDEC system, and individuals. The relative handiness of FEDEC, as well as its likely absence of usage fees, would seem to pose terrific problems for financial institutions. However, the threat would be mitigated by several factors.

FEDEC accounts would bear no interest, nor would the system make loans or offer collateral services. Thus, funds would not likely be left for long in FEDEC accounts before being transferred to commercial accounts. Additionally, because all transactions in the cashless environment would be for exact amounts, much of the cash circulating outside banks would find its way into commercial accounts after it had been exchanged for federal electronic currency. This includes billions of idle dollars kept by retailers for "change."

Speed would play a role as well. FEDEC receipts by merchants, obtained by transfers of dollars from customers' FEDEC accounts to merchants' FEDEC accounts, would be transferred to financial institutions immediately, for merchants would thus earn interest on the funds as early as possible. Such transfers might be effected automatically as a feature of integrated payment-accounting systems.

Nevertheless, the convenience, economy, and security of electronic currency, as well as the unpopularity of fees charged by banks, are likely to motivate individuals who today hold non-interest-bearing or low-interest checking accounts to convert their funds to electronic currency. Thus, the threat persists that a percentage of demand accounts would be lost to the government system. Again, even this threat is limited.

Presumably, FEDEC would be designed to emulate tangible cash. Therefore, it would not work in every payment scenario. Today, account holders typically pay the great majority of their monthly bills by mailing off checks. Because FEDEC, at least in its initial stage, would lack a means for making non-face-to-face payments, this practice would continue. Demand-account funds to cover the checks would remain at about the same levels as today. At most, some people would shift a small portion of their checking-account funds to their FEDEC accounts for use in face-to-face payments—or perhaps to download onto smart cards; but as long as the FEDEC system lacked non-face-to-face service, the great bulk of today's checking account funds would remain in place. Indeed, financial institutions, through the FSTC, are testing newly designed electronic (paperless) checking devices that consumers may find quite attractive. Some of the transaction models offer customers multiple payment options.[3] In general, the FSTC is working on a comprehensive electronic infrastructure to facilitate secure electronic transactions via existing banking systems. These include avenues accessible by merchants via counter terminals, as well by the growing millions of Americans who already own modem-equipped computers. New electronic checking systems, which would eliminate paper handling and avert today's growing forgery problem, might provide a means for secure non-face-to-face electronic payments.

FEDEC would appear to clash head on with private debit-card systems, for FEDEC (as envisioned by this author, at least) would comprise a debit-card system itself. However, debit-card systems are simply an adjunct to commercial bank accounts, and as explained above, many individuals would desire to retain funds in such accounts to earn interest and to use commercial payment systems for remote payment of bills, among other reasons. Even in face-to-face scenarios, at the grocer, for example, a consumer might opt to access funds by using a bank debit card rather than paying with FEDEC funds. Private debit-card systems might compete with FEDEC in additional ways, perhaps by offering features that the government system lacked. For example, developments are underway that tie ATM/POS networks to the Internet. Thus, consumers might make debit-card purchases directly over the Internet, something that might be impossible in FEDEC.

Because the FEDEC system would not provide credit, its impact on credit-card volume should be minimal. People will continue to buy on credit, and the funds involved in credit-card payments would remain in the private sector. The 52 percent of credit-card users who now take advantage of float[4] would continue doing so, for as long as industry offered it.

FEDEC would definitely clash with private sector e-cash, for FEDEC would simply preempt the field. FEDEC itself might employ the smart-card format for small payments and specialized applications. Except where employed in closed-environment systems (e.g., schools, prisons), private-sector e-cash systems could hardly compete with a universal, charge-free, government electronic currency. Yet, judging by the size of today's e-cash market, its loss would be nearly insignificant.

The attempt would be made to structure and design FEDEC to facilitate and emulate today's ratio of bank money and cash reserves. But if, despite the just-described saving factors, transforming cash were to result in a significant shift of money stock to electronic currency, financial institutions could be allowed to borrow the difference back from the Fed at an appropriate discount rate.

The true impact of federal electronic currency on the general bankcard industry would turn on FEDEC's design, its systemic breadth, and, as stated, whether it might be used in non-face-to-face settings. An issue could arise as to which type of "money" government should use in making direct deposits of government benefits, wages, and invoice payments. If FEDEC is to strictly emulate cash, which in today's world necessitates transfer of possession, then it should not logically be used for direct electronic deposits, since that is impossible with cash. The attempt to emulate tangible cash by limiting FEDEC to face-to-face scenarios will run into other problems as well: In an attempt to limit FEDEC to face-to-face usage, FEDEC payments made outside the POS scenario—those made by individuals via handheld, home, or public terminals—could conceivably be designed to require the physical presence of the payee, as by requiring the engagement of the payee's FEDEC card in the same terminal or the entry of a biometric.

Allowing the payee merely to enter a payee's account number in the payer's terminal would extend the use of FEDEC for remote payments. The latter possibility might have a profound effect not only on how individuals would pay each other but also on how they would pay their bills and in which medium they might store their funds.

It is conceivable that tomorrow's "cash" might be adaptable to the Internet. Members of a future cashless society would think it a bit pointless, if not backward, to limit FEDEC within the functional confines of paper bills and coin. But these are tomorrow's concerns. At FEDEC's inception and in the foreseeable future, no compelling reason would exist for government to integrate e-currency with the Internet or even to provide non-face-to-face payments in electronic currency. It must be emphasized that the chief motivations for ending cash are reduction of cash-handling costs and crime prevention; merely removing tangible cash from circulation would achieve that much.

CONCLUSION

The creation of electronic bankcard systems a quarter century ago brought the realization that cash might someday be entirely displaced by electronic forms of money. Consumers quickly adapted to convenient new bankcards, and today credit and ATM/debit cards are commonplace around the globe, with the typical American carrying several. Yet cash still dominates as the most frequent method of payment, accounting for some 85 percent of transactions in the United States, where production of currency and coin is actually on the rise. To meet demand, and with an eye to the future, the Treasury Department is investing millions of dollars in new equipment to increase production of bills and coins.

Individuals who use bankcards for most of their purchases may question why the fabled cashless society is so slow in arriving. The answer lies in the fact that industry has never set out to make society cashless. Cashlessness is merely a potential by-product of electronic funds transfer (EFT) systems. Notwithstanding pervasive deployment of bankcard networks, industry has never attempted to replace or even seriously suggested replacing all tangible cash.

Nor has the federal government taken active interest in making the United States cashless, preferring instead to relegate consumer EFT to the private sector. Government's role is merely that of a regulator, protecting consumers on the one hand and facilitating industry on the other. Indeed, officials would likely react to any anticipated demise of cash more as a threat than a matter of progress. This is because cash, despite its archaic form and though electronic monies offer incomparable efficiencies and conveniences, is the basis of the Federal Reserve System. Were cash entirely supplanted by private-sector e-monies, banking and monetary controls might be lost, and the economy would sail uncharted waters. Minor concern did, in fact, arise in the United States around 1995, when "e-cash" made its debut. At that time experts were estimating that in two or three years 25 million Americans would be transacting in e-cash. This triggered a series of congressional hearings, and officials pondered the likelihood and consequences of a cashless, or at least a "less-cash," world. Many experts dismissed such predictions as hyperbole. Indeed, e-cash has not materialized in the United States, and the threat has waned.

Still in an experimental stage, e-cash is a worldwide phenomenon that some regard as an avenue to a cashless era. Millions of individuals in Europe and the Far East have begun transacting in "e-cash," a relatively new EFT payment medium that emulates actual currency. Used across the merchant's counter and in vending machines and for payment of bus and train fares, e-cash can also facilitate speed-through payments of bridge and highway tolls and even interpersonal transfers of "money." Moreover, PC-based versions of this type of "money" can be transacted at long distance over the Internet.

The increasing technological means for replacing cash evidence that we are in the midst of a worldwide transformation of physical currency. E-cash is but one of several unfolding electronic payment systems with the necessary capacity. Awesome advancements in electronics, computers, and communication make this possible. Enormous potential profits in new monetary structures drive industry to make it happen, while convenience and efficiency make the public an eager partner in this historic electron-ification of cash.

To a banker, an economist, an investor in an e-cash company, or a student of the history of money, this transition is pretty exciting stuff. As an ordinary citizen, however, one may view the coming electronification of cash as merely another modern marvel providing a higher degree of handiness. Amid the endless development of ever-novel precision elec-tronic devices being marketed today, from complex calculators to hand-held global positioning devices, with many such advanced items selling for as little as a few dollars, e-cash may evoke a yawn.

Our intimacy with cash, carrying it in pocket and purse, and our fa-miliarity with it in our daily routines renders it so ordinary and innocuous as not to be worth a thought. The customer's tender of cash and the clerk's return of change is an ancient payment procedure woven into our culture and history. Pieces of metal and paper, with fixed denominations and a government's seal stamped and inscribed on them, have been passed back and forth as money in transactions for millennia. Greek and Roman coins, and Chinese paper notes were used much as they are today.

Awareness about the relative function of cash was shaken a bit several decades ago by predictions that cash would be replaced by electronic bank-cards. Americans first transacting with new mag-stripe credit cards began to comprehend the implications of a "cashless society." Looking back, the concept could have been termed "the electronic-money society" or simply "the e-money society," except that these terms do not convey the same meaning as "cashless society." What caught everyone's imagination at that time, of course, was the freedom from having to carry, count, and exchange currency and coin and an end to the nuisance of making change. This made so much sense that many Americans anticipated a swift demise of cash. Though expectation of a cashless society has diminished, its potential benefits far exceed the limited convenience that Americans then envisioned.

The personal nuisance of using cash, relative to bankcard transactions, is the least of its detriments. The continued use of cash is a huge burden on the economy. Commercial stocking, counting, transporting, and securing of cash are often reported to cost between 1 and 2 percent of the GDP.

The worst feature of cash, however, is that simply being present in a neighborhood grocery, fast-food store, bank, supermarket, or other establishment where cash is used and kept exposes cashiers, clerks, and customers to physical harm or even death. The chance of an occurrence of a violent cash crime depends on the type of business and the particular location, but robbery can happen anywhere—and it does. About 1.5 million people are subjected to robberies and attempted robberies each year in the United States, according to an in-depth study conducted several years ago.[1]

Robbery, by definition, is a violent crime. Indeed, over half of its victims are attacked, with one in twelve suffering serious injuries from being shot, knifed, beaten unconscious, raped, or worse. About 2,000 Americans are murdered each year during robberies.[2] Robbery is just part of the picture, for personal victimizations also occur during burglaries and other cash-inspired or cash-related crimes.

Most of America's crime is dependent on the existence of cash. Some crimes, as with almost all robbery, would not occur without cash. In other types of crimes, the use of cash insulates criminals from detection, as in receiving stolen property and in illegal drug sales.

Cash does not cause crime. But, currency in cash registers, bank drawers, wallets, purses, and the dresser beckons the criminally minded as bait attracts animals. The good news is that as tempting and useful as cash is to criminals, it is also their point of vulnerability. The cash-crime nexus, in light of electronic money technology, presents a highly effective new approach to crime prevention.

Distracted by today's e-money dynamism, with hundreds of schemes in play, and dazzled by EFT efficiencies, it is easy for its players, including government, to disregard other important potential benefits. On the infrequent occasions when economists and electronic funds experts discuss

the possibility of true cashlessness, hardly any mention is made of its potential for reducing crime. When mentioned at all, the subject is treated
as an incidental benefit of the bigger economic show. Although proponents of electronic payment media often remind us that plastic is safer to
carry than cash, the fact is that even a high-percentage reduction in circulating cash would fail to achieve a proportionate reduction of crime.
Sums involved in cash crimes are typically small. Crime would still thrive.

Public discussion about crime and bankcards typically dwells on the
prospect that e-money would be used in counterfeiting, fraud, tax evasion,
and money laundering. Far greater concern exists about new types of theft
and fraud crimes that might be conducted in electronic money than ap-
preciation for its potential to eliminate crimes involving cash. Reports of
wire-transfer and credit-card frauds easily capture public attention. Some
individuals mistakenly equate crimes that would be prevented through
the disuse of cash with those that might be conducted in the electronic
medium replacing it. Thus, it is common to hear someone say, "The crooks
will just steal credit cards instead of cash." This fails to consider a major
point, that EFT crimes almost always lack the violence factor so common
in cash crimes.

Crime prevention in a cash-free environment could prove very effective. If tangible cash no longer circulated, Americans would discover that
robbery had become rare and that illegal drug sales had plummeted.
Crooks would soon discover they were being caught quicker, and most
would be deterred. Criminal-court logjams and prison overcrowding
would substantially diminish. Not only would those who operate cash
registers, drive taxis and buses, and handle money in banks benefit, but
transforming cash to an electronic medium promises to improve the quality of life for tens of millions of law-abiding Americans as well. The benefit
would extend those who reside in crime-ridden neighborhoods, where
turf wars often imprison residents in their own homes, where many residents cannot walk their streets for fear of becoming victims of robbery
attacks. Citizens not directly victimized would benefit in the pocketbook,
by being relieved of the enormous cost of cash crime in the form of insurance premiums, taxes, and personal security outlays.

Several observers over the years, impatient with the slow arrival of the
prophesied cashless society and eager to realize its crime-reducing benefits, have suggested accelerating cash's demise by simply abolishing cash
and allowing bankcard systems to fill in for it. Unfortunately, they failed
to address the substantive issues involved or to explain what type of system would actually replace cash. Clearly, this is far too complex a matter
to be approached in that manner.

In the purely economic picture, the crime prevention and economic
benefits of transforming currency into an electronic medium are inextricably related. The dividend of crime prevention would likely exceed $200

billion a year and might run at several times that, benefitting virtually every American—rich, poor, young, old, working, or retired—through victim-of-crime savings, reduced justice-system cost savings, and increased revenues from the underground economy. Adding in the increased efficiency of no longer having to process tangible cash reveals a sum so enormous that it alone warrants making cashlessness a national mandate.

America has all the components necessary to make its currency electronic: proven technologies, off-the-shelf time-tested products, efficient communication networks already in place, highly capable industries, and a bankcard-knowledgeable public. It would be unreasonable to condition the proposed monetary conversion on easy implementation, on foolproof security, on absolute prediction of favorable economic consequences in every aspect, or on irrefutable proof that crime rates would decline. The only guarantee in the offing is that forbearance and indecision by government, and its continued deference to the private sector will deny generations of Americans the profound benefits of cashlessness.

NOTES

PREFACE

1. Donald Gleason, president of the Smart Card Enterprise unit of Electronic Payment Services, Inc., is quoted as saying "Cash is a nightmare. It costs money handlers in the US alone approximately US$60 billion a year to move the stuff." From "E-Money (That's What I Want)," by Steven Levy, viewable at website *http://www.mcs.com/sorkin/wired/emoney.html*. Alvin Toffler states "the costs of printing, distributing and processing money—estimated at a couple of percentage points of the gross domestic product—are an invisible drag on the economy and a hidden tax on capital." Source: *American Banker*, May 21, 1996, via *NewsPage*, website address: *http://www.newspage.com*. In 1998, Toffler's assertion would put the cost somewhere between $75 and $150 billion a year.

Such estimates strike some people as unbelievable. Harvey Rosenblum, vice-president of the Dallas Federal Reserve Bank, expressed doubts about the oft-recited estimate of cash usage costing America "between one and two percent of the GDP."

However, evidence indicates that a $60 billion estimate for the direct costs of cash may not be off the mark. A 1998 in-depth study by the Food Marketing Institute entitled "EPS Costs: A Retailer's Guide to Electronic Payment Systems Costs," states that the [grocer] retailer's average cost in a point-of-sale (POS) cash transaction in the United States is $.0834, a figure that includes pertinent business overhead; applying this $.0834 figure to the nation's more-than 550 billion cash transactions (for all but a tiny fraction are at POS), would account for some $46 billion in costs. But, cash handling in some industries is more expensive; for example, in vending-machine and taxi industries, thus the POS cost is somewhat higher. The Fed and Treasury Department together spend about $1 billion producing, shipping and receiving currency and coin ($889 million in 1997), and this does not include anti–money-laundering outlays. Depository banks spend about another billion dollars shipping cash to and from the Fed, while banks and various other businesses spend some $1 billion in filling out currency transaction reports (CTRs). Add to all this the cost of cash stolen from citizens, which may run around $10 billion (see Chapter Six), and the $60 billion figure seems quite plausible.

If the full cost of cash's role in crime and the underground economy is added in, the bottom line soars. This goes beyond direct "handling and processing" costs; yet, the illicit aspects are undeniable features of cash usage. As developed in this book, they add at least $185 billion to the overall cost of using cash. When included in the calculation they easily substantiate a cash-cost estimate of "two percentage points of the GDP."

2. U.S. Patent Number 5,455,407, issued October 3, 1995.

3. Mark Bernkopk, "Electronic Cash and Monetary Policy," *First Monday, Peer-Reviewed Journal on the Internet*, (web address: *http://www.firstmonday.dk/issues1/ecash/index.html*), March 1998.

INTRODUCTION

1. GAO/T-GGD-97-146, p. 3.

2. Food Marketing Institute, "Retailers Guide to Electronic Payment Costs, 1994."

3. Hearing notice, U.S. House of Representatives, Subcommittee on Domestic and International Monetary Policy Hearing, "The Future of Money," July 25, 1995.

A number of EFT notables testified, including David Van Lear, president of Electronic Payment Services; David Chaum, CEO of DigiCash, BV; William Melton, CEO of CyberCash, Inc.; Rosalind L. Fisher, executive vice president, Visa USA; Heidi Goff, senior vice president, Mastercard International; and Scott Cook, chairman of Intuit, Inc. Government experts who testified before the subcommittee in October of 1995 included Alan Blinder, vice chairman of the Board of Governors of the Federal Reserve System, and Eugene A. Ludwig, Comptroller of the Currency, as well as the heads of the Financial Crimes Enforcement Network (FinCEN), National Institute of Standards and Technology, National Security Agency, U.S. Mint, and Secret Service.

4. Ibid.

5. "In a nutshell, the Mint has proposed that the Treasury Department take the lead in identifying and addressing policy issues related to stored-value and smart cards as substitutes for currency." Statement of Philip Diehl to the said House Committee, October 11, 1995, p. 3. This proposal calls for an initial study group composed of representatives from federal departments, the Federal Reserve, and private industry.

6. Statement of Alan S. Blinder to the House Subcommittee on Domestic and International Monetary Policy, October 11, 1995, p. 2.

CHAPTER 1

1. U.S. Department of Justice, Federal Bureau of Investigation, *Crime in the United States, 1996* (Washington, D.C.: U.S. Department of Justice, August 1997), p. 26.

2. U.S. Department of Justice, Bureau of Justice Statistics, *Sourcebook of Criminal Justice Statistics, 1996* (Washington, D.C.: U.S. Department of Justice, November 1997), p. 139.

3. *Crime in the United States, 1996.*

4. *Sourcebook of Criminal Justice Statistics, 1996*, p. 3.

5. *Sourcebook of Criminal Justice Statistics, 1996*, "Justice System Direct and Intergovernment Expenditures." Table 1.3 p. 4, gives figures for 1993 (which have increased steadily) as follows: Federal—$18,591,000, States—34,227,000, and Local Governments—$52,562,000.

6. From the government's census of fatal injuries. *San Francisco Chronicle*, October 2, 1993, p. A3.

7. *Crime in the United States, 1996*, p. 8, showing Larceny Theft comprising 58.6%, Robbery 4%, and Burglary 18.6% of all crimes.

8. Marilyn E. Walsh, *Strategies for Combatting the Criminal Receiver (Fence) of Stolen Goods* (Washington, D.C.: U.S. Government Printing Office, 1976), p. 123. This coincides with a computer analysis of data collected in the National Crime Victimization Survey 1991, U.S. Department of Justice, Bureau of Justice Statistics (unpublished), which revealed that in nearly 18 percent of all crimes in which something was stolen, the item taken was either cash, a pocketbook, or a billfold. Cash by itself was stolen in 7.5 percent of crimes; purses were stolen in 3.5 percent; and wallets were taken in 5.7 percent.

9. U.S. Department of Justice, Bureau of Justice Statistics, "Personal and Household Crimes, 1990," in *Bureau of Justice Statistics Bulletin* (Washington D.C.: U.S. Department of Justice), Table 89.

10. *Crime in the United States, 1996*, p. 29.

11. U.S. Department of Justice, Bureau of Justice Statistics, Bureau of Justice Statistics special report, "Robbery Victims" (Washington D.C.: U.S. Department of Justice Statistics, April 1987), p. 1.

12. This figure is from a victim-of-crime cost study published in *Health Affairs*, Winter 1993, p. 193. The actual figure given for 1993 was 1,480,000 robberies and attempts.

Though robbery rates have decreased in most of the United States over the last few years, the National Crime Victim Survey (NCVS) for 1996, the latest NCVS report available for this book, indicated 1,134,000 robberies and attempts in 1996; it separately indicated 318,000 purse snatchings/pickpocketings in that year, which, when added to robbery, totals 1,452,000.

13. *Crime in the United States, 1996*, Table 2.14, p. 21.

14. U.S. Department of Justice, Bureau of Justice Statistics, "Household Burglary," in *Bureau of Justice Statistics Bulletin*, 1985, p. 1.

15. The $300 billion figure is based on high-end estimates of annual money laundering and assumes that virtually all of it comes from illegal drug sales. "State and Local Money Laundering Control Strategies," U.S. Department of Justice, National Institute of Justice, October 1992, p. 1. The $50 billion figure is from the Office of National Drug Control Policy (ONDCP), as cited in the FY1996 proposed budget, Section 4.

16. *Crime in the United States, 1996*, p. 27, states that 24 percent of all robberies were of commercial houses and financial institutions. The *Sourcebook of Criminal Justice Statistics, 1996* reveals approximately 1.3 million robberies that year.

CHAPTER 2

1. Howard Anderson, *Upside*, "Showdown Over E-cash," January 1996.

2. Tower Group report, *Smart Cards in the US: An Infrastructure Cost Analysis*, February, 1997.

3. See report by Killen and Associates, *Non-Bank's Smart Card Strategies: New Opportunities to Increase Sales and Profits*, April 10, 1997.

4. Tower Group report.

5. From an advertisement for World Trade Clearinghouse, Ltd. (WTC), on the Internet circa September 1995. Website address: *http://www.btmar.com.80/mall/ shops/?????/wtd.???*

6. *ABA Banking Journal*, June 1995.

7. On-line statistics from National Automated Clearinghouse Association from a "U.S. Payments" graph, 1998. Website address: *http://www.acha.org*

8. U.S. Bureau of the Census, *Historical Statistics of the United States, Colonial Times to 1970*, Bicentennial Edition, Part 2 (Washington DC: U.S. Government Printing Office, 1979), p. 992. Also, U.S. Department of Commerce, Bureau of Economic Analysis, "Currency in Circulation, Table 3," URL: *www.bea.doc.gov/bea/ ai/0797bp/table3.htm*.

9. Edgar L. Feige, *The Underground Economies* (Cambridge University Press, 1989), p. 5.

10. Testimony before the House Subcommittee on Domestic and International Monetary Policy regarding "Consumer Implications of Electronic Banking and Commerce," March 7, 1996.

11. *American Banker*, November 8, 1993, p. 24.

12. This percentage is the relationship between the total number of violent crimes, 1,864,168, as indicated in the FBI's *Crime in the United States, 1994*, and the total number of murders, rapes, and robberies attributable to cash, 623,889 (2,072 murders, 3,000 rapes, and 618,817 robberies).

13. U.S. Bureau of the Census, *Statistical Abstract of the United States, 1993* (113th edition) (Washington D.C.: U.S. Government Printing Office, 1993), p. 502.

14. U.S. Government Printing Office, *Sourcebook of Criminal Justice Statistics, 1996*, November 1997, p. 1.

15. *Crime in the United States, 1996*, pp. 70–74.

16. Ibid., p. 27.

17. U.S. Bureau of the Census, *Statistical Abstract of the United States, 1997*, 117th edition (Washington, D.C., 1997), Table 332, p. 211. At the website address: *http:/ /www.census.gov*.

18. Ibid., Section V: "Drugs in America," p. 280.

19. Bureau of Justice Statistics, National Crime Victim Survey 1996, "Changes 1995–96 with Trends 1993–96," November 1997, p. 1. At the Website address: *http://www.ojp.usdoj.gov.bjs.cvictgen.htm*.

20. Ibid., p. 3.

21. Ibid., p. 5.

22. For example, in 1991 there were 13.5 robberies for every 1,000 black persons, as opposed to 4.4 for whites and 7.4 for other racial categories. U.S. Depart-

ment of Justice, Bureau of Justice Statistics, "Criminal Victimization 1991," ibid., p. 2.

23. U.S. Department of Justice, Bureau of Justice Statistics, "Executive Summary," NCJ-163917, June 1997, p. 1.

24. *Sourcebook of Criminal Justice Statistics, 1996,* Table 1.2, p. 3.

25. *Sourcebook of Criminal Justice Statistics, 1996,* November 1997, pp. 1, 4.

26. Government Accounting Office, GAO/T-GGD-97-146, Appendix II, "Coin and Currency Usage in the United States," p. 21. See also Martin Mayer, *The Bankers: The Next Generation* (New York: Truman Tally Books/Dutton, 1997), p. 451.

27. *Crime in the United States, 1996,* p. 202.

28. Martin Mayer, *The Bankers: The Next Generation,* p. 77.

29. "Thinking Globally, Acting Locally," Visa International, 1989, p. 3; and "The Evolution of a Full-Service Consumer-Payment System," Visa U.S.A., March 1990, pp. 1, 10.

30. *American Banker,* May 6, 1997.

31. *POS NEWS,* June 1994, p. 6.

32. Government Accounting Office, GAO/GGD-93-1, "Money Laundering," pp. 2, 3.

33. The President's Commission on Organized Crime, "Interim Report to the President and Attorney General, The Cash Connection: Organized Crime, Financial Institutions, and Money Laundering" (Washington D.C.: U.S. Government Printing Office, 1984), pp. vii–viii.

34. GAO/NSAID-91-130, "Money Laundering," p. 8.

35. *San Francisco Chronicle,* April 9, 1994, D1.

36. GAO/NSAID-91-130, pp. 57–58.

37. 31 C.F.R. Sec. 103.29 (1990); 31 U.S.C. Sec. 5325 (1988), effective August 13, 1990.

38. GAO/GGD-94-45FS, "Money Laundering," p. 7.

39. GAO/NSAID-91-130, p. 38.

40. Ibid., quoting the testimony of Henry R. Wray, Director, Administration of Justice Issues, General Government Division, GAO, before the Committee on Banking, Finance and Urban Affairs, House of Representatives, May 26, 1993.

41. Ibid.

42. *Notre Dame Law Review,* 66: 863, 864.

43. The Bureau of Labor lists the following categories as areas of underground economic activity: Grocery sales from stands; clothing sales, alterations, mending, laundry, and ironing; personal care, including hair cuts, hair care, and cosmetics; private lessons, such as tutoring, piano, or guitar instructions; driving, child care; vacation rentals; tickets to sporting events or concerts; used books and textbooks; door-to-door magazine sales; used furniture and appliances; appliance repair; cleaning and domestic help; lawn mowing and gardening; furniture repair or reupholstering; carpet cleaning; moving and storage; painting and wallpapering; plumbing, electrical, and carpentry services; wood, coal, and charcoal sales; garbage and trash removal; used vehicles, boat and boat equipment sales; car washing; car maintenance, such as grease jobs, oil changes and tune-ups; tire and battery sales; car parts sales; parking and towing.

44. Motorists in Belgium can pay parking meters in this manner by using smart cards. Martin Mayer, *The Bankers: The Next Generation*, p. 148.

45. "Estimates of Income Unreported on Individual Income Tax Returns," IRS Publication 1104 (9–79).

46. Ibid., p. 18.

47. Helen Sinclair, President, Canadian Bankers Association, in a speech to the Canadian Club, February 19, 1990.

CHAPTER 3

1. According to NACHA, the number of cash transactions in the United States in 1997 was 550 billion.

2. *San Francisco Chronicle*, April 4, 1993, B2.

3. Source: International Reciprocal Trade Association web site: *http://www.irta. net/index/html*.

4. Ibid.

5. *Contra Costa Times*, March 23, 1993, p. 6D.

6. See Lewis D. Solomon, *Rethinking Our Centralized Monetary System: The Case for a System of Local Currencies* (Westport, Conn.: Praeger Publishers, 1996).

7. Jack Weatherford, author of *The History of Money*, emphasizing the nuisance, cost, and obsolescence of cash, suggests that the Treasury Department simply stop producing currency and coin. *USA Today*, April 26, 1997.

8. Stuart M. Speiser, "Abolish Paper Money and Eliminate Most Crime," *American Bar Journal*, vol. 61 (1978), p. 47. Leon M. Lederman, "To Reduce Crime, Eliminate Cash," *New York Times*, April 27, 1981.

CHAPTER 4

1. *POS News*, June 1994, p. 6.

2. This was a presentation at Washington University in St. Louis in May, 1995. It was reviewed by the Journal of *Money, Credit and Banking* in February 1997. It was also the subject of the "Research Scan" column of *American Banker* on May 9, 1997. I read a truncated version of the *American Banker* column that appeared on *NewsPage*, May 6, 1997. *Newspage's* website address: *http:// www.newspage.com*.

3. *American Banker*, David A. Balto, Federal Trade Commission, May 8, 1997.

4. *Rethinking Our Centralized Monetary System*, p. 68.

5. *Electronic Money Flows: The Moulding of a New Financial Order*, edited by Elinor Harris Solomon, Yoshihari Oritani, and other authors (Boston: Kluwer Academic Publishers, 1991), pp. 119–120.

6. David F. Linowes, *Privacy in America: Is Your Private Life in the Public Eye?* (Urbana: University of Illinois Press, 1989), pp. 109–111.

7. Yet, Thomas C. Melzer, president of the Federal Reserve Bank of St. Louis, says that issuers of new stored-value products "would probably consider themselves lucky to earn the 1% of value that is typical of traditional travelers checks." Harvey Rosenblum, senior vice president and director of research at the Dallas

Federal Reserve Bank, comments that such financial incentives have not been thought through and are unlikely to be profitable. *American Banker*, May 6, 1997.

8. *Los Angeles Times*, August 26, 1994, pp. 23, 64; citing source as *Bank Rate Monitor*.

9. *Kiplinger Personal Finance Report*, January 1995.

10. PIRG Home Page, Internet, *http://www.pirg/org*, August 8, 1996.

CHAPTER 5

1. See "Will That Be Cash, Check, Charge, or Interest?" by economist Adam M. Zeretsky, *Regional Economist*, Federal Reserve Bank of St. Louis, April 1996.

2. "Visa Chip Card Services for Emerging Markets, Chip Offline Pre-Authorized Card Service Overview," Visa International, December 1997.

3. Newspage, website address: *http://www.newspage.com*, April 27, 1998.

4. *Payments Monthly*, June 1992, p. 2.

5. *POS News*, February 1993, p. 8. Also, on March 1993, p. 7, describing Buy-pass Inc.'s "Spirit," a handheld POS device on which waiters conduct debit transactions at tables.

6. Web site: *http://www.intellect.com.au/*.

7. Peter Harrop, *The Future of Payment Media* (London: Financial Times Business Information, 1989), p. 145. Also, see *QST Magazine*, March 1994, p. 50, stating that such a terminal is "very close."

8. See Jeffrey Rothfeder, *Privacy for Sale* (New York: Simon and Schuster, 1992), for examples.

9. Application data, when cross-checked, could unveil thousands of fugitives, illegal aliens, and other missing persons.

10. Feige, *Underground Economies*, pp. 82–96.

11. Committee on Government Operations, Privacy and the National Data Bank Concept, H.R. Rep. No. 1842, 90th Congress, 2nd Sessions, 1–3 (1968). Referred to as the "Ruggles Report."

12. The Privacy Act of 1974 and its amendments may be viewed via the Internet at *http://www.epic.org/privacy/laws/privacy_act.html*.

13. *American Automatic Merchandiser*, November 1990, p. 14.

14. *USA Today*, April 26, 1997, by Jack Weatherford, author of *The History of Money*.

15. Ibid.

16. *POS News*, January 1993, p. 1.

17. Christopher W. Logan and Mark G. Menne, "Implementing an Electronic Transfer System for the Food Stamp Program: Information for State Agencies," Abt Associates, Inc., 1990, p. 4.

18. *Federal Register*, vol. 57, no. 63 (April 1, 1992), Rules and Regulations, pp. 11218–11259.

CHAPTER 6

1. Bureau of Justice Statistics Bulletin, "Household Burglary," January 1985, p. 5.

2. *Health Affairs*, p. 193.

3. *Sourcebook of Criminal Justice Statistics, 1996*, p. 3.

4. *Crime in the United States, 1996*, Table 2.14, p. 21.

5. Peter Reuter, Rand Corp., "Hawks Ascendant: The Punitive Trend of American Drug Policy," RAND/RP-153, 1992, p. 21.

6. From the President's Proposed Federal Budget for 1996, "Justice Outlays."

7. Ibid.

8. Mathea Falco, *The Making of Drug-Free America* (New York: Time Books, 1992), p. 176.

9. Peter Reuter et al., "Money from Crime: A Study of the Economics of Drug Dealing in Washington, D.C.," Rand Corporation, June 1990, pp. 15–17.

10. "Estimates of Income Unreported on Individual Income Tax Returns," IRS publication 1104 (9–79), p. ii.

11. U.S. Department of Justice, National Institute of Justice, "State and Local Money Laundering Control Strategies" (Washington, D.C.: U.S. Department of Justice, October 1992), p. 1.

12. See "How Big Is the Irregular Economy?" *Challenge*, November–December 1979.

13. "Income Tax Compliance Research," Net Tax Gap and Remittance Gap Estimates, IRS Publication 1415, April 19, 1990, p. 1.

14. Ibid., p. 2.

15. "IRS Income Tax Compliance Research: Supporting Appendices to Publication 7285," IRS Publication 1415, July 1988, p. A-6.

16. "Estimates of Income Unreported on Individual Income Tax Returns," IRS Publication 1104 (9–79).

17. *Underground Economies*, p. 41.

18. "Estimates of Income Unreported on Individual Income Tax Returns," p. 4.

19. *San Francisco Chronicle*, March 3, 1993, p. A16.

20. *San Francisco Chronicle*, April 12, 1994, p. A5.

21. Abt Associates, Inc., "Unreported Taxable Income from Selected Illegal Activities," vol. 2 (March 31, 1983), p. 253.

22. Ibid., pp. 253–303.

23. Abt Associates, "Unreported Taxable Income," p. 255.

24. "Justice Expenditure and Employment, 1990" in *Bureau of Justice Statistics Bulletin* (Washington, D.C.: U.S. Department of Justice), p. 1.

25. *Sourcebook of Criminal Justice Statistics*, Table 1.3, p. 4.

26. *Statistical Abstract of the United States 1997: The National Data Book* (Washington, D.C.: U.S. Department of Commerce, Bureau of the Census, 1997) Table 577, p. 371, for 1994.

27. "Survey Estimate of the Economic Cost of Crime to Victims" (Washington, D.C.: U.S. Department of Justice, Bureau of Justice Statistics, 1991), Appendix 4.

28. Bureau of Justice Statistics, "The Costs of Crime to Victims: Crime Data Brief," NCJ-145865, February 1994, p. 1.

29. "Victim Costs and Consequences: A New Look," National Institute of Justice Research Report, January 1996.

30. "Victim Costs of Violent Crime and Resulting Injuries," Ted R. Miller, Mark A. Cohen, and Shelli B. Rossman, *Health Affairs*, Winter 1993, pp. 186–197.

31. Ibid., p. 188.

32. "Robbery Victims," Bureau of Justice Statistics Special Report, p. 1.

33. *Health Affairs*, "Victim Costs of Violent Crime," p. 188.

34. Ibid., p. 193.

35. This is calculated by multiplying the nation's 757,000 completed robberies (*Sourcebook of Criminal Justice Statistics, 1996*, Table I, p. 3) by $873, which is the average value of property stolen during robberies (*Statistical Abstract of the United States, 1997* (Washington, D.C., 1997), Table 300, p520321, p. 205.

36. "What America's Users Spend on Drugs," technical paper, Office of National Drug Control Policy, June 1991, p. 23.

37. "Hawks Ascendant," pp. 30–32.

38. *San Francisco Chronicle*, October 24, 1992, p. A7.

39. *Making of Drug-Free America*, p. 133.

40. "Bank Robbery," U.S. Department of Justice, Bureau of Justice Statistics Bulletin, p. 2.

41. *Making of Drug-Free America*, p. 83.

42. *Statistical Abstract of the United States: 1997*, Table 800, p520321, p. 205. This indicates a 1995 average loss in robbery as $873. The figure for robbery is $1,259.

43. Admittedly, this figure does not correspond to figures produced in the National Crime Victimization Survey, supra, which in 1991 showed an overall economic loss to victims of crime of only $19.2 billion. The reason for the gross discrepancy is not clear.

44. *San Francisco Chronicle*, January 10, 1994, A3.

CHAPTER 7

1. Arthur R. Miller, *The Assault on Privacy* (Ann Arbor: University of Michigan Press, 1972), p. 25.

2. 277 U.S. 438 (1928).

3. 389 U.S. 3347 (1967).

4. 488 F.2d 193 (1973).

5. *NAACP v. Alabama*, 357 U.S. 449 (1958).

6. 410 U.S. 113 (1973).

7. 5 U.S.C., Sec. 552a (1988).

8. Ibid. Sec. 552(e) (1).

9. Ibid. Sec. 552(e) (10).

10. Ibid.

11. Ibid.

12. Ibid.

13. The Privacy Protection Study Commission (established under section 5 of U.S. Public Law 93–579 June 1, 1977, and ceased to exist September 30, 1977, pursuant to Public Law 93–579). "Personal Privacy in an Information Society," 346, at 362, note 2.

14. 425 U.S. 435 (1976).

15. 12 U.S.C. Sections 3401–22 (1988 and Supp. II 1990).

16. GAO/IMTEC-90-70BR, "Government Computers and Privacy," p. 24.

17. Ibid., p. 31.

18. 31 U.S.C. 5313(a). 139 IRS Form 4789.

19. U.S. General Accounting Office, GAO/GGD–91–53, "FinCEN," p. 4.

20. Ibid.

21. U.S. General Accounting Office, GAO/GGD–91–53, "FinCEN," pp. 1–2.

22. Final Rule, 56 Fed. Reg. 12,446 (1991).

23. "This World," *San Francisco Chronicle*, March 13, 1994, p. 5.

24. *New York Times*, May 4, 1979, A19, col. 1.

25. David Burnham, *The Rise of the Computer State* (New York: Vintage Books, 1984) pp. 33–34.

26. See *Harmelin v. Michigan*, 111 S. Ct. 2680 (1991).

27. Robert Nisbet et al., ed. by Irving Howe, *1984 Revisited* (New York: Harper and Row, 1983), p. 189.

28. Johanno Strasser et al., ed. by Irving Howe, *1984 Revisited*, p. 160.

29. Alexander Dallin et al., ed. by Peter Stansley, *On Nineteen Eighty-Four* (W. H. Freeman and Co., 1983), pp. 194–195.

30. U.S.C. 2519 (1).

31. GAO/IMTEC–90–70BR, "Government Computers and Privacy," p. 10.

32. Linowes, *Privacy in America*, p. 82.

33. Source: National Automated Clearinghouse (NACHA).

CHAPTER 8

1. U.S. Department of Justice, Federal Bureau of Investigation, *Crime in the United States 1991* (Washington DC: U.S. Government Printing Office), Table 24, p. 201.

2. *The Costco Connection*, August 1993, p. 11.

3. *The Nilson Report*, January 1993, p. 1.

4. *Atlanta Journal*, December 11, 1995.

5. *Contra Costa Times*, January 10, 1994, A260.

6. *American Banker*, January 12, 1990, p. 4.

7. See U.S. Dept. of Agriculture, Food and Nutrition Service, "Nutrition Program Facts," December, 1997. Website address: *http://www.usda.com*.

8. Harrop, *Future of Payment Media*, p. 30.

9. 15 U.S.C. Sec. 1693–1693r.

10. 15 U.S.C.S. Sec. 1693g(a) (2).

11. *Contra Costa Times*, March 15, 1994, D1.

12. Harrop, *Future of Payment Media*, p. 122.

13. Mayer, *The Bankers: The Next Generation*, p. 124.

14. *Computer Reseller News*, March 24, 1997, p. 30.

15. "78th Annual Report," Board of Governors of the Federal Reserve System, 1991, p. 228.

16. *Crime in the United States, 1996*, p. 4.

CHAPTER 9

1. Harrop, *Future of Payment Media*, p. 80.

2. Source: NCR Corporation, via *NewsPage*, April 24, 1998. NCR's website address: *http://www.ncr.com*.

CHAPTER 10

1. Only about one-third of the approximately $400 billion in U.S. currency circulates in the United States.

2. The American Bankers Association says the matter has been overblown and that there are "only" seven or eight ATM robberies a day, not many in comparison to the total number of ATM transactions.

3. *http://www.llnl.gov/fstc/projects/commerce/public/epay/des.htl.*

4. Bureau of the Census, *Statistical Abstract of the United States: 1997*, Table 800, p. 520.

CONCLUSION

1. Based on 1,480,000 victimizations per year. As reported in *Health Affairs*, Winter 1993, p. 193. See Chapter 1, note 12.

2. Department of Justice, *Crime in the United States, 1996*, p. 13.

SELECTED BIBLIOGRAPHY

BOOKS

Feige, Edgar L. *The Underground Economies*. New York: Cambridge University Press, 1989.

Harrop, Peter. *The Future of Payment Media*. London: Financial Times Business Information, 1989.

Linowes, David F. *Privacy in America: Is Your Private Life in the Public Eye?* Urbana: University of Illinois Press, 1989.

Mayer, Martin. *The Bankers: The Next Generation*. New York: Dutton, 1997.

Miller, Arthur R. *The Assault on Privacy*. Ann Arbor: University of Michigan Press, 1972.

Oritani, Yoshihari et al. *Electronic Money Flows: The Moulding of a New Financial Order*, edited by Elinor Harris Solomon. Boston: Kluwer Publishers, 1991.

Rothfeder, Jeffrey. *Privacy For Sale*. New York: Simon & Schuster, 1992.

U.S. Department of Justice, Bureau of Justice Statistics. *Sourcebook of Criminal Justice Statistics, 1996*. Washington D.C.: U.S. Department of Justice, November, 1997.

U.S. Department of Justice, Federal Bureau of Investigation. *Crime in the United States, 1996*. Washington D.C.: U.S. Department of Justice, August, 1997.

ARTICLES

"Financial Privacy." *Northwestern University Law Review*, vol. 86 (1992).

"In the Shadow of 1984: National Identification Systems, Computer Matching, and Privacy in the United States." *Hastings Law Journal*, vol. 35 (1984).

Miller, Ted R., Mark A. Cohen, and Shelli B. Rossman. "Victim Costs of Violent Crime and Resulting Injuries." *Health Affairs* (Winter 1993).

"Money Laundering." *American Business Law Journal*, vol. 30 (1992).

"Note-Money Laundering." *Notre Dame Law Review*, vol. 66 (1991).

Reuter, Peter. "Hawks Ascendant: The Punitive Trend of American Drug Policy." RAND/RP–153. Santa Monica: Rand Publications (1992).

U.S. Government Accounting Office. "Government Computers and Privacy." GAO/IMTEC–90–70BR (1990).

U.S. Government Accounting Office. "FinCEN." GAO/GGD–91–53 (1991).

U.S. Government Accounting Office. "Money Laundering." GAO/NSAID–91–130 (1991).

U.S. Government Accounting Office. "Money Laundering." GAO/GGD–93–1 (1993).

INDEX

About the Author

DAVID R. WARWICK is an investor, researcher, and writer living in Santa Rosa, CA. He holds an LL.B. and a J.D. from Hastings College of the Law and has practiced plaintiff's personal injury law. He later turned his attention to real estate development, then to entrepreneurship in retail electronics, importing, and security hardware manufacturing. He has a patent pending for a means to make electronic bill payments via ATM and Internet terminals. Mr. Warwick is author of "The Cash Free Society," an important article published in *The Futurist* in 1992, and of other writings for the National Council on Crime and Delinquency. He has also aired his views on National Public Radio and regional television.

DATE DUE

23July05			